A History of Russia

Roger Bartlett

First published 2005 by
PALGRAVE MACMILLAN
Houndmills, Basingstoke, Hampshire RG21 6XS and
175 Fifth Avenue, New York, N.Y. 10010
Companies and representatives throughout the world

PALGRAVE MACMILLAN is the global academic imprint of the Palgrave Macmillan division of St. Martin's Press, LLC and of Palgrave Macmillan Ltd. Macmillan® is a registered trademark in the United States, United Kingdom and other countries. Palgrave is a registered trademark in the European Union and other countries.

ISBN-13: 978–0333–63263–5   hardback
ISBN-10: 0–333–63263–X   hardback
ISBN-13: 978–0333–63264–2   paperback
ISBN-10: 0–333–63264–8   paperback

This book is printed on paper suitable for recycling and made from fully managed and sustained forest sources.

A catalogue record for this book is available from the British Library.

A catalog record for this book is available from the Library of Congress.

10	9	8	7	6	5	4	3	2	1
14	13	12	11	10	09	08	07	06	05

Printed in China

A HISTORY OF RUSSIA

PALGRAVE ESSENTIAL HISTORIES
General Editor: Jeremy Black

This series of compact, readable and informative national histories is designed to appeal to anyone wishing to gain a broad understanding of a country's history.

Published

Further titles are in preparation

Series Standing Order

1–4039–3811–3 hardback
1–4039–3812–1 paperback

If you would like to receive future titles in this series as they are published, you can make use of our standing order facility. To place a standing order please contact your bookseller or, in case of difficulty, write to us at the address below with your name and address and the name of the series. Please state with which title you wish to begin your standing order. (If you live outside the United Kingdom we may not have the rights for your area, in which case we will forward your order to the publisher concerned.)

Customer Services Department, Macmillan Distribution Ltd
Houndmills, Basingstoke, Hampshire RG21 6XS, England

Contents

Maps

Tables

Illustrations

Preface

Russia presents difficult choices to anyone writing a general history, especially within a limited space. How should one slim volume encompass one-sixth of the world's land surface? A multi-ethnic realm with over a hundred languages? A polity in which for centuries some nine people out of every ten were peasants, who have their own separate stories? A society whose culture ancient and modern has been rich, multifarious and deeply influential? A political and military structure with a major role in international affairs whose values for most of the twentieth century presented challenges across the globe to hegemonic Euro-American norms and assumptions? I have tried first to present a coherent and balanced chronological narrative, to make sense of development over time. I have tried to outline the broader topics mentioned above, but constraints of space focus this account on Great Russia: fuller treatments of wider issues are mentioned in the suggestions for Further Reading. The principal themes reflected here which have concerned me as an historian have been Russia's rise as a territorial and military power; the nature of its political systems; the development and modalities of modern Russian culture and thought; and the relationship between the vast peasant population and the ruling elites in what, following Gerd Spittler, I call here the 'peasant state'.

There are choices to be made, too, of analytical tools and terminology. My own understanding of the historical process will be apparent from the text, but concepts I have avoided include that of 'backwardness' – value-laden, misleading and teleological in its application to Russia. In speaking of social groups I have eschewed class categories, especially preferring the term 'elite' to 'ruling class' – while nevertheless acknowledging the latter's analytical power. In the modern period I have tried particularly to do justice to the debate around 'totalitarianism' and other views of Stalin's Russia.

I have many debts to acknowledge. This book is written almost without footnotes or references; but I am keenly aware of how much I depend, like a pygmy standing on the shoulders of giants, on the research and analysis of other scholars whose work has informed my own knowledge and judgments. Partial indication of the more modern sources appears in Further Reading. More specifically, I thank those friends and colleagues who have generously helped with advice, information and critical comment – Sergei Bogatyrëv, Ed Boyle, Pete Duncan, Lindsey Hughes, Emma Minns, Susan Morrissey, Bob Service and Dennis Shaw; and Geoffrey Hosking and Wendy Rosslyn, who read the draft text in its entirety – Wendy has also had to live with the project for far too long. Lindsey Hughes opened her private art and architecture collection to me. All these interventions have nurtured and strengthened the embryonic text: I am deeply grateful. But for the new-born child I must claim exclusive parental responsibility. Its godparents, finally, my editors at Palgrave, Terka Acton and Sonya Barker, have been exemplary in their encouragement, and astonishing in their forbearance: to both my warm thanks and appreciation.

The book is dedicated to all my Russian friends, through whom the Russian world has come alive for me.

Nottingham

Acknowledgements

I am indebted to Routledge Publishers and Sir Martin Gilbert for the reproduction of maps from Martin Gilbert, *The Routledge Atlas of Russian History* (Routledge 2002, ISBN 0415281180HB; 0415281199PB), and for Map 8 to Professor John T. Alexander (from his *Autocratic Politics in a National Crisis: The Imperial Russian Government and Pugachev's Revolt*, Bloomington and London 1969). The British Library gave permission to reproduce Figures 6–8 from J. A. Atkinson, *A Picturesque Representation of the Manners, Customs and Amusements of the Russians* ... (London 1812); the Stedelijk Museum, Amsterdam, to reproduce Figure 12; and Ullstein Bild, Berlin, to reproduce Figure 10 from C. Obolensky, comp., *The Russian Empire: A Portrait in Photographs* (London 1980). Professor Lindsey Hughes generously made available items from her personal collection (Figures 3, 5, 13 and 15). Remaining illustrations are my own.

Note on Transliteration, Names and Dates

For transliteration of Russian terms the Library of Congress system has been used, omitting soft and hard signs, and diacritics except the diaeresis on letter *ё* (indicating *yo* as in 'yonder' – Potëmkin: Pot-yomm-kin *not* Pot-emm-kin). In words beginning with 'soft' vowels, *i-* becomes *y-* (Yaroslavl *not* Iaroslavl). Proper names largely keep their original spellings, except for modern monarchs familiar in anglicised forms. Readers will sometimes meet the Russian patronymic, used as a second name: Ivanovich/Ivanovna indicates 'son/daughter of Ivan'. Dates follow the Julian calendar until 1918, the Gregorian thereafter. Peter I introduced the Julian calendar in Russia in 1700; most of Europe went over soon after to the Gregorian calendar, only adopted in Russia (by the secular authorities) in January 1918. Julian dates are often designated Old Style (OS), Gregorian – New Style (NS): the difference was 11 days in the eighteenth century, 12 in the nineteenth, 13 in the twentieth: thus the October Revolution (25 October OS, 1917) took place on 7 November NS.

Biographical dates are usually given in the text or the index.

Introduction:
the Geographical Setting

Russia's history and development have been critically shaped (like those of most countries) by its location and geography. For centuries the largest country on the planet, it spans Europe and Asia. Its position on the flat East-European plain places it on the periphery of the European peninsula, and left it historically open to attack but also able to expand. For much of its history Russia has been a frontier society; it has been marked by a constant imperative of defence, by steady growth of territory and empire, and by a continual movement of outward colonisation and settlement. A vast, poor country with a harsh climate, Russia has been remarkably successful over time in mobilising its resources for national survival.

*   *   *

The earliest state of the Eastern Slavs, Rus, centred upon the city of Kiev, emerged in the ninth and tenth centuries. Its lands lay between the Baltic and Black Seas and the Dnepr (Dnieper) and Volga rivers, astride the Eastern European plain. The location and nature of this area of settlement have had a decisive influence on the history of Rus and of Russia. Placed on the forested north-eastern edge of what would later become Europe, the new state was also inextricably tied into the life of the steppe which was open to Asia. The East European plain forms part of a great lowland corridor running from the Carpathian mountains in Romania to the low Ural range and on across western Siberia, ending with the Central Siberian Plateau beyond the River Yenisei: an immense flat land merging Asia with Europe, scarcely interrupted by any higher relief. Mountains rise only around its periphery. These lowlands have been given various names: the most recent synthesis, by David Christian, calls them Inner Eurasia, and contrasts them with the more fertile, settled and developed coastal lands of Outer Eurasia which encircled them. 'Inner Eurasia' is a coherent historical region, comparable to 'Europe', or 'Africa', or 'India'. Across this vast territory, climatic and ecological conditions forced choices and strategies on peoples who settled it which differentiated their societies fundamentally from those of China, India, or Southern and Western Europe. Many of them were pastoralists, herdsmen and horsemen, mobile over huge distances and also peculiarly suited by their lifestyle and organisation to warfare. In the forested north-west, however, farming had been practised for millennia, and it was greatly expanded by large-scale population movements from about AD 500 onwards.

The early history of the region is of migration, invasion and state-building by successive warrior races; Rus was one of many polities which rose and fell in Inner Eurasia. Some nomadic peoples combined transhumance with settlement, and built great cities at the centres of the empires they created. Russians in the nineteenth century sometimes identified themselves with the Scythians who settled the Pontic steppes north of the Black Sea in the first millennium BC, while Poles thought of themselves as the Sarmatians who displaced the Scythians about the time of Christ. The state of Rus was subjugated by the last and greatest of the steppe warrior nomads, the Mongol soldiers of Chingiz Khan, in the thirteenth century; and subsequent Russian rulers claimed the inheritance of the Mongol successor khans of the Golden Horde, as well as that of Byzantium. This political and cultural lineage was reinforced geographically by Muscovite Russia's later expansion into Siberia and Imperial Russia's into Central Asia.

The steppes lay open to other invaders too. Germanic tribes, such as the Goths, whose homeland lay near the Baltic, spread south and west across Europe in the great migrations of the fourth and fifth centuries AD. They moved, like the nomads, under pressures of population growth, economic need, or invasion by other peoples; some became first the auxiliaries, and then the destroyers of Rome. Not only Germans but Slavic populations originated in Eastern Europe, the Slavs somewhere near the Carpathians. Archaeological finds show early Slav settlements in the middle Dnepr and Dnestr area at the end of the pre-Christian era; slowly they spread further through what is now Ukraine and northwards towards the Baltic, mixing with resident Baltic and Finnic tribes. Slavic settlers also fanned out through Central Europe and into the Balkans.

Slavs first appear in the written record as warriors who in the sixth century AD crossed the Carpathians and moved eastwards, reaching Greece and Asia Minor. In AD 626 an army of Slavs allied with Central Asian Avars besieged Constantinople. In the eighth century the Slavs in what is now Central Europe reached equilibrium with Germanic neighbours further west, and a stable Slav–German frontier emerged along the Elbe and Saale rivers and into Bohemia. Southern Slavs established themselves in the Balkans and absorbed the Turkic Bulgars. The western branch of settlement crystallised into Slav Poland and the Czech kingdom. Rus, the first organised state of the eastern Slavs, emerged on the north-eastern periphery of what became Christendom and then Europe, and was one of the polities drawn into the Christian community in the ninth and tenth centuries. But its openness to the vast expanses of Inner Eurasia meant that its history, and especially its early history, was bound up as much with Asia as with Europe. The 'Eurasian' school of Russian historians claimed that this location produced a Russian civilisation quite distinct from that of European neighbours. In fact, Rus and Russia became an integral part of Europe and its civilisation as that developed in the second millennium AD. Even so, Russia's involvement in the events of Inner Eurasia and its eastern heritage have formed a fundamental component of its history and culture. Another, different and influential, approach to these geographical facts and Russia's location in respect of the European peninsula was the 'heartland' concept of Halford Mackinder, which sought to define the geopolitics of expansion.

Russia's position in the Eurasian lowlands also helps to explain the country's huge size: already at the end of the fifteenth century it was one the world's largest territorial states, and it continued to expand right up to the twentieth century. Even after 1991, when the Soviet Union split into separate parts, the core area of the Russian Federation, including Siberia, still occupies far more space than any other country: some 17,075,000 km.², about one-eighth of the world's land surface. Average population density, however, has always been low in comparison with the rest of Europe or even North America: it is currently 9 per km.². Russia is also continental, part of the Eurasian land-mass, unlike peninsular Central and Western Europe. While it now has extensive coastlines, these lie principally in the Arctic north or in the Pacific far east; and its topography and climate are unlike the varying and broken relief and more temperate climates of its western neighbours. Russia's territorial vastness and harsh climatic conditions carry inescapable consequences. One fundamental and perennial feature has been a weakness of provincial administration, the centre's difficulty in controlling and administering peripheral areas. The economy, and communication, travel and transportation, are similarly affected. Especially before the nineteenth century, which brought the telegraph and the railway, both government and commerce were limited by the sheer distances to be confronted across more than 8000 km. and 10 time-zones, and the vagaries of the seasons. Rivers were the major arteries of communication – they made possible the development of Rus. But rivers have their problems: rapids, shallows, spring floods and late summer drought, the winter freeze and dangerous, ice-block-filled thaw. In the long winters, packed snow and ice could provide an ideal sledging surface: travel was often easier than summer journeys over unmade rutted tracks or corduroy roads. Yet frosts and thaws fracture even well-paved surfaces. Spring thaw and autumn rains brought the worst travelling conditions of all, when tracks and roadways disappeared under water or dissolved in mud. Even in the modern period, with new methods and materials, road maintenance has remained an insuperably resource-expensive problem in many parts of the country.

The geography of Eastern Europe and Inner Eurasia combines northerly location with a cold, relatively dry, continental climate. The vegetation zones of the area reflect these characteristics. The far north, around the Arctic Circle, is tundra: a region of permafrost, with average temperatures about −10°C and snow-cover for most of the year, supporting sparse low trees and scrub, mosses and lichen. South of the tundra begins forest: the *taiga*, or boreal forest, vast coniferous woodlands – the world's largest softwood timber reserves – with some deciduous species, growing on poor, leached and often marshy soils. The taiga, stretching from the west right across Siberia, harboured animals which provided early Russia with a fabulously rich store of furs – as later in North America, the fur trade was a powerful stimulus to exploration and settlement.

Further south, the taiga merges into mixed forest of conifers – pine and spruce – and deciduous beech, maple and oak (much of these now cleared), which stretched as far south as Kiev and as far east as the Urals. Here too the soils, although richer, are relatively poor and with the short summer season and predominantly summer rainfall make agriculture difficult. Nevertheless, the mixed forest zone became the heartland of Rus and Muscovy. It is here that the main rivers of European Russia rise, giving inhabitants of the territory, and its rulers, valuable lines of communication. Forest offered protection against attack, whether from the steppe to the south, or from enemies further west. And from early times the forest was the determining context of Russian settlement and culture. The great nineteenth-century historian Vasilii Kliuchevskii wrote, looking back:

Right up until the mid-eighteenth century the life of most of the Russian people passed in the forest zone of our plains. The steppe invaded this life only in evil episodes, Tatar invasions, Cossack rebellions. As late as the seventeenth century, to a Westerner travelling from Smolensk to Moscow, Muscovy appeared an endless forest, in which towns and villages were simply larger or smaller clearings. ... The woodlands offered many benefits to the Russian who lived in them, economically, politically, even morally. They provided him with a house of pine or oak, heated it with birch and aspen wood, and lit it with birch tapers. The forest provided shoes of lime-tree bast, a variety of household utensils. ... The forest was the safest place of refuge from external enemies, taking the place of mountains and fortresses. The state itself, whose predecessor Rus had failed because it was too close to the steppes, could flourish only in the north, far away from Kiev, under the protection of the forest. ... [But at the same time,] the forest was always a burden for the Russian. In olden times, when there was too much of it, its thickets blocked roads and paths, reclaiming with their importunate outgrowth the meadows and fields cleared by painful work, and threatening man and domestic beasts with wolf and bear. Nests of robbers flourished in the forest, too. And the heavy labour with axe and fire to clear burn-land for farming was vexing and exhausting. ... The Russian never loved his forest.

Further south, on a line from Kiev through Tula, Riazan, and Kazan, the forest thins out into wooded steppe – ranges of grassland, interspersed with stands of deciduous woodland, which run for 2500 km. from the Carpathians to the Urals and eastward to the Yenisei. In the south, the wooded steppe gives way in turn to the grasslands of the open steppe, Russia's 'wide-open spaces'. These stretch down to the Black Sea, and further east shade into salt steppe and arid semi-desert north of the Caspian. The steppe soils are principally black earth (*chernozëm*), rich and fertile, providing great agricultural productivity despite low rainfall, across a long triangle 4000 km. from Ukraine into western Siberia. These lands were the grazing and hunting grounds of the migrant nomadic peoples. And for many centuries they remained a no-man's land, disputed frontier territory and the arena of steppe politics, in which Kievans, Muscovites, Poles and Lithuanians interacted with steppe invaders such as Pecheneg and Polovtsy, later with the Tatar heirs of Chingiz Khan and in Imperial times with other nomadic groups such as Kalmyk and Kazakh. Well into the eighteenth century, Muscovites, Poles and Ukrainians faced the Crimean Tatar descendants of the Mongols and other steppe peoples, who rode out into what Muscovites referred to as the 'wild field', raiding, plundering, and seizing Russian and Polish prisoners for the slave markets of the Crimea and Constantinople.

Thus for Kievan, Muscovite and Imperial governments, right into the modern period, the steppes were both threat and opportunity. They held the prospect of imminent destruction from powerful invaders: early rulers were bound into the diplomatic and military imperatives of Eurasian steppe politics, and defence and fortification were constant preoccupations. The eastern borderlands also represented an uncontrolled and unsettled space to be filled and exploited, with immense possibilities for expansion and trade. Russia was a frontier state, and for far longer than, say, America: the expanding frontier is one of the perennial features of Russian history. The relative emptiness of Siberia, conquered from its native peoples and from Tatar descendants of the Mongols in the sixteenth and seventeenth centuries, and the dangerous volatility of the southern 'wild field', required constant policing and defence, perpetually draining resources. Unlike America, moreover, Russia had to deal with frontier assimilation in the east and south while also confronting powerful rival neighbours elsewhere. This situation forced Russia's rulers to mobilise all their resources at an earlier stage, and more systematically, than most of their European counterparts. The costs over the centuries, in constant insecurity, population lost or diverted, in high defence expenditures and economic development foregone, were huge – although so were the opportunities. Siberia still retains many frontier features. The southern steppe frontier in what is now Ukraine closed when all land there was settled in the early nineteenth century; but later in the century, after the conquest and pacification of the Caucasus, Russian expansion further south-east opened a huge new frontier region beyond the Volga and into Central Asia. Russia's steady advance south-eastward in the nineteenth century alarmed the rulers of Britain's colonial possessions; Central Asia and Afghanistan became an arena of the 'great game' of empire and colonial expansion, and British imperialists saw Russia increasingly, though unrealistically, as a threat to British India.

Russian expansion was driven by economic and security issues, and the lack of boundaries or of powerful opposition; in some cases, like Britain, its rulers acquired territory 'in a fit of absence of mind'. But for some parts of the Russian population, frontier territories had a quite different significance. Peasants seeking new land to farm migrated (legally or illegally) to frontier areas. The frontier was also a refuge, a wilderness retreat for fugitives from the oppressively controlled Russian centre. Peasant dreams of a better life gave rise to utopian stories of lands beyond the reach of authority, like the mythical *Belovod'e* (Land of the White Water), lying somewhere in the Siberian Far East or Japan. Frederick Jackson Turner's dubious thesis of the American frontier as 'safety valve' and crucible of the nation has also been applied to Russia. Slav runaways and Tatar brigands gathered in the wild southern grasslands and settled on the great rivers, adopting the mobile, military lifestyle of the steppe nomads in order to survive: from them emerged the Cossack 'hosts' (militarised communities) of the southern steppes. The term 'Cossack' derives from a Turkic root meaning 'free man'. The untrammelled spaciousness of the Muscovite medieval frontier guaranteed freedom (*volia*) to the Cossacks in somewhat the same way that settlers and cowboys would later range armed, and self-reliant, on the North American prairie. *Volia*, one of two words for 'freedom' in Russian (the other, *svoboda*, conveys freedom under the law), also denotes 'will' or 'will-power'. *Volia* meant freedom to exercise one's own will, the ability to live under no other person's command. The early Cossacks were essentially a violent law unto themselves. Russian peasants, enserfed in the sixteenth and seventeenth centuries and denied ownership of the land they tilled, also yearned for *volia*, which for them meant freedom from interference by estate-owner or government. Russian religious dissenters, fleeing the official Church after the schism of the seventeenth century, likewise sought sanctuary on the periphery, often hiding in the forests and mountains of northern Russia and Siberia. In the mid-twentieth century Soviet explorers occasionally discovered hidden Siberian Old Believer (dissenter) villages whose inhabitants had no knowledge of the Bolshevik revolution and subsequent events.

The great river systems intersect both the forest and steppe zones. The flatness of the land did not break up watersheds and allowed huge waterways to develop. The Dnepr (2285 km.) is exceeded in length in European Russia only by the Volga, Europe's longest river (3700 km.), which links Moscow and the north-west with the Caspian Sea, while a short portage from Volga to Don gives access to the Sea of Azov, the Black Sea and the Mediterranean. Not surprisingly, attempts were made early on to link the Volga and Don; the project was only completed in 1952. Siberia's rivers eclipse even those of European Russia: the Yenisei (4090 km.), the Ob with its tributary the Irtysh (5410 km.) and the Lena (4,400 km.) rise near the Mongolian and Chinese borders and flow into the Arctic Ocean. For organisational purposes their northward flow is in the wrong direction – what Soviet planners saw as a 'defect of nature'; but their tributaries run conveniently east and west. In the southern part of the Russian Far East the Amur with its tributary the Ussuri (4510 km.) forms much of the border with China.

These rivers freeze over for much of the year, as do the seas bordering the old heartland of Rus and Russia in the north – the White Sea and the Baltic. Elsewhere, for much of Russian history, the territory was landlocked, the Pacific coast so distant as to constitute a largely separate economic sphere. Access to temperate seas, to opportunities for uninterrupted sea-borne trade and international communication became an aspiration of Russia's Muscovite and Imperial rulers. Rus's ability to send trading flotillas and sometimes military expeditions across the Black Sea was an important factor in Kievan relations with Byzantium. Beyond Constantinople lay the Mediterranean, accessible only in the late eighteenth century. Russians first reached the Pacific in the seventeenth century, while modern bases on the Baltic were acquired only in the eighteenth.

The lands of Rus lay athwart some of the greatest trading routes of the time. The 'road from the Varangians [Vikings] to the Greeks [Byzantines]' ran from the Baltic through the river systems of the Lovat-Volkhov and Western Dvina across the divide of the Valdai hills and adjacent uplands to the Dnepr, the Black Sea and the Bosphorus. The Volga offered a route for north-European traders to the markets of Baghdad, Arabia and later China. Novgorod, one of the oldest Rus cities, became rich through linking north-European commerce to the markets of Asia. Russia's contribution to this commerce was principally products of the forest – furs, game, honey, wax, timber – to which were later added hemp, flax, tallow and naval stores. After the conquest of Siberia, explorations of its fabulous mineral resources began. But Siberian mineral wealth was difficult to exploit. It was (and is) hard to reach, to turn into useable forms, and to deliver to centres of trade or consumption. In the eighteenth century Russian iron from the Urals, barge-borne along the waterways, could be bought more cheaply in Constantinople than in St Petersburg.

The way in which commerce and the economy developed also crucially affected the profile of Russian society. Rus, which built its prosperity to a considerable degree on long-distance trade, was relatively urbanised for its time. The Mongol conquest disrupted many commercial connections, and Muscovite Russia evolved as a more enclosed, agrarian economy, whose towns functioned more often as administrative centres or military strong-points: weak development of the market, and the autonomy of noble estate economies, did not support urbanisation or city independence. Into the nineteenth and twentieth centuries, Russian towns remained comparatively few, poor, and of little political significance; this has been a critical factor in the (under)development of civil society and the evolution of Russian political culture.

The facts of Russia's size, geography, geology and climate have thus imposed critical constraints on Russians' way of life, and on the country's development. Throughout their history Russians have had relatively poorer resources, greater security problems, and faced harsher conditions than almost any other major state in the Old or New Worlds. In this environment it is more difficult to live, work and to mobilise resources for survival in a competitive world. This is still a problem in the twentieth and twenty-first centuries, if less challenging than in the tenth and eleventh. It is in fact a problem shared by all Inner Eurasian societies, which differentiated them from the coastal societies of Outer Eurasia. In Christian's words: 'The societies that did most to shape the history of Inner Eurasia did so because they evolved successful ways of concentrating or mobilising the scarce human resources of a region of relatively low natural productivity.' In this hostile environment, the successive states of the Eastern Slavs have nevertheless proved themselves immensely successful. Russia became and has remained the largest territorial state in the world, with an economic and military potential which continues to make it a great power, even after the loss of its superpower status in 1991.

I

The Origins to 1300: Kiev and Sarai

The first East-Slav polity, Rus, centred in Kiev on the River Dnepr, emerged in the ninth century AD and became a major state of medieval Europe, especially after conversion to Eastern Christianity in 988, a step which influenced decisively its cultural and political orientations. In the thirteenth century Rus was conquered by the Mongol forces of the descendants of Chingiz Khan, and became part of the Mongol Empire. The Mongol rulers of the Khanate of Kipchak (the Golden Horde), the most westerly part of the Empire, made their capital Sarai, on the Volga.

KIEV RUS

The Origins of Rus

The origins of Kiev Rus are obscure. During the ninth century the Slav tribes of the region came to have as princes and rulers representatives of people named Rhos or Rus. The exact origin and identity of these Rus, and the process whereby they became leaders of a new political structure based on Novgorod and Kiev, remain unclear. The so-called Norman question has provoked controversy ever since it was first raised in the eighteenth century. Its starting point was an entry in the Russian Primary Chronicle or Tale of Bygone Years , the principal indigenous source for early Russian history. Written down in various stages in the eleventh twelfth centuries by monks based in Kiev, and designed to glorify the contemporary ruling dynasty, the Chronicle is an invaluable record from a time for which few sources exist, but a complex and difficult document. Under the years 859–62 the Chronicler noted that the local Slav and Finnish tribes, who had previously rejected Rus demands for tribute, found themselves so much at loggerheads that they decided to call upon the outsiders as arbiters and rulers:

> *859.* The Varangians from beyond the sea imposed tribute upon the Chuds, the Slavs, the Merians, the Ves, the Krivichians. But the Khazars imposed it upon the Polianians, the Severians and the Viatichians, and collected a squirrel-skin and a beaver-skin from each hearth.
> *860–62.* The tributaries of the Varangians drove them back beyond the sea, and, refusing them further tribute, set out to govern themselves. There was no law among them . . . And they began to war one against another. They said to themselves: 'Let us seek a prince who may rule over us and judge us according to law.' They accordingly went overseas to the Varangian Russes: these particular Varangians were called Russes, just as some are called Swedes, and others Normans, Angles and Goths, for they were thus named. The Chuds, the Slavs and the Krivichians then said to the people of Rus, 'Our whole land is great and rich, but there is no order in it. Come to rule and reign over us.' They thus selected three brothers [Riurik, Sineus and Truvor], with their kinsfolk, who took with them all the Russes, and migrated.

This tale, comparable to the story of the creation of Rome by Romulus and Remus, or the *Anglo-Saxon Chronicle*'s account of Hengist and Horsa, is a typical foundation myth. Other sources and archaeological evidence make clear, however, that warriors and traders called Rhos or Rus had indeed established themselves by this time in north-eastern Europe, and attempts have been made to identify a real prototype for the legendary leader Riurik, who was to give his name to the Kievan and Muscovite Russian dynasty. The Rus were of Scandinavian origin and came into the region to trade and raid, attracted especially by the supplies of silver drawn at this time from the markets of the Arab world. From the eighth century onwards, Scandinavian Norse society experienced a wave of expansion which took Vikings in their longships across the world, as raiders, explorers and merchants. Over some two centuries, Vikings reached or settled in North America, Iceland and Greenland, the

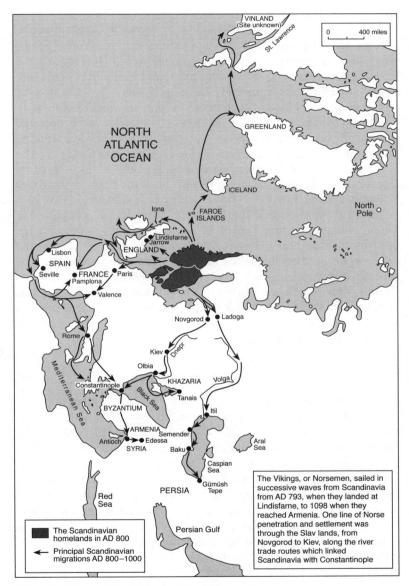

Map 1 Viking Migrations, AD 800–1000

© Sir Martin Gilbert, *The Routledge Atlas of Russian History* (London and New York, 2002), no. 11.

British Isles, France, Spain, the Sicilies, Armenia. Vikings provided the 'Varangian Guard' of the Byzantine Emperors in Constantinople. 'Varangians' likewise penetrated eastward in search of Asian goods, which they acquired in the markets of the Volga Bulgars and the kaghanate of Khazaria; their traces are found in the Slav lands too. These armed traders apparently developed more permanent links with Slavic and Finnish populations during the ninth century. In return for tribute, the Varangians offered protection from nomadic attack and competing Varangian raids, and in time became princes, ruling over tribal societies with their retinues (*druzhina*). The newcomers initially founded strong-points in the north. Riurikovo Gorodishche (Riurik's Town), a significant settlement on the River Volkhov, at Lake Ilmen, has been identified as a probable first base of the Rus. According to the Primary Chronicle, on accepting the Slavs' invitation Riurik settled in the city of Novgorod, and his brothers ruled in nearby towns. On their deaths Riurik became sole ruler; when he died in 879 or 882, the Chronicle reports, he was succeeded by his young son Igor, initially under the regency of Oleg (Helgi), who established himself in Kiev around 880. Igor was killed by rebellious tributaries in 945 and his widow Olga (Helga) ruled in Kiev until the accession of her son Sviatoslav, the first Riurikid ruler with a Slavic name, in 962.

Sviatoslav, Vladimir and the Conversion of Rus

By the time of Sviatoslav (962–72) Kiev Rus, now centred upon the middle Dnepr, had become a significant power. It was able to confront the other powers of the region, the Volga Bulgars, the Khazars, and even the Byzantine Empire. The empire or kaghanate of the Khazars was a conglomerate multi-ethnic state; its centre lay between the Black Sea and the Caspian. Its capital in later years was Itil, on the Volga above Astrakhan, but its writ ran far to the north and west, as well as south into the Caucasus. The Khazars took tribute from Slav tribes on the Dnepr, and Kiev was probably initially a Khazar town, or garrisoned by Khazar troops. They combined tribute-collecting increasingly with trade, and even with wealth from mining. Khazar dominance created a *pax khazarica* in the southern steppe in the eighth century, which also facilitated Slav migration. After briefly accepting Islam, the Khazar elites adopted Judaism as their state religion in 861. The Khazar empire had complex relations with Byzantium in the south; it was also a significant influence on the emergent Rus state.

In the 960s Sviatoslav expanded his territories, subjugating Khazar tributaries on the Oka and Volga rivers. He captured southern Khazaria, too, and in 965 destroyed Itil, which led to the collapse of Khazar power. The Rus dominated the whole Volga-Caspian trade route, as well as the Dnepr and the Pontic (Black Sea) steppes. But the fall of Khazaria freed the southern steppe for the nomadic Pechenegs, who, ironically, now became a greater threat to Rus, sometimes allying with its princes, often threatening them, able to besiege Kiev in 969. At the same time Sviatoslav sacked the capital of the Volga Bulgars, Bolgary; and, at the request of the Byzantine Emperor, he turned south-west and defeated the Danubian Bulgars. But his conquests were fragile. Plans to consolidate his hold on the Danube were frustrated by the Byzantines, and on his way home Sviatoslav was killed by Pechenegs: following nomadic custom, they made his skull into a drinking cup.

Rus relations with Byzantium throughout the tenth century were marked by both conflict and collaboration, and are reflected in Arab and Byzantine as well as Kievan sources. The first Varangian Rus attack on the Eastern Empire had been mounted in 861. Others, to gain booty and favourable commercial opportunities, followed in 907, 941 and 971, leading to successive treaties regulating Byzantine–Rus relations and Rus trading rights in Constantinople (911, 944, 971). In 957 Olga personally led a delegation to the Byzantine capital, where she was received by the Emperor Constantine VII, who was well aware of the new power to the north. Byzantium remained of immense cultural importance to Rus even in its decline, up to its capture by the Ottoman Turks in 1453.

The death of Sviatoslav led to fierce battle between his sons in 977 for control of his inheritance. One was killed and the youngest, Vladimir, fled to Scandinavia and the protection of the king of Norway. He returned with a Varangian war-band and successfully took control of Kiev, assassinating his half-brother Yaropolk. The reign of Vladimir Sviatoslavich (980–1015) marked the final consolidation of Kiev Rus from a congeries of tributary tribes into a relatively coherent polity. He both completed the consolidation of his lands and established himself as Great Prince and their unquestioned master. Vladimir developed Kiev as his capital, and founded new towns and settlements in its hinterland, peopling them with settlers

Map 2 Kiev Rus in the Ninth Century

© Sir Martin Gilbert, *The Routledge Atlas of Russian History* (London and New York, 2002), no. 12.

from further north. He also expanded the rudimentary forms of central administration which Olga had introduced in place of older tribal arrangements. Besides using officials responsible directly to the prince, Vladimir followed his father in assigning different parts of the realm (principal cities and their territory) to different sons: each prince, with his own military retinue, became responsible for revenue collection, civil order and defence. In the reign of Vladimir's son Yaroslav (the Wise, 1019–54) the first law-code was issued, the *Russkaia Pravda* (*Russian Truth* or *Russian Justice*), which formed the basis of Russian civil law for several centuries to come, in conjunction with Church law derived from Byzantium.

Rus was initially a pagan state, whose peoples worshipped Slav and Finnish deities, and on his accession Vladimir set up a pantheon on a prominent site in Kiev. The Rus elites, however, were not untouched by religious currents around them. While the Khazar rulers practised Judaism, and the spread of Islam reached the Volga Bulgars in the early tenth century, Christianity was gaining ground throughout southern and eastern Europe. In the Balkans the Byzantine monks Cyril and Methodius had translated scriptures and liturgy from Greek into Glagolitic, a newly devised written form of Slavonic, and converted the Danubian Bulgars in 864. Poland accepted Christianity from Rome in the 960s, as did the Hungarian Magyars *c*.985. Further north, the Danish king Harald Bluetooth converted in 965, the Norwegians in 993. Byzantine Christianity was already familiar to the Rus: in 867 the Byzantine Patriarch Photius had established a diocese to minister to Slav and Varangian converts. On her visit to Constantinople in 957 Olga had accepted Christian baptism, and following a Rus embassy to the Holy Roman Emperor at Frankfurt, Otto I sent a Catholic bishop to Kiev in 960. But Olga's initiative provoked opposition among the pagan Kievan elite: her son Sviatoslav feared that his retinue would mock him if he converted. It was left to Sviatoslav's son, Vladimir, to undertake this momentous step, for himself and his people, in 988.

The famous account in the Primary Chronicle, under AD 987, portrays Vladimir's decision as the result of a spiritual search: after visits by proselytising representatives of the monotheistic faiths (Muslim Bulgars, Jewish Khazars, Catholic Germans, Orthodox Greek Byzantines), he sends out emissaries to enquire further. The latter, unimpressed with their first encounters, are overwhelmed by the glory of Byzantine Christianity: 'The Greeks led us to the edifices where they worship their God, and we knew not whether we were in heaven or on earth. . . . We only know that God dwells there among men, and their service is fairer than the ceremonies of other nations: for we cannot forget that beauty.' However, the conversion was more probably the consequence of practical factors. The monotheistic religions espoused by powerful neighbours were attractive instruments of political integration and social control. Conversion could bring *rapprochement* with the cultural and economic power-centre of Byzantium. In 987 Emperor Basil II faced a serious rebellion, and desperately needed a powerful ally. In return for decisive military assistance, Vladimir insisted upon an alliance and the hand of an Imperial princess: but for Anna Porphyrogenita, Basil's sister, marriage to a barbarian would have infringed both Byzantine tradition and Imperial law, unless he first converted. In 988 Vladimir gained his princess, was baptised and married, and returned to Kiev to overthrow the pagan pantheon. He cast off his concubines and multiple wives and, according to the Chronicle, ordered the population of Kiev to undergo compulsory mass baptism in the Dnepr. Kiev Rus became a Metropolitanate of the Eastern Church, with bishoprics in Belgorod, Novgorod and Chernigov, its Metropolitan appointed by the Patriarch of Constantinople.

The conversion of Rus to Christianity was a triumph both for Vladimir and for Byzantium, which now extended its influence far to the north. The conversion had immense significance for Russia. Vladimir committed Rus to the Christian world, to what would later become Europe. Its culture was to be derived from Byzantium. Anna was accompanied to Kiev by a retinue of Greek clergy, and Vladimir fetched Greek master-craftsmen, who built the Church of the Tithe (991–6) in Kiev, the first major Christian structure of Rus. It was followed by Cathedrals of St Sophia in Kiev and Novgorod. With these architectural monuments came the Byzantine arts of the fresco and the icon. The Byzantine princess brought with her not only the majesty and religion of Byzantium, but also its literate culture, artistic forms, political and legal norms, and the Eastern monastic tradition. The new metropolitanate developed a written language of its own, Church Slavonic, derived from the Cyrillic Glagolitic alphabet; and the Rus gained access to Byzantine religious and secular texts and chronicles. The medieval Russian code of Church law known as the *Book of the Helmsman* (*Kormchaia kniga*) was a Byzantine compilation. In time Kiev Rus produced its own literary culture, with

The spread of Christianity led to the division of the Slav world. The Croats (in AD 700) and the Poles (in AD 999) were converted to Roman Catholicism. The Serbs (in AD 700), Bulgars (AD 865) and Russians (AD 988) were converted to Eastern(Orthodox) Catholicism, This led in particular to strong antipathy between Russians and Poles, and also between Serbs and Croats.

The spread of Eastern, or Orthodox, Catholicism, under Constantinople's authority by AD 1000

Western,or Roman, Catholicism

Areas under Muslim, or Islamic, rule

0   400 miles

Map 3   The Slavs and Christianity

© Sir Martin Gilbert, *The Routledge Atlas of Russian History* (London and New York, 2002), no. 15.

texts such as the historical *Sermon on Law and Grace* (*c*.1050) of Metropolitan Hilarion. From a somewhat later period, probably the late twelfth century, dates the most famous work of early Russian literature, rediscovered in 1810, the epic *Lay of Igor's Host* (*Slovo o Polku Igoreve*), which provided the subject of Borodin's opera *Prince Igor*. However the adoption of Byzantine rather than Roman Christianity hindered the spread of Latin, and the creation of a Slavonic church vernacular meant that the Rus were relatively little exposed to the Greek language.

Vladimir's choice of Eastern, Orthodox rather than Western, Roman Catholic Christianity had other far-reaching consequences. After the schism between the Eastern and Western Churches of 1054, Rus was distanced (though not so completely as often thought) from cultural and intellectual developments in Catholic Europe. Tensions between Orthodox and Catholic later played a significant role in relations between Russia and western neighbours, especially Poland. Orthodox liturgy and theology were of immense importance in the development of Russian culture and world-view. The Byzantine tradition emphasised ritual, prayer and the adoration rather than the theological construction of God. Intellectual enquiry developed late and learning remained monastic: apart from Ohrid (Macedonia) in the ninth century, the Orthodox lands produced no universities until the early modern period. After the decline of Constantinople, no single centre could claim the universal authority which Rome exercised in the Catholic lands. Orthodox traditions also deeply influenced Russian arts, notably in the dominance of icons, which are not representational paintings but symbolic depictions intended to draw both the painter and the viewer into the realm of the spiritual and divine. Representational and secular forms of art came late to Russia. Orthodoxy frowned likewise on instrumental music: the subsequent magnificent choral tradition of Russian sacred music coexisted with official persecution of folk instruments played by the wandering minstrels (*skomorokhi*), and determined resistance to European instrumental music, until the time of Peter I. Of equal significance was the Eastern tradition of monastic life, which found its fullest expression in the communities of Mount Athos in Greece. The earliest Kievan monastery, the *Pecherskaia Lavra* (Monastery of the Caves), was founded by the Athonite monk and later Saint, Antonii, at Kiev *c*.1050. Monasteries became principal centres of spiritual life and of learning and culture. In time they also provided a crucial focus of colonisation and settlement on the far peripheries; they became major landowners; and with the building of massive masonry walls they doubled as fortresses and refuges in times of conflict (Figure 1). Despite Vladimir's decisive actions after his conversion, and the influx of Byzantine personnel and cultural influences which crucially shaped the lives of the Rus elite, Christianity spread slowly among the popular masses. Initial active opposition – in Novgorod an uprising took place against the desecration of pagan idols – was short-lived. But pagan beliefs and local customs died hard, and in Rus as elsewhere the new religion tolerated and in some cases adapted itself to older belief systems: reverence for spirits of the forest and the home, ancestor worship, animistic and magical practices. This syncretism, which characterised Russian popular religion even into modern times, has sometimes been called 'dual belief' (*dvoeverie*). Institutional Christianity nevertheless imposed itself without difficulty in Rus as the official system, and provided both the basis for a

Figure 1 Monastery/fortress: like many others, the well-fortified Pokrovskii Monastery (nunnery) at Suzdal also served as refuge and gaol

From the personal collection of the author.

common state-wide culture, and the theoretical justification for the rule of the Kievan and Muscovite princely house of Riurik.

The population over whom the Riurikid princes consolidated their sway was overwhelmingly rural: peasants who lived principally by agriculture. Although Rus was a slave-owning society, the peasantry were free; they supported themselves, and the urban populations and urban-based elite, by slash-and-burn agricultural techniques and by cultivation, principally of cereals, in forest clearings, supplemented by animal husbandry. They also fished, hunted and gathered produce (berries, mushrooms, nuts, honey and wax) in the forest. Households, which had individual landholdings, were usually grouped into villages or hamlets, and formed part of a territorially-based commune or local association (*verv* or *mir*), sharing common land and amenities. The communes bore general or collective responsibility for the payment of taxes and discharge of other legal obligations by individual members or families.

Besides its essentially rural base, Rus also came to possess a significant urban society, reflecting the importance of commerce in its development: probably 13–15 per cent of the population lived in its relatively numerous and well-developed towns. The largest cities of Rus stood comparison with major cities elsewhere in contemporary Europe. They were the seats of princes and Church dignitaries, who had large households; these persons sometimes also owned estates in the countryside. The majority of the urban population consisted of artisans, small-scale traders and free unskilled labourers. Between them and the elite stood wealthier merchants, both native and foreign, while the lowest rungs of the social ladder were occupied by dependent workers and slaves. The towns also had communal organisations, town assemblies (*veche*). The relationship of the prince and his retainers to the townsfolk was of central importance: while the Great Prince assigned cities to individual princes, the latter had to rely on their townsfolk for efficient routine administration. Moreover, the druzhina alone was rarely sufficient on campaign without reinforcement by the local population and its militia. Sometimes princes fell out with their townspeople and were ejected; sometimes the veche would elect or invite a prince to rule it. Novgorod in particular developed a strong tradition of local autonomy, with elected urban leaders (*posadniki*); and the veche bell of Novgorod became a symbol of its independence.

Conflict arose not only, on occasion, between prince and townsmen, but also between members of the ruling house. By assigning cities or principalities with their lands to his sons (their 'appanage' [*udel*] or personal estate), Vladimir sought to strengthen Kiev's central hold over outlying regions, to consolidate the new religion there, and especially to avoid the renewal of fratricidal strife. Under Vladimir's descendants a clear system of succession emerged among the Riurikid princes, not unlike that practised in other steppe communities. All brothers of the royal blood shared in ruling the country. The senior prince held Kiev and the title of Great Prince;* the others received portions according to seniority, and would move up to another seat on the death of an elder relative or for similar reason. The principle of collateral succession and the rotation of seats provided a clear rule of succession and a method of providing for all sons and their retainers. Significant grey areas remained, however: seniority could be measured by various criteria. Cracks soon appeared in the system, and after Vladimir's death the problem became increasingly difficult as the Riurikid clan diverged into ever-more branches and sub-branches. In 1097 the leading princes met at the town of Liubech in an attempt to negotiate the problems of succession. They were only partly successful. Their internecine feuding should not be seen as something peculiar to Rus: it compares with wars in, say, Saxon and Norman England, France or Scandinavia in the same period. However, right up to the Mongol conquest in the thirteenth century, princely rivalry remained a major source of strife and disunity, and the tradition continued under the Mongols too, until a new unified polity emerged under the Great Princes of Moscow in the fifteenth century.

Under Vladimir and Yaroslav and their successors, to the reign of Vladimir Monomakh (Great Prince 1113–25), Kiev Rus remained a unitary state. Its status and integration into the contemporary world is illustrated by the frequent marriage alliances which its princes made with other ruling families across Europe – English, French, German, Hungarian, Lithuanian, Mongol, Polish, Scandinavian, and the Byzantines. The architecture of the principal cities also testified to the majesty of the Kievan rulers: thus Yaroslav celebrated his final defeat of the Pechenegs in 1036 with a major construction

---

* The term *Velikii kniaz* is translated here as Great Prince when it refers to the ruler. In the Imperial period, when the ruler was titled *Imperator* or *Tsar*, his brothers received the title *Velikii kniaz*, translated as Grand Duke.

Table 1   The Principal Rulers/Great Princes of Rus

[Riurik]		Yaropolk	1132–39
Oleg	c.880–912	Viacheslav	1139–46
Igor	912–45	Yurii Dolgorukii	1149–57
Olga, regent	945–62	Andrei Bogoliubskii	1157–74
Sviatoslav	945–72	Vsevolod	
Yaropolk	972–80	'of the Big Nest'	1176–1212
Vladimir (St Vladimir)	980–1015	Yurii	1212--38
Sviatopolk the Damned	1015–19	Yaroslav	1238–46
Yaroslav the Wise	1019–54	Sviatoslav	1246–48
Iziaslav	1054--78	Andrei	1248–52
Sviatoslav	1073–76	Aleksandr Nevskii	1252–63
Vsevolod	1078–93	Yaroslav	1264–71
Sviatopolk	1093–113	Vasilii	1272–76
Vladimir Monomakh	1113–25	Dmitrii	1277–94
Mstislav	1125–32	Andrei	1294–1304

programme in Kiev, centred upon the new Cathedral of St Sophia, and other magnificent stone churches still survive from the eleventh and twelfth centuries. But as the Kievan economy changed and grew, the relative significance of individual cities and princely holdings altered, and over the following century Kiev Rus evolved effectively into a federal union of principalities, each increasingly associated with a different branch of the dynasty: in 1237 the number of principalities was 15. The princes of different areas developed their own regional power and expanded diplomatic relations with the foreign power centres nearest to them, and Kiev's importance gradually declined.

The Pre-eminence of Vladimir-Suzdal

As part of these developments, in the twelfth century a new focus of power emerged in the north: the region of Vladimir-Suzdal. The city of Vladimir was founded on the Kliazma river in 1108 by Yurii Dolgorukii ('Long Arm'), prince (1125–57) of Rostov and Suzdal and briefly Great Prince of Kiev. Other towns and local frontier posts soon followed, among them Moscow, first mentioned in the Chronicle under 1147. Under Yurii Dolgorukii's son and successor Andrei Bogoliubskii (1157–74), Vladimir-Suzdal grew in importance. Andrei strengthened Vladimir with major fortification works and beautified it with stone churches, including the lovely Church of the Veil or Intercession on the Nerl river (Figure 2). During wars over the Kievan succession, in 1169 Andrei's troops took and sacked Kiev: but he chose to stay in the north rather than occupy the Kievan seat himself, and also attempted, though unsuccessfully, to transfer

Figure 2 The Church of the Intercession, on the River Nerl near Vladimir

From the personal collection of the author.

the metropolitanate to Vladimir. The sack of 1169 has traditionally been seen as a landmark event, indicative of the fragmentation of the Kievan state. More recently scholars have argued that Bogoliubskii in fact went to war to preserve the traditional succession system, and that 1169 marks less the decline of Kiev than the growing strength of the different regions within Rus at this time, for which Kiev nevertheless still represented the political centre. At least it is clear that the divergent interests and constant internecine rivalry of the Riurikid princes absorbed valuable resources, and undermined the unity essential to face external threats.

THE MONGOLS: THE 'TATAR YOKE'

The Mongol Conquest of Rus

Besides their relations with each other, and with neighbouring settled rulers, the Rus princes faced the danger of the steppe. War against nomad armies was a persistent feature of Kievan life. After the fall of Khazaria, Rus fought protracted wars against the Pechenegs. In 1055 the Kipchak Cumans or Polovtsy appeared in the steppe, and remained a major threat for the next two centuries. In 1096 they attacked Kiev and burnt the Caves Monastery. The defeat at their hands of Prince Igor Sviatoslavich of Novgorod-Seversk in 1185 inspired the *Lay of Igor's Host*. Relations later became more cooperative, including alliances and intermarriage. But the Rus proved powerless before the last and greatest of the steppe invaders, the Mongol cavalry of Chingiz Khan.

The empire of the Mongols – or as the Rus sources somewhat incorrectly called them, Tatars – was constructed with remarkable speed during the thirteenth century. In 1215 they took Beijing, completing their conquest of China. Then they advanced further west. Mongols first appeared in the western steppe in 1223, when a large army led by Chingiz Khan's grandson Batu swept through Rus territory, decisively defeated a coalition of Rus and Polovtsy at the Kalka river, and disappeared again. The Rus princes failed to unite or to strengthen their territories in the face of this powerful, unknown enemy. In 1229–36 the Mongols mounted successful attacks on the Polovtsy and the Volga Bulgars but in 1237 they turned back to Rus. They swept all before them, destroying the northern Rus princes at the battle of Sit in 1238 and conquering south-western Chernigov and Galicia the following year. Kiev fell in 1240, although major Rus centres in the north (notably Novgorod, which submitted without being overrun) escaped the destruction visited on the south. The Mongols possessed huge numbers, superior weaponry including heavy siege machinery, excellent military organisation and mobility, and they benefited from the unreadiness and disunity of their Rus opponents. By 1242, when the Mongol advance halted, all Rus was subjected, and their armies were pressing upon Poland and Hungary.

In 1242 the Great Khan died, and Batu turned back to Karakorum in Mongolia, to take part in the Mongol succession process. Rus remained the most westerly part of the Mongol conquests: the westward advance was not renewed. On his return, Batu organised his domain into a separate khanate within the Mongol Empire, called among other names Kipchak (Desht-i-Kipchak), but known in later Russian and European sources as the Golden Horde. Besides the former Rus principalities it included a huge swathe of the southern steppe, from the Danube east into the northern Caucasus, and beyond the Volga to the Aral Sea. Its capital was Sarai on the lower Volga, which over the following century grew into a major city with great buildings and an elaborate water supply, and became an international centre of trade and diplomacy. Rus was not of major importance in the overall Mongol scheme of things. The Kipchak khanate was subordinate to the Great Khan in Karakorum, and its politics reflected those of the Mongol Empire and its own ruling factions.

The devastations of the Mongol conquest produced major shifts of power and population in Rus. Many inhabitants of older centres fled: cities such as Moscow and Tver took in the fugitives. Nevertheless the essential structures remained in place. Although many individual princes had been killed, the ruling Riurikid house survived, and largely continued its previous customs. However, princes now ruled at the pleasure of the khan, who issued a patent (*yarlyk*) confirming their rights, usually in a face-to-face ceremony at Sarai. In 1243 Prince Yaroslav of Vladimir paid homage in this way, and was confirmed as Great Prince of both Kiev and Vladimir: the central seat of Riurikid power now moved finally from south to north-east. Some princes were sent on the far more arduous journey to Karakorum to receive confirmation, or to be judged. The Orthodox Church retained its place and role in Rus society, and was patronised by the new overlords, who were tolerant in religious matters and treated it favourably as regarded taxation and land-holding.

The Mongols largely lived in the steppe, and usually intervened in the affairs of Kievan princes and cities only to assert their will and to raise tribute in taxes and levies. Mongol rulers made specific demands of all subject peoples. They required provisions and support troops for their armies, and maintenance of the extraordinarily efficient Mongol post system (*yam*). They enforced censuses, and payment of taxes accordingly, with the provision of hostages; governors were appointed to ensure submission and good order; and the prince was compelled to appear in person before the khan. The burdens imposed were very considerable, in both money and manpower: Rus towns paid taxes and tribute, their soldiers fought in Mongol armies, and their men built Mongol cities. However, Rus princes were able to manage their own lands in collaboration with Mongol prefects (*baskaki*) and other officials; they were also drawn into Mongol affairs, some living for long periods at Sarai, and they could equally make use of Mongol power in their own interest. Skilful use of Mongol patronage was one of the bases for the later rise of Moscow. Under Mongol suzerainty the princes also maintained their own military forces and conducted military operations, against each other and external enemies.

The Chingisid Kipchak khans were soon accepted by the Rus princes as their legitimate suzerains. Princely authority was now determined among Riurikid rivals by the grant of the khan's yarlyk. Byzantium remained outside the sphere of Mongol conquest and adopted a policy of accommodation and alliance with Sarai, which meant that Rus religious opposition to the conquerors, who accepted Islam definitively in the early fourteenth century, did not develop until much later; the Mongols for their part protected the Kievan Church. The career of Aleksandr Nevskii, prince of Novgorod and Vladimir, a heroic figure of Russian history and legend, provides a graphic illustration of the relationship between Riurikid princes, their cities, and their new suzerains. Elected by Novgorod in 1236 as its prince, he defended its territories against major threats from the west: Swedish expansion was a long-standing danger, and in 1240 Aleksandr won his soubriquet 'Nevskii' with a victory over Swedish forces on the River Neva, at the eastern end of the Gulf of Finland. Two years later he blocked the advance of the crusading Teutonic Knights of Livonia in a battle on the frozen Lake Peipus (in present-day Estonia). These battles, which secured the western Rus borderlands, gave Nevskii the image of a saviour of Rus, and subsequently

Map 4   The Republic of Novgorod, 997–1478

© Sir Martin Gilbert, *The Routledge Atlas of Russian History* (London and New York, 2002), no. 18.

led to his canonisation (1547), and in modern times under Stalin to his celebration in Sergei Eizenshtein's famous patriotic film *Aleksandr Nevskii*. After his father Yaroslav's death in 1245, Nevskii made visits to the Horde and Karakorum which resulted first (1246) in the allocation to him of southern Russia, including Kiev; after a second visit, a Mongol army drove his rebellious brother out of Vladimir, and he received the yarlyk as Great Prince (1252). He maintained his position by continuing close cooperation with and obedience to the Mongol overlords, in which he was supported by the Metropolitan, and by making frequent visits to the Horde. His loyalty to Sarai, which is much less clearly reflected in his legend as saint and national saviour than his feats against western enemies, won him the confidence of the khan and strengthened his hand in dealings with his subjects and other princes; it also provided protection for his lands from any harsher Mongol intervention.

Appanage Rus

The Mongol domination, later often called the 'Tatar Yoke', under which the Rus lands lived for more than two centuries (c.1240–1480), completed the fragmentation of the Kievan state. The growing separation of the principalities before the conquest, especially the division between north-east and south-west, was now accentuated, and under Mongol impact the princely holdings of each branch of the dynasty splintered further, subdividing into smaller appanages. Some south-western territories of the Kievan state in time came under other lordships: in 1349 Poland acquired most of the former Rus principality of Galicia, while Lithuania gained Polotsk, Kiev itself, and other southern lands. The unity of the Orthodox Church was also threatened: the new Polish and Lithuanian overlords, soon both Roman Catholic, were naturally interested in bringing Church government more closely under their own control. In 1299 the Metropolitan of Rus, head of the Church in all the Rus lands, moved his seat informally from Kiev to Vladimir, and during the following century repeated attempts were made to establish separate metropolitanates in the now Polish and Lithuanian Orthodox territories. The declaration of Muscovite autocephaly in 1448 (see below) brought divisions among these Orthodox in the south; in 1596 a considerable number accepted the Union of Brest which created the Ukrainian Greek Catholic (also known as Uniate)

Church, whose members acknowledge the supremacy of the Pope in Rome but, like the other Eastern Catholic Churches, retain their own liturgy. The Ukrainian Greek Catholic Church has continued to exist on territory divided and subsequently redivided among several powers (Austria, Poland, Muscovite and Imperial Russia/the Soviet Union), all of which have encouraged or persecuted it according to their own purposes.

The dispersion of Kiev Rus territories marks a hiatus; the continuity of Russian history at this point has been a matter of controversy. From the Muscovite and Russian point of view, an obvious line of connection lay in the continuing rule of the Riurikids and the integrity of the Russian Orthodox Church: the ruling house of Rus survived under the Mongols, and as the suzerain's power waned, the Riurikid princes of Moscow, with the support of later Metropolitans, gradually 'gathered the Rus lands' into the Muscovite Russian state, which looked back to Riurik as its founder. The same view prevailed in the Russian Empire and Soviet Union. Soviet historians consistently wrote, for instance, of the later 'reunification' of Kiev with Russia in 1667, when it was ceded by Poland-Lithuania at the end of the Thirteen Years' War (1654–67). Alternatives have been propounded, however, to the Great-Russian historical narrative. Territorially, the Muscovite state never coincided exactly with Rus. The annexation of Kiev in the seventeenth century was the result of the incorporation into the Muscovite empire of the Hetman Ukraine, the land of the semi-autonomous Cossacks. In the nineteenth century, when nationalist feeling stirred in the Russian Empire, the first Ukrainian nationalist group to emerge called itself the Society of Cyril and Methodius, looking back to the 'apostles of the Slavs' with whom Kiev's Christian culture was associated. The Greek Catholic Church has retained many adherents. The millennium of the conversion in 1988 brought great rivalry between those who saw it as Russian, and those who claimed it as a Ukrainian celebration, and the latter viewpoint sees itself justified by the (re)creation of an independent Ukraine in 1991.

The role of Lithuania and Poland as successor states of Rus was also important. Lithuania, the closest western neighbour of Rus, was spared Mongol invasion, and successfully resisted encroachments from Sweden and the knightly Teutonic Order of Livonia. In the fifteenth century it became a major power and later the largest state in Europe, stretching from the Baltic to the Black Sea; it might have absorbed Rus but for the latter's Mongol overlords. It was able to withstand Mongol pressure, involve itself in the politics of the declining Golden Horde, and gain territory at the Horde's expense. It converted to (Roman) Christianity rather later than most other polities of the region, when its Great Prince Jagiello married the Polish queen in 1386. Lithuanian princes had close dealings, and diplomatic and marriage ties, with their Rus neighbours, and *boyars* (senior members of aristocratic houses) from each community joined the other's elite. Poland also benefited (as we have seen) from the break-up of Rus. Subsequently, in 1569, in the face of growing Muscovite power, Poland and Lithuania amalgamated under Sigismund II to form a Polish-Lithuanian 'commonwealth' including much of the formerly Rus south-west. Most of these lands were incorporated into the Imperial Russian state only in the eighteenth century, 400 years after they passed out of Rus jurisdiction.

Under Mongol rule the Riurikid princes continued to vie for position in Rus. Nevskii was one of the most successful, and the ultimate winners in these complex manoeuvrings were the descendants of Nevskii's younger son, Daniil of Moscow (d. 1303): the Daniilovichi. According to the traditional rules governing the Riurikid succession this line, a cadet branch, had no right to the Great Princely title. Its princes nevertheless successfully demonstrated their value as servitors to the khans, and manipulated the politics of Horde–Riurikid relations to establish themselves on the Great Princely throne. This involved a prolonged struggle with other Riurikids opposed to them, in which Mongol military forces played an important part. After a tussle with Tver, their tenure of the Great Princely title became permanent with the grant of the yarlyk about 1327 to Ivan Daniilovich Kalita, otherwise known as Ivan I of Moscow.

2

1300–1600
Moscow and Novgorod: The Emergence of Empire and Absolute Rule

Under the Daniilovich princes, Moscow subordinated all rival principalities and became the political centre of Rus. The Moscow princes
vastly expanded their territorial holdings, initially at the expense of
Rus rivals, then by the conquest of successor khanates of the Golden
Horde, which broke up in the fifteenth century: the foundations of
empire. As a result of bitter civil wars in the mid-fifteenth century,
and the ideological myth-making of Moscow churchmen, a new
theory and practice of absolute princely rule emerged, the foundation
of autocracy, which was taken to its extreme in the reign of Ivan IV,
the Terrible. In the process the oligarchical city republic of Novgorod,
representative of a different political model, was crushed and
absorbed. This period also saw the establishment of peasant serfdom.

THE PRINCIPALITY OF MOSCOW

The Rise of Moscow

During the period 1300–1550 Moscow rose from minor principality
to seat of the Tsar of All Rus. Moscow was an unlikely candidate for
pre-eminence among the principalities of Rus: a late foundation, a
minor town within the established principality of Vladimir-Suzdal,
and the seat of a cadet Riurikid line. The reasons for its rise have

been much debated. Its princes' ability to retain the support of the khans was a critical factor. Mongol favour depended upon loyalty, active support of the khan's interests, and regular delivery of tax-based tribute and gifts, and in this the Daniilovichi were very successful: Ivan I (nicknamed 'Moneybags') assumed responsibility for collecting Rus tribute, a task previously performed by Mongol officials. Moscow's princes also wielded the khan's favour against competitors, especially the principality of Tver. The Tver princes became increasingly powerful under the Mongol domination, and had a better dynastic claim to the Great Princely throne: conflict and rivalry lasted into the fifteenth century. The Daniilovichi were successful in expanding their territorial holdings, accumulating lands by marriage, inheritance and purchase as well as by direct military intervention. Partly by the good fortune of timely deaths in the family, they managed for a considerable time to avoid the quarrels and fragmentation of holdings which resulted elsewhere from collateral succession claims and the distribution of appanages to princely sons. Their marriage policy forged family ties with both allies and competitors, whose support as well as whose lands they could then claim. And geography favoured them too. Moscow was better situated in terms of communications and commerce, and more secure from attack, than many (though not all) of its rivals. Moreover the Daniilovich princes husbanded their resources carefully and attracted new servitors and population from other areas.

They likewise benefited from the support of the Church. In 1326 the seat of the Metropolitan of Rus was transferred to Moscow, when Metropolitan Pëtr (Peter) took up residence there: in a contested election the Moscow princes had supported his candidacy. On Pëtr's death he was buried in Moscow and canonised, his tomb becoming a shrine which conferred great prestige on the Muscovites; thereafter all Metropolitans resided in the city. The close relationship between

Table 2   The Daniilovich Rulers of Muscovy

Ivan I Moneybags	1328–41	Vasilii II, the Blind	1425–62
Semën, the Proud	1341–53	Ivan III, the Great	1462–1505
Ivan II, the Meek	1353–59	Vasilii III	1505–33
Dmitrii Donskoi	1359–89	Ivan IV, the Terrible	1533–84
Vasilii I	1389–1425	Fëdor I	1584–98

Orthodox Church and princely power, which worked greatly to Moscow's advantage, was enhanced when the Russian Orthodox Church became effectively autocephalous in 1448. In 1439 Constantinople and Rome had agreed the Union of Florence, under which the Eastern Orthodox Church acknowledged papal authority. Metropolitan Isidore of Moscow had subscribed to it, but the ensuing Russian Church Council rejected the union and disavowed Isidore, and a subsequent synod elected a new Metropolitan without reference to Constantinople. When Byzantium fell to the Turks five years later, this was seen as divine punishment; Moscow remained as the bearer and upholder of 'true' Orthodoxy.

Moscow's princes also benefited from the wisdom of other churchmen, notably St Sergii of Radonezh (1314–92), the greatest figure of the early Russian monastic tradition. Sergii's famous hagiographic biography, written in the early fifteenth century, recounts his initial personal search for spiritual advancement as an isolated ascetic and forest hermit. His piety soon attracted followers, however, and led c.1335 to the founding near Moscow of the Holy Trinity (later Trinity-Sergius) Monastery, of which he reluctantly became abbot and which subsequently became the centre of the Russian Orthodox Church. Most early Rus monasteries were urban, and monastic vows had not precluded the pursuit of previous secular activities. Sergii now inspired a remarkable series of remote cenobitic (communal) monastic foundations. His disciples and colleagues went out into the wilderness and repeated the pattern of the Holy Trinity settlement. Within a century some 150 new monasteries emerged across northern Rus, as far as the White Sea, where the great Solovetskii (Solovki) monastery was founded c.1450. These centres reflected a spiritual renewal marked by the advent of Byzantine hesychasm, a movement deriving from Mt Athos which emphasised individual prayer and devotion as means to closer communion with God, and which found ready expression in ascetic life. Sergii's dedication of his initial chapel and his monastery to the Holy Trinity reflected the hesychasts' particular concern with the three manifestations of the divine. The 'Old-Testament Trinity' is likewise the subject of the masterpiece of Andrei Rublëv (c.1360–c.1430), Russia's greatest icon-painter. Rublëv was for a time a monk in the Trinity-Sergius monastery and one of a remarkable group of masters working in this period, which is a high point of Russian religious art.

However, Sergii's energies were applied to secular as well as spiritual ends, and his counsel was sought by princes. The Church's support was critical in Rus moves towards independence from the Mongols as the Golden Horde, and the whole Mongol Empire, fell into decay. The gradual development of agriculture in the Horde's lands undermined its ability to train and maintain adequate armies; its original nomadic organisation failed to adapt sufficiently to provide firm control over its diverse subject populations or to prevent internecine in-fighting among its elites; and it also came under external attack. The first notable military victory of Rus over Mongol troops arose from power struggles within the Horde. In 1380 Dmitrii Ivanovich of Moscow (1359–89) led a Rus coalition against the Mongol commander Mamai at Kulikovo Field, on the upper Don river. As Mamai was not descended from the Chingisid line, he could be seen as an illegitimate usurper in the Horde. Stories about the role of Sergii of Radonezh – that he blessed the army and sent monks to lead the Rus troops – appear to be later pious inventions, but the Church evidently approved of the enterprise. Mamai's Lithuanian allies failed to appear, and the Rus won a famous victory, which gave Dmitrii great prestige and the soubriquet 'Donskoi'. In fact the battle was not of great practical significance. The Chingisid Tokhtamysh, who took power in the Horde, reasserted Mongol authority and Dmitrii was unable to prevent him sacking Moscow in 1382. But Kulikovo Field destroyed the record of Mongol invincibility, and showed that the balance of power was changing. It also consolidated the position of the Daniilovichi as the dominant Riurikid branch. Mongol power remained formidable, able to assert its overlordship and continuing right to tribute: in 1408 Mongol troops besieged Moscow again when Vasilii I Dmitrievich (1389–1425) temporarily refused payment. A few decades later, however, the Kipchak khanate finally fragmented into a series of successor states, of which Rus was effectively one. Its Tatar population split into the separate khanates of Crimea (1430), Kazan on the middle Volga (1436), and Astrakhan at its mouth (1466), together with Sibir beyond the Urals, leaving the so-called Great Horde, the rump of the Golden Horde. The Great Horde continued to live a nomadic existence in the steppe, based on Sarai, until in 1502 it was taken over and absorbed by the Crimeans, the most powerful and longest lived of the successor khanates.

As Mongol dominance waned, the family stability which had favoured the Daniilovichi deserted them. In the absence of collateral claimants, Dmitrii Donskoi had effectively established a system of vertical succession in Moscow; but in 1431 the title of his young grandson Vasilii II (1425–62) was challenged by an uncle. There followed years of civil war and fluctuating fortunes among the Daniilovichi themselves and their allies and opponents, both domestic and foreign: struggles which may be compared to the roughly contemporary Wars of the Roses in England. In the course of these events Vasilii II was taken captive, and blinded, but he finally emerged victorious in the 1450s. In the process the political balance of power was transformed. Moscow gathered more principalities and its dominance in Rus became unquestionable, as did the exclusive succession rights of its princes: vertical succession became the norm. Previously independent appanage princes became Muscovite servitors. In the course of his wars Vasilii made extensive use of Tatar troops who took service under him and in 1452 he granted the appanage or 'khanate' of Kasimov on the Oka river to Kasim, brother of the khan of Kazan: the first significant grant by a Rus prince to a Tatar serviceman.

In 1462 Vasilii died and was succeeded by his son Ivan, who had acted as co-ruler with his blind father. Under Ivan III (the Great, 1462–1505) and his son Vasilii III (1505–33) Moscow completed the formation of what became the Muscovite state. Ivan disregarded the authority of Sarai in the matter of his investiture as Great Prince, withstood two punitive Mongol expeditions sent against him, and in 1480, in the face of tribute demands, formally repudiated Mongol suzerainty. His Mongol opponents allied with Lithuania, while Ivan sought the support of the Crimean khan. The opposing armies met on opposite sides of the river Ugra, a tributary of the Oka; but the Lithuanians did not appear, and the Mongols, failing to cross the river, finally withdrew: the 'stand on the Ugra' has traditionally been taken to mark the end of the 'Tatar Yoke'.

The Consolidation of the Muscovite State and the Fall of Novgorod

Under Vasilii II and Ivan III the territory under Moscow's control more than tripled, to encompass more than 1,000,000 km^2. This involved the subordination and absorption of competitor principalities. Appanages whose rulers had opposed Moscow were abolished, and their servitors assimilated. Other principalities retained formal independence, but now Moscow controlled their administration and resources. Tver, Moscow's greatest Rus competitor, acknowledged Muscovite superiority, but was finally crushed in 1485 when Ivan discovered that it had made a secret alliance against him with Lithuania.

Another casualty was Novgorod. Novgorod's location on a river feeding into the eastern Baltic gave it close contact with international trading networks: beside its Scandinavian links, it was the most easterly depot of the Hansa. Economic success had made it a conduit for the silver coin which paid the khan's tribute, and enabled it to build up a huge empire in the north, stretching from the White Sea to the Urals. Novgorod had a cosmopolitan population, with special residential and trading areas for foreign traders, and a highly literate culture using writing tablets of birch-bark, which have been found by archaeologists in great numbers. Visiting merchant ships brought heterodox trends and ideas, like those of the rationalistic Novgorod *strigol'niki* ('shaven ones') condemned as heretics in the early fifteenth century. Heterodoxy simmered on: some decades later, in the 1470s, another major Novgorod heresy denied the divinity of Christ and the temporal power of the Church. These 'Judaisers' accused the Archbishop of Novgorod, Gennadii, of simony, leading him to set in train translations of authoritative texts, including the first complete Slavonic translation of the Bible (1499), and to flirt with the practices of the Inquisition, in order to combat heresy. The city's political vitality matched its lively cultural life, and its economic strength enabled it to take an independent line towards the Riurikid princes. Under its own boyars and elected leaders, its veche was an instrument of real power. At the same time its westerly location enabled (or compelled) it to pursue a balancing strategy between western powers, especially Lithuania, and the power centres of Rus. However, despite its economic resources, Novgorod failed to develop the military strength to withstand the growing might of Moscow; and like Tver 14 years later, in 1471 it aroused Ivan's wrath by making a treaty with Lithuania. Ivan moved against Novgorod; in 1475 the city rose again in an unsuccessful revolt, which led in 1478 to definitive defeat and the exile of many leading families, aristocrats and merchants, to other towns. The Muscovites demonstratively carried off the veche assembly-bell. The exiles' lands were redistributed to servicemen from the Muscovite centre, thus emasculating Novgorod society and replacing oppositional elements with outsiders loyal to Ivan. In 1495, after redirecting foreign trade through

Livonian Narva, Ivan expelled Novgorod's foreign Hanseatic merchants and confiscated their stores. Novgorod's lesser neighbour and sister-city Pskov, which had a similar political structure, remained independent only a little longer, being annexed by Vasilii III in 1510. Thus the oligarchical-republican city-state alternative to centralised 'autocratic' power was snuffed out in Russia; much later, in the Imperial period, an idealised Novgorod and its veche became symbols of lost liberty.

Once Moscow had consolidated its hold over the former principalities of Rus, it was left facing external competitors and opponents: principally Lithuania and the Tatar khanates. With Lithuania, the dominant regional power during the decline of the Horde, Moscow conducted a successful policy according to circumstance. At times it was treaty and alliance – in 1494 Ivan III married his daughter to Aleksandr of Lithuania, who acknowledged his newly-proclaimed title of 'lord (*gosudar*) of all Russia'; at times it was conflict and hostilities – in 1500 Ivan declared war on his son-in-law on the pretext of defending his daughter's Orthodox religion. These hostilities, which also involved Livonia and Sweden, were concluded by an advantageous ten-year truce in 1503. In 1517 and again in 1526 the Holy Roman Emperor Maximilian, who allied himself with Vasilii III, sought to mediate between Moscow and Lithuania. (The Imperial ambassador on these occasions, Sigismund von Herberstein, by birth a Slovene, wrote one of the first European accounts of Muscovy, *Rerum moscoviticarum commentarii* . . . [*Notes on Muscovite Affairs,* 1549], a detailed description which informed European views of the country for years to come.) Mediation could only temporarily calm the rivalry of the two powerful neighbours, although the balance tipped increasingly in favour of Muscovy, and the issue was not resolved until the eighteenth century.

Relations with the khanates followed a similar pattern. In terms of real power the Ugra confrontation was no more significant than Kulikovo Field a century before: Ivan had already established his relative independence, and after 1480 Moscow continued to pay tribute to the khan of the Great Horde, but as a symbolic act and at a much reduced rate. Moscow was closely tied in to the politics of the post-Mongol steppe. The most powerful of the Tatar successor states was the Crimea; the nearest, the khanate of Kazan. Crimea was a valuable ally and dangerous opponent. For much of his reign Ivan III was able to maintain friendly relations with the khan, as a counterweight to Lithuania. When the Crimea absorbed the Great Horde in 1502, it laid legitimate claim to the inheritance of Sarai, and also became the recipient of Moscow's tribute. Vasilii III's interventions in Kazan politics alienated the Crimeans, who remained hostile to Moscow for most of the sixteenth century: defence of Muscovy's southern boundary consequently became one of the fundamental military concerns of the state. In 1523 the Crimean khan declared himself a vassal of the Ottoman Sultan, thus bringing the formidable Turkish power much closer to the arena of steppe politics: a Crimean army which invaded Muscovy in 1541 included Ottoman janissaries and cannoneers. Kazan was a softer target. Moscow was already a party in the political squabbles of the Kazan elite, seeking to influence the election of the khans. The appanage khanate of Kasimov became a forward position for Moscow's influence, an early example of what was to become a standard Russian tactic of subverting and conciliating elites in territories which Russia wished to absorb. In the first decades of the sixteenth century the Muscovite court established increasing dominance in the politics of Kazan.

The Muscovite Court and Army

The Muscovite Court, made up of a small number of great families or clans, formed the nucleus of the prince's armed forces and provided his council and administrators. The greatest families were distinguished by their entitlement to the rank of boyar, usually held by individual male members for life, the title passing within the clan according to seniority: boyar rank was also within the gift of the prince. Boyars were the prince's advisers, and filled senior military and administrative offices. The Boyar Council (or *Duma*, as some later scholars called it), which appeared at this time, initially had a restricted membership, but as Muscovy and its administrative functions expanded, its numbers grew, and further 'duma ranks' appeared below that of boyar (*okolnichii* 'sub-boyar', *dumnyi dvorianin* 'court gentryman', and others). The prince was expected to consult his boyars, and his decisions and decrees were confirmed and thus validated by his councillors. The *dvor* was sufficient for the administration of the principality of Moscow under the Mongols. But the consolidation of Muscovite independence and hegemony, and territorial expansion, could only be achieved through radical changes in internal organization and military capacity. In the words of Marshall

Poe: 'What had been in 1450 a tiny collection of warriors managing a protection operation in the forests and on the trade routes of north-eastern Rus became by 1650 a large administrative system ruling a huge empire.' The growing requirements of literate administration were met by council clerks and scribes: most Muscovites were and remained illiterate. Initially, tasks of regional and local government were assigned to individual servitors. The prince appointed civilian and military governors, with broad functions and powers, who were expected to maintain and remunerate themselves through gifts and levies from the local population (so-called *kormlenie*, 'feeding' – officials were rotated to prevent excessive exploitation). By 1500 Muscovy had 15 regional civilian governors (*namestniki*) and some 100 *volosteli* or rural governors, who had a local remit.

At the same time, the assertion of Moscow's dominance over its rivals facilitated the expansion of its armed forces: the prince's Court absorbed the retinues of defeated enemies, neutral neighbours and impoverished princely allies, and evolved into a discrete military body with separate organisation. As Moscow's star rose, moreover, so ever more warriors wished to serve its rulers. Rus boyars and servitors had a long-established right to choose which prince they served, and could move freely from one Riurikid court to another. New servitors also came from Lithuania (and further west), and from the Tatar khanates. A significant influx of Tatar nobles entered Muscovite service during the fifteenth and sixteenth centuries: Tatar princely or Chingisid rank was respected in Moscow, and many of the great Russian clans (some 17 per cent in the seventeenth century) looked back to Tatar ancestors. Moscow's Tatar allies, particularly Kasimov, added further strength to what was becoming a Muscovite army drawn from the whole country.

The expansion of the armed forces required the support of servitors, and the social integration of newcomers. The issue of support was resolved by the introduction of a new land-holding system. The estates confiscated from the exiled Novgorod elite in 1478 provided a land-fund which Ivan III now distributed among Moscow servitors in conditional service tenure, as *pomest'e* estates. In contrast to the *votchina* (lands hereditary within the clan) of the great families, pomest'e land was given specifically to enable service. The entitlement of the servitor depended on his rank, and the proportion of entitlement which he actually received depended on the availability of suitable empty holdings. The pomest'e was hereditary, though it

Map 5   The Rise of Moscow to 1533

© Sir Martin Gilbert, *The Routledge Atlas of Russian History* (London and New York, 2002), no. 25.

could be removed from a family in the absence of further servitors, and was designed as an income base – together with some payment in cash – to provide the serviceman with subsistence and equipment. It also gave him jurisdiction over the peasants who worked the lands of his holding, from whom he drew revenue and for whom he administered justice and provided protection. Ivan's large-scale distribution of Novgorod land is usually considered the beginning of this practice as a system. It has been called the 'first Muscovite service revolution', laying the foundations of an organised and centralised service structure. Once the provisioning of servitors had been assured, the duty of military service was extended to larger numbers: lesser ranks, including provincial servitors known as *deti boyarskie* (literally, 'boyar children'), were included among those directly obliged to fight for the Prince. Unlike votchina lands, pomest'e estates were usually small, but over the following century the new 'middle service class' of pomest'e-holders differentiated itself increasingly from the mass of the population and assumed an elite mentality: all servitors were members of the privileged higher section of Muscovite society.

This type of service land-grant was common in Asia, in the Mongol and Islamic tenure system known as *iqta*, and the Turkish *timar*, which were designed to support military forces while ensuring administration of newly conquered territories. (The larger question of possible Mongol influence on the development of Muscovite institutions in general has been much debated.) Iqta presupposed a stable, sedentary peasant labour force. However, the Rus and Muscovite peasant practised slash-and-burn agriculture, which required movement to new land when existing clearings became exhausted. Peasant mobility was therefore a potential problem for the *pomeshchik* (holder of a pomest'e): already in the Muscovite law-code (*Sudebnik*) of 1497 some restriction was placed on the right of peasant tenants to leave their land. Nevertheless, the pomest'e system rapidly established itself, and remained a fundamental structure of Russian society right up to the nineteenth century.

A further problem facing the Great Prince was the status of high-ranking incomers. Distinguished newcomers had to be received at court with appropriate honour, without displacing or offending loyal servitors from old-established families. The Great Prince also needed a ranking system as a basis for appointment to military and civil office, as rivalry grew over the limited number of appointments. The requirement was met by a complex system of 'service precedence' (*mestnichestvo*). This calculated service seniority in terms of extended-family or clan status (genealogical relationship to the prince), clan service record (previous offices and service of family members) and individual standing (position within the clan). It proved a cumbersome system, especially since acceptance of a position lower than that formally deserved could influence all subsequent rankings of the clan's members: precedence disputes were numerous. But the system largely served its purposes of conciliating previously independent families to the service and authority of the Great Prince, and of providing an acceptable hierarchical structure within which service could be organised, at least until the end of the seventeenth century. It also had the effect of institutionalising competition among the elite and making them more dependent for status and advancement upon the Prince who stood above them all. Both the pomest'e and the mestnichestvo systems required special record-keeping in order to function properly, and their introduction produced new state offices which formed part of the increasingly complex administration of the Muscovite court.

While welcoming outsiders, the Muscovite princes successfully constrained their own elite Rus retainers, who had the traditional right to choose their princely master. As independent Rus princes became fewer, the ability of servitors to move from one court to another became increasingly limited, until finally the only real service alternatives to Moscow were Lithuania and the Tatar khanates; but these foreign options were now seen as apostasy by the Church and treason by the Great Prince. The Muscovite princes in any case adopted the Mongol doctrine that all land belonged to the ruler. The departure of a boyar was contested for the first time in 1375, when Dmitrii of Moscow confiscated the lands of a defector to his rival Tver. By the time of Ivan III there was nowhere to go, and a charge of treason would taint the entire extended family or clan. Although the question remained a residual problem for rulers until the end of the dynasty, with the Crown sometimes requiring oaths, signatures or hostages against defection, in practice the boyar 'right of departure', a guarantee of servitors' independence, had disappeared.

The Muscovite Great Princes of the late fifteenth and early sixteenth centuries thus acquired larger military forces over which they had greater control. They also engaged in the common

European practice of hiring foreign mercenaries. The numbers they could command are uncertain, perhaps a total available strength at the beginning of the sixteenth century, including baggage personnel and auxiliaries, of 70,000. Military administration and finance at this period appear to have remained fairly rudimentary, but the appearance of new military officials and taxes suggests active engagement, even a militarisation of local government. These developments also reflect the fact that Moscow was being drawn into the so-called 'military revolution', the Europe-wide development of gunpowder weapons. In the sixteenth and seventeenth centuries this brought major changes across Europe in army formations, field tactics, fortification and siege methods, and consequent change in governments and society. The earliest recorded reference to gunpowder weaponry in Rus is the reported use of a cannon by the defenders of Moscow against Tokhtamysh in 1382. Ivan III was able to summon gunmakers (together with a variety of other specialists) from the Italian lands, who established a cannon-foundry and powder-yard in Moscow. Infantry firearms also appeared – harquebusiers participated in the 'stand on the Ugra' – but they were of less value in the Tatar style of warfare favoured by Muscovite commanders, which emphasised cavalry mobility and rapid movement. Siege work relied on old-fashioned blockade until in 1514 Vasilii III made an effective artillery assault on the walls of the fortress of Smolensk – a political football between Moscow and Lithuania – which he duly captured, with other border areas, from the Lithuanians. Despite these advances, it was only from the mid-sixteenth century that the full effects of the gunpowder revolution made themselves felt.

The Ideology of Muscovy

During the period of Mongol domination, while the princes of Rus acknowledged the suzerainty and legitimate supreme authority of the khan at Sarai, under the Great Khan at Karakorum, in religious matters Rus looked to the authority of Byzantium and the Patriarch of Constantinople, and the Byzantine accommodation with the Kipchak khanate gave sanction to the khan's power as the will of God. In Byzantine tradition the Emperor was a hieratic figure governing in close 'symphony' with the Patriarch, who deferred to him in secular but not in Church affairs. In the later fifteenth century, as both centres of authority declined, and Rus asserted its independence – from

Constantinople in 1448 and from Sarai after 1462 (Ivan III's investiture) – the Great Princes and their supporters sought theoretical and symbolic demonstrations of their own pre-eminent and sovereign power. In 1472 Zoe (Sophia) Palaeologa, niece of the last Byzantine emperor and ward of the Pope, was given by her guardian in marriage to Ivan III. Rome was once more hoping to achieve a reunion of the Eastern and Western Churches. The marriage has often been seen as providing Moscow with justification for claims to an Imperial Byzantine heritage, though this is not borne out in contemporary sources. The connection to Rome nevertheless served to further aggrandisement. After the civil wars the Great Princes had begun a considerable construction programme in Moscow, and in 1475 Ivan III used his new contacts to employ an Italian, Aristotle Fioravanti (also his cannon-master), to construct a great new Cathedral of the Assumption: further building in the Kremlin followed, also by Italian architects, and the Kremlin itself was refortified. Ivan also adopted the symbol of the double-headed eagle; and in 1493 he began to use the title *gosudar* (lord), a term which now became a standard expression of sovereign power.

The Rus Orthodox Church strongly supported this stance. By the fifteenth century it had become a powerful institution, both politically and economically. It supported the Muscovite princes, and also sought to secure its own authority. The late fifteenth century was a time of great religious ferment. The Church calendar measured time from the beginning of the world, calculated to be 5508 BC, and its 7000-year span was to end in 1492; even after this date had passed, many still expected the end of the world, and a tense millenarian mood was widespread. Moreover, Muscovite Russia lacked any concept of the state separate from the personal power of the prince, which was theoretically unlimited and divinely sanctioned (though Byzantine doctrine, known in Muscovy, allowed advisers and churchmen to oppose a ruler who disobeyed God's will). The Church promoted a vision in which the Tsar represented a living icon of God, and the Muscovite Orthodox empire an icon of the heavenly kingdom.

The growing power and independence of Moscow raised questions also about the role of the Church in society. As a result of land grants and pious donations, the Church had become a major landowner. The issue of Church wealth became linked with that of its relationship to the prince. One train of thought, connected particularly with Iosif, abbot of the Volokolamsk monastery, advocated close association of the Church with Muscovite princely power, and also justified the Church's possession of wealth as a guarantor of its social role. On the other hand Iosif's contemporaries, the monk Nil of Sora and his followers, saw the Russian Church more as part of the universal Church, and preached poverty, humility and asceticism in the style of hesychasm. Traditional views of these different emphases as a dramatic clash between 'possessors' and 'non-possessors' within the Church may be exaggerated, but it is clear that the Great Princes acted to restrain Church accumulation of land from diverting their own resources (though without undertaking anything like Henry VIII's secularisation of English monasteries), while at the same time maintaining the close association of princely and ecclesiastical authority.

The debate over Church property gave expression to another important doctrine which appeared at this time, that of 'Moscow the third Rome'. An epistle, probably written by the monk Filofei in the early sixteenth century, declared that 'two Romes have fallen, the third [Moscow] stands, and a fourth there shall not be'; the image subsequently reappeared in documents connected to the 1569 establishment of the Patriarchate. Much is obscure in these texts, but it seems that Rus was here proclaimed as the successor of the first two embodiments of Imperial Christian power, or at least as the new protector of the Christian realm. However, research has suggested that Filofei's epistle was not intended as a political declaration of Muscovite manifest destiny, but was rather a polemical religious paean to the ruler's power which also called on him to be godly and respect the integrity of the Church, lest the 'third Rome' fall: it was possibly a reaction to Catholic propaganda, or to perceived Muscovite encroachment on Church prerogatives in Novgorod. Consequently, and contrary to historiographical tradition, the doctrine had little contemporary political resonance, although it may have contributed to popular Messianism; it was, however, taken up again in nationalistic intellectual circles in the nineteenth century.

The Church hierarchy was interested in supporting a view of Moscow's place in the world which justified Church status and accorded with Church teaching. From 1448 onwards, Church writings – chronicles and other texts – increasingly suggested an opposition between Mongol (Muslim) and Rus (Christian) power. Churchmen sought to create and impose their own Christian vision of Rus and its past, in which the 'Tatar yoke' was a disastrous infidel oppression visited by God upon the Rus for their sins, and after the (in this view) divinely sanctioned fall of Constantinople and its Emperor, the newly independent Muscovite princes remained sole bearers of the Imperial Orthodox tradition. Muscovite political independence and power thus received divine confirmation. Church writings also stressed the alleged continuity of political authority from Kiev Rus to Moscow. In 1492 the Metropolitan began to refer to the Great Prince as *samoderzhets* (independent sovereign ruler, 'self-upholder' or 'autocrat', corresponding to the Greek *avtokrator*). And at the turn of the century there appeared in Church sources a fictitious genealogy linking the house of Riurik to the family of Augustus Caesar, and a 'Legend of Monomach' which related how the Byzantine Emperor Constantine Monomachos sent regalia, and particularly an Imperial 'crown of Monomakh', to the Great Prince of Kiev Vladimir Monomakh, thereby suggesting if not a *translatio imperii* (transfer of empire), then at least a continuity, between Constantinople, Kiev, and Kiev's putative successor Moscow. The anonymous writer disregarded gross chronological and genealogical discrepancies, as well as the Central Asian provenance of the crown in question (still preserved in the Treasury of the Moscow Armoury). The term *tsar* (emperor), previously used of the Mongol khan, the Byzantine Emperor and Old Testament kings, was also applied to the Great Princes of Moscow in Church utterances of this period, although it was not common in secular usage until the reign of Ivan IV. On his conquest of the Tatar successor khanates in the 1550s, Ivan IV did begin to claim the authority of the Mongol khans. The efforts of the tiny handful of churchmen and their associates who wove these representations of the tsar and his status were extremely successful: in popular and elite consciousness the tsar's person became hallowed and inviolate, his power unquestionable.

In seeking to justify the Great Prince's authority in religious and quasi-historical terms, the publicists and ideologues of Moscow projected an image of absolute majesty and unlimited power. The prince was seen as owner of all the lands under his rule, which formed his 'patrimony'. Moreover the rudimentary administrative arrangements of the Muscovite government provided no institutional check upon princely power; nor (after the demise of Novgorod) were there any other bases of political authority, such as great cities with independent rights. In his *Notes on Muscovy* (1549), Herberstein wrote of the Muscovite Great Prince that in the sway which he holds over his people, he surpasses the monarchs of the whole world. . . . He uses his authority as much over ecclesiastics as lay-men, and holds unlimited control over the lives and property of all his subjects: not one of his councillors has sufficient authority to dare to oppose him, or even differ from him, on any subject. They openly confess that the will of the prince is the will of God.

The English merchant-diplomat Giles Fletcher, author of another influential account of Muscovy (1598), asserted that 'The state and forme of their government is plaine tyrannicall.' This was the image of Muscovite political authority which subsequently became dominant elsewhere in Europe, and gave rise to the view of 'autocracy' as a despotic and oppressive form of absolutism. In strict terms *samoderzhets* indicates simply a fully independent ruler and is rendered in diplomatic translations by 'sovereign'. It is important to look closely at what is being described here, because the political system which emerged from the civil wars of the fifteenth century and was consolidated in the sixteenth fundamentally determined the political development of the country thereafter. The absolute power of the prince, set above all others at his court, became the guarantee of the stability and survival of the society. Compared to the courts from which the foreign observers came, Muscovite practice was certainly personally oppressive, and elite servitors had few explicit prerogatives which set them apart from their lesser fellows. They were liable to ill-treatment, including physical violence and beating, which was considered unacceptably dishonouring for aristocrats of other nations. From the fifteenth century onwards it became normal (until the eighteenth) for servitors to call themselves the prince's 'slave' (*kholop*). Great Princes could behave ruthlessly, and brutally, in dealing with those who opposed or displeased them; and in consolidating their control over the former lands of Rus and creating the pomest'e system, they established their right to demand service from all parts of the population, a requirement systematised and made explicit in the ordinances of Ivan IV.

Recent scholarship has, however, increasingly questioned the traditional stereotypes of autocratic despotism. The ceremonial display and religious ritual constructed around the prince certainly contributed to this impression of absolute power. The social ethics of the time condoned considerable physical cruelty (as Ivan III demonstrated), although the same can be said of other contemporary societies. But in practice the Muscovite political system functioned essentially through consensus between the prince and the ruling elite, on whose collaboration the running of the country depended. The elite accepted princely authority as divinely sanctioned, and also as the source of the status and well-being which it enjoyed; elite nobles vied with each other to gain the best 'place' for their family in court affairs, rather than seeking to compete with, confront or extort rights from the prince – Muscovy knew nothing like Magna Carta. Muscovy had its own well-developed ideas about honour, centred on the extended family or clan, concepts which defined the status and loyalties of the elite and themselves became a force for social integration. The rhetorical term 'slave of the ruler' carried as much the sense of 'your humble servant' as of true slavery, nor was elite slavery on the Turkish pattern ever developed in Muscovy. The prince in turn was normally expected to listen to his servitors, and to apportion power and wealth equitably among them. As the Patrikeev case showed, an overmighty family could be toppled. In 1499 the boyar Prince Ivan Patrikeev, the most prominent of Ivan III's courtiers, was arrested and tonsured, while his sons were imprisoned: balance was restored. Nor was it the case that great-princely 'patrimonial' dominance normalised arbitrary treatment of property: while Great Princes had the power to confiscate property, and did so in cases of treason or insubordination, traditionally they acknowledged the votchina rights of their servitors, and at least until the reign of Ivan IV the great and lesser families were relatively independent in their management of their estates. The prince's power was limited theoretically, by divine justice and custom, and practically, by the need to work together with his elite. Over time there also came into existence collective structures – local communities and their courts, the 'assembly of the land' which appeared in 1549 – which allowed some freedom of action at local levels and the articulation of sectional interests. Likewise the importance of the personal element (individuals as well as clans) has been stressed: in the political structure which evolved in the Muscovite period and persisted after it, power lay less in institutions than with persons.

IVAN IV

The Early Years

Questions of ideology and of political power in the emergent Muscovite state were posed most sharply in the reign of Ivan IV, the Terrible (1533–84: Russian *Groznyi* means Terrible in the sense of 'Dread', Awe-inspiring). Ivan is one of the most enigmatic of Russia's rulers. His personality and his actions have provoked widely differing interpretations, in part at least because they were so unusual and extreme, in part because evidence concerning them is fragmentary and inconclusive. He has been considered the essence of despotic tyranny, a worthy predecessor of Stalin; an illiterate sadist, or simply mad; an intellectual on the throne, a 'Renaissance prince', inviting comparison with other European rulers of the sixteenth century, particularly Henry VIII of England.

Vasilii III's elder son by his second marriage, Ivan came to the throne in 1533 as a child aged three. His inability to exercise Great-Princely power destabilised the newly consolidated political equilibrium, and during his minority the tensions among the elite which mestnichestvo had been designed to curb broke out in full force. Until Ivan reached his majority in 1547, principal boyar clans fought viciously for dominance, also involving the leaders of the Church. Especially prominent were the Shuiskii family, descended from the Suzdal Riurikid line, the Lithuanian Glinskii family of Ivan's mother Elena, and the Belskiis, also originally from Lithuania. If Ivan's minority was insecure, his reign began inauspiciously too: fires in Moscow led to riots in which an uncle was lynched. Throughout his life, security and loyalty would be crucial issues.

At 16 Ivan came of age and asserted his prerogatives. In January 1547, in a splendid ceremony redolent of Byzantine rites, Metropolitan Makarii crowned him Great Prince, and at the same time Tsar of all Rus. The coronation had only one precedent – most previous princes had not been ceremonially crowned – and the new title implied equality with Byzantine and Mongol rulers. The ceremonial reflected both the growing power of the Muscovite state, and the continuing theoretical claims made for it by its Church leadership. Metropolitan Makarii, personally close to Ivan since his installation in 1542, instructed him on his prerogatives and duties; and during the reign new ecclesiastical literary and artistic works were compiled to glorify the high lineage and God-given sanctity of Ivan's royal house. Links with Kiev and the ruler's role as protector of Orthodoxy were emphasised by the creation of many new saints, including former Riurikid princes – Aleksandr Nevskii was one. Relations with the Tatar khanates, particularly Kazan, were increasingly represented by the Church as an Orthodox crusade against the infidel. Makarii's view, which built upon the doctrines and myth-creations of his predecessors, was theocratic: the tsar was God's representative and servant on earth and as such endowed with absolute and unquestionable political power, which, however, he must use wisely and virtuously. His person and his power thus became hallowed: Ivan's reign marks the final stage in the sacralisation of the Russian monarchy. Another, complementary, view of rulership was offered by Ivan Peresvetov, a minor nobleman who had served in the Ottoman Empire. As well as recommending the virtues of Turkish military organisation, Peresvetov advocated solving the problems of boyar anarchy and social governance through absolute royal power and exemplary severity. Ivan IV's practice as ruler developed both these approaches. He came to believe himself responsible only to God, and distinguished between his own mortal sinfulness and the power of the divinely appointed ruler, accountable to no human authority.

Shortly after his coronation, Ivan confirmed his position as ruler by marrying, as tradition required. He took as his wife Anastasia Romanova, a member of the aristocratic Iurev-Zakharin family, which now gained predominance at Court. In the first years of his reign, Ivan also favoured a number of reform-minded and less aristocratic advisers, including the Metropolitan. At the same time he found other ways of communicating with the elite. Meetings with senior clerics and laymen from 1549 led to the emergence of a new institution, which historians later named the *zemskii sobor*, 'Assembly of the Land' ('land' meaning those communities which lived upon it). This consultative assembly had some limited resemblance to estates-general in other European countries, though it was not truly representative, lacked powers of its own and convened irregularly, at the prince's will. But it was a valuable sounding-board for the Tsar, enabling him to mobilise support and resources. Assemblies of the Land continued to meet until the later seventeenth century. Simultaneously the Tsar and his advisers turned their attention to the Church, summoning a Church council in 1551 known as the 'Hundred Chapters' (*Stoglav*) to address problems of Church governance and relations with the Crown, as well as to confirm Church teaching.

Ivan and his advisers used these mechanisms to implement an ambitious domestic policy aimed at restructuring central and local administration and mobilising military power more effectively. The Tsar's administrative reforms have been called a 'bureaucratic revolution': a term also notably applied by Geoffrey Elton to the work of the contemporary English Tudors. During the sixteenth century discrete organs of state government and administration evolved from the previous general administrative structure of the Muscovite Court. The trend towards centralised control overcame both the residual territorial fragmentation resulting from the appanage system and the differences of law among the various lands which the Great Princes had brought under their rule. (In northern Russia, for instance, territories were run by largely autonomous communes; Smolensk and other western towns used Lithuanian law.) Ivan's measures of the late 1540s and 1550s completed the foundation of a functional centralised administrative system based upon government departments or 'chancelleries' (*prikazy*), staffed by professional civil servants, successors of the functionaries of the prince's court and the Boyar Council. In 1550 a new law code (*Sudebnik*) was issued, which clarified administrative procedures. Ivan also sought, less successfully, to further changes in local administration begun in the 1530s, by limiting *kormlenie* and creating relatively autonomous local administrative offices, especially for tax collection. The new central chancelleries were initially poorly defined, sometimes had overlapping jurisdictions, and provided only basic administrative capacity; and there were few effective institutional links between central offices and the localities. But the system was adequate to the principal functions of government, particularly the organisation of finance and military service.

Ivan's measures were equally important in the military sphere. He sought to streamline the army command and defuse precedence disputes. His 'thousander reform' of 1550 aimed to create a core military elite by distributing landed estates around Moscow to 1000 select permanent servitors – though it is unclear how far this was realised in practice. The 1556 'Code of State Service' articulated the duties of these and of lesser, provincial, servitors, and established in law the principle that 'all land must serve'. While all nobles had long since owed service to the crown, the new code was a landmark, laying down precise service norms. Henceforth Muscovy was a 'service state' in which all classes of the population bore specific obligations. Ivan also took account of the increasing importance of gunpowder weaponry: while his principal forces remained cavalry armed with bows and cold steel, in 1550 he created the first permanent Muscovite infantry musketeer force, *streltsy* ('shooters'), drawn from the urban populace and based mainly in the capital. These troops were salaried but, like the pomeshchiki, also had their own economic base, working in peacetime as smallholders, craftsmen or petty traders. They made a major contribution to Moscow's military effectiveness, and in addition provided forces for guarding and policing purposes; by 1560 they numbered about 10,000. Ivan also created a special 'Cannon Chancellery' to oversee the training of bombardiers, and supplies for the increasingly important artillery. And it was in his reign that Moscow first made serious attempts to harness the Cossacks of the southern steppe for the defence of the southern frontier. Cossacks, despite their independence, had to rely on neighbouring communities for such things as weaponry, and would collaborate with the highest bidder – Poles, Crimeans or Muscovites. Ivan engaged the Don Cossacks as irregulars in his wars with Kazan, and in 1570 issued a charter which confirmed their landholdings on the Don in return for permanent frontier service.

War, Expansion and Empire

The military reforms ran parallel to growing military activities against Kazan. Muscovite intervention in the khanate's troubled affairs had become increasingly direct, and the new Tsar and his advisers finally decided to subjugate it. In 1552 a huge Muscovite army with 150 heavy cannon besieged and captured Kazan, despite desperate Tatar resistance. Pacification of the rest of the khanate took five years, but the conquest fundamentally altered the whole regional balance of power: many lesser Tatar rulers now acknowledged Muscovite suzerainty. It brought a major acquisition of important territory, and opened the way for further expansion eastwards, and south towards the Caspian – the khanate of Astrakhan at the mouth of the Volga fell to Ivan four years later. In one sense, Ivan's conquests merely consolidated an existing situation: Muscovy already had Tatar servitors and a client khanate in Kasimov, and had long played king-maker in Kazan. In political terms, however,

1552–6 marked a watershed. Muscovy now ruled an empire of ethnically diverse populations with their own political and cultural traditions; the integration and conciliation of such new subjects was to become a permanent problem of Russian government. The triumph was marked by the construction of a great Orthodox cathedral in Kazan, and of the Cathedral of Intercession on the Moat, universally known as St Basil's Cathedral, on Red Square in Moscow (1555–61: Figure 3).

After the conquest of Kazan and Astrakhan, Ivan faced a choice. He could follow up his successes with an assault on the Crimea; and some moves were made in that direction. But the Crimea was a powerful enemy – the khan invaded Muscovy in 1555 in response to the Kazan events – and also a distant territory extremely difficult to attack: subsequent Russian attempts succeeded only in the eighteenth century. Ivan therefore turned his attention north-westwards, towards Livonia, the decayed and crumbling state of the Teutonic Knights. His initial goals were apparently limited: the imposition of tribute. But the geopolitical potential was much larger: the conquest of Livonia would give Muscovy new commercial opportunities on the Baltic. In 1553 English explorers led by Sir Richard Chancellor, seeking a north-eastern sea passage to China, had found their way to Moscow, and Elizabeth I of England created a Muscovy Company to trade with Ivan's realm. Ivan welcomed the English, his first major European trading partners, and gave them exclusive privileges. But since the Baltic was controlled by other, largely hostile, powers, all their commerce passed through the White Sea – the new port of Archangel was founded in 1585. The long Livonian War (1555–83) began brilliantly for the Muscovites, and they maintained their advance even after the intervention of Poland, to whom the Livonian knights made submission and which merged with Lithuania in 1569 to become the Polish-Lithuanian Commonwealth. But all the major Baltic powers joined in the grab for Livonia. Finally the Poles created a coalition with Sweden and the Crimea against Moscow, and the war ended in defeat, loss of Muscovite gains, and the exhaustion of the country.

The westward advance was halted. Simultaneously, however, Moscow was expanding eastwards, into Siberia. Tatar power had kept Siberia out of reach: the way was barred by Kazan and the khanate of Sibir beyond the Urals. However, Sibir was destroyed not by the Tsar's armies, but by a band of adventurers led by the Cossack Yermak Timofeevich. Yermak, who had fought in the Livonian War,

Figure 3   Cathedral of the Intercession on the Moat, Moscow (1555–61), commonly known as St Basil's Cathedral. The cathedral, actually nine chapels in one, was popularly named after Vasilii, a Moscow *yuródivyi* or 'holy fool'. The fantastic and unusual onion domes were added around 1600, and additional decoration in the seventeenth century

From the personal collection of Professor Lindsey Hughes.

was initially employed by the merchant Stroganov family, who held huge land-grants and salt-works at Solvychegodsk in the far north-east, former Novgorod territory, which they controlled essentially as a private fiefdom under the tsar. In 1581–3 Yermak defeated Khan Kuchum and overran Sibir, quickly taking control of the whole Ob river basin – Kuchum had no answer to the Cossacks' muskets. Yermak drowned escaping from the Tartars in 1585, but the opening into Siberia had been made: by 1639 Muscovites had reached the Pacific, and established strong-points which assured their dominance over the whole vast territory. Expansion continued on the Pacific sea-board of North America, finally meeting French and Spanish expansion from the south. Russia retained Alaska until 1867. Only in the south-east, on the Amur river, did the Muscovites come up against a serious power: the Chinese Empire. Here the Chinese were, and remained, far stronger than the Russians: a century after Yermak's conquest the first Russo-Chinese treaty (of Nerchinsk, 1689) acknowledged the Chinese position, while regulating new trade relations between the two sides.

Yermak was a freebooter, comparable to the Spanish explorers and conquistadors who opened up America in roughly the same period, allowing state power to follow after them. The native peoples whom he found in Siberia were similar in cultural terms to the native North Americans – who may have entered North America over a land-bridge from Siberia in pre-historic times. The attitudes of the conquerors were not dissimilar; the local Siberian populations were placed under tribute (*yasak*) and set to work for the new overlords. Russians at least have been less prone to racism against indigenous populations than other European colonisers. Siberia stood in the same relation to the European Russian centre as the overseas dominions of the sea-borne empires, and its resources and peoples have been exploited in similar ways. Before the twentieth century the clearest parallel to the notorious exile system established there was the British institution of penal transportation to North America and Australia. Since the territory was contiguous to the metropolitan region, however, the possibility of separation and independence was much slighter, even though in the nineteenth century a 'regionalist' movement with separatist overtones developed. Geographically Siberia is comparable to Canada. Its initial attraction (like that of North America) was its furs: *yasak* was largely levied in pelts, and the Muscovite Court derived huge revenues from this treasure.

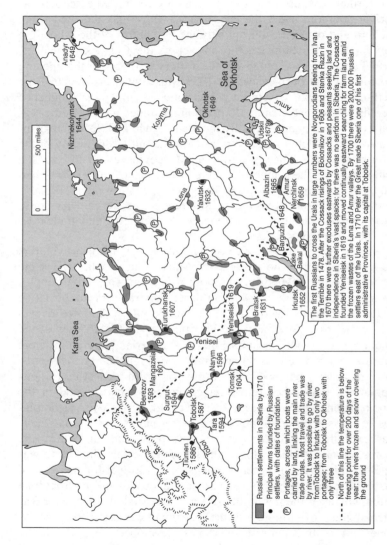

The first Russians to cross the Urals in large numbers were Novgorodians fleeing from Ivan the Terrible in 1478. After the Cossack risings of Bolotnikov in 1606 and Stenka Razin in 1670 there were further exoduses eastwards by Cossacks and peasants seeking land and independence in Siberia's vast spaces; for there was no serfdom in Siberia. The Cossacks founded Yeniseisk in 1619 and moved continually eastward searching for farm land amid the frozen wastes of the Lena and Amur valleys. By 1700 there were 200,000 Russian settlers east of the Urals. In 1710 Peter the Great made Siberia one of his first administrative Provinces, with its capital at Tobolsk.

Russian settlements in Siberia by 1710

● Principal towns founded by Russian settlers, with dates of foundation

Ⓟ Portages, across which boats were carried by land, linking the main river trade routes. Most travel and trade was by river. It was possible to go by river from Tobolsk to Irkutsk with only two portages; from Tobolsk to Okhotsk with only three

‑‑‑‑ North of this line the temperature is below freezing point for over 200 days of the year: the rivers frozen and snow covering the ground

Map 6   Eastward Expansion, 1478–1710

© Sir Martin Gilbert, *The Routledge Atlas of Russian History* (London and New York, 2002), no. 33.

Terror and the Oprichnina

The early years of the Livonian War coincided with major political turbulence in Moscow and with change in Ivan's personal behaviour. In 1560 the Tsar cast two of his principal advisers into disgrace. Later that year, Ivan's wife Anastasia, to whom he was deeply attached, suddenly died; as in many early-modern cases of sudden unexplained death, poison has been suspected. Ivan's relations with his elite now became progressively more strained. In 1562 he disgraced several leading boyars on flimsy charges, demanded onerous guarantees of loyalty from those he pardoned, and in 1563 and 1564 ordered the execution of still more. Metropolitan Makarii died (of natural causes) in 1563. The tone of Court life became less orderly and more debauched, and the same year Ivan introduced a new element by taking as wife a Circassian princess, Maria Temriukovna, whose father had recently entered Muscovite service. (In all Ivan was to marry seven times.)

Life at Court was becoming uncertain, even dangerous, and some Muscovite servitors began to defect to the Polish and Lithuanian enemy. The most notable of these defectors was Prince Andrei Kurbskii: high-born and well-connected, a prominent military commander, he may have felt himself personally in danger, or feared being held responsible for Muscovite military failure. In 1564 he fled to Poland, and from his foreign retreat wrote to Ivan, indicting the Tsar's cruelty to his subjects, and justifying his own departure. Ivan replied with a furious denunciation of Kurbskii and all traitors, including his former counsellors, and an assertion of his God-given absolute power, to which all subjects must submit. The Ivan–Kurbskii correspondence has been the subject of great controversy in recent years, since the American historian Edward Keenan alleged that the documents were a seventeenth-century forgery; but most historians accept their authenticity. At least it can be said that the ideas expressed in Ivan's supposed letters are consistent with his subsequent behaviour.

In December 1564, Ivan suddenly left Moscow for a country estate, and a month later announced to the Metropolitan and the stunned elite that he intended to abdicate, driven from the throne (he claimed) by the disobedience and treachery of boyars and clerics. The theocratic theory so successfully advanced by his clergy left no alternative to the rule of the 'anointed' tsar, and his courtiers at once begged him to return, promising him a free hand with traitors. Ivan returned on his own conditions: he divided the country into two separate administrations, an *oprichnina* (a 'state apart') under his own control, and the rest, the *zemshchina* (the 'realm of the land') administered by members of the Court and Boyar Council. From his new power base, Ivan waged war against perceived opponents. He created a local army of servants of the oprichnina (*oprichniki*), who wore black cloaks and carried symbolic dogs' heads and besoms on their saddles. Banishment and confiscation of property, torture, execution and murder, including members of victims' families, were visited on successive groups within the elite, and caught up many lesser persons. The new Metropolitan, who protested at Ivan's conduct, was deposed by a kangaroo court and strangled in prison. The oprichniki destroyed the recently established Foreign Suburb of Moscow, said to have housed some 4000 foreigners (mainly military men and their dependents). Prince Vladimir of Staritsa, a kinsman sufficiently close to Ivan to contest the throne, and the focus of a previous crisis in 1553, was forced to take poison, together with his family. Ivan sent to Elizabeth of England to ask for a promise of asylum, which was granted (though the Queen politely refused his offer of reciprocity). Novgorod, by now entirely subordinate to Moscow but suspected of treason by the Tsar, was sacked and subjected to a murderous reign of terror; Pskov nearly suffered the same fate. Meanwhile, the Livonian War was dragging on, and in 1571 a second front was created when the Crimean Tatars invaded and burned Moscow. The oprichnina army failed to prevent them; Ivan reacted by turning on the oprichniki themselves, whom he made responsible. By reuniting the oprichnina and zemshchina armies, he was able to drive off the Tatars when they repeated their invasion the following year. After its failure, the oprichnina was wound up as a separate administration in 1572.

The significance of the oprichnina has been much debated. It has been seen as a systematic if chaotic attempt to strengthen royal authority against overmighty nobles and dissenting subjects; as an imagined return to the form of appanage government, or the replication of the Spanish Inquisition or a steppe khanate; as an outlandish but consistent attempt to give reality to the symbolism of Orthodox Wisdom theology; as an extreme expression of personal insecurity and paranoia (probably the most plausible explanation), even insanity. But Ivan's doings were so bizarre and bloodthirsty, and so relatively few reliable sources have survived, that it is diffi-cult to reach a judgment. The episode brought no permanent changes to the social or political structure of the country, and some victims were soon reinstated. Nevertheless, the terror did not end in 1572. For the rest of his reign Ivan continued to pursue real or imag-ined traitors, with waves of arrests and executions, and he again threatened abdication in 1575.

THE DEVELOPMENT OF SERFDOM AND THE END OF THE DYNASTY

The violence and disruption of Ivan's later years, together with the growing burdens of war, as well as plague and epidemics which struck in the 1570s and 1580s, exhausted the country. All classes suffered, but particularly the peasantry, who became increasingly indebted to their landlords. Many peasants now fled their homes: when Giles Fletcher travelled from the White Sea to Moscow in 1588 he passed through whole regions of largely deserted villages. Some peasants moved to the security of big estates, went to the Cossacks, or eastwards to new lands opened by the conquest of the Volga khanates; some sold themselves into slavery to persons who could provide for them. Military servitor-landowners, especially the lesser pomeshchiki, saw their labour force and material security disappear-ing; in some cases of desperation they themselves abandoned their lands. During the civil wars Vasilii II had granted some monasteries the power to restrict their peasants' right of departure to two weeks on either side of St George's Day (26 November), when the annual agricultural cycle was completed. This restriction was applied to all peasants in the Sudebnik of 1497 – thereby also confirming their right to move elsewhere at that time, provided they had fulfilled their obligations to their landlord. Now, in response to servitor petitions and to this threat both to the treasury and the army, the government took radical steps. It instituted a land census to establish exact oblig-ations of tax and service, and in the 1580s introduced 'forbidden years', initially one year at a time, during which the labouring peas-ant population was forbidden to leave its place of residence. In the early 1590s a further decree made the prohibition on movement indefinite. This tied peasants permanently to the land and gave effec-tive control over them to the servitors on whose estates they lived, who were also allowed to reclaim those leaving illegally. The development of the central administration in the sixteenth century made possible for the first time some tracking of peasant mobility. In 1597 a time limit of five years was imposed on claims against runaways, but in 1607 the government of Vasilii Shuiskii extended it to 15 years – short periods favoured wealthy landowners who could attract fugitives and block claims for their return, while longer periods gave lesser owners more time to target errant peasants. In 1649, under pressure from the middle service class, the limit was abolished altogether. Serfdom now replaced former free contractual relations. Wherever servitors held estates, the peasants were legally bound to the soil. Only in the far North and Siberia, where there were no pomest'e lands, did the peasantry remain free of landlord control (although all peasants had tax and service obligations to the state).

At this time (c.1600) landlords' peasants still technically enjoyed personal freedom, once their labour or rental obligations had been met. They were still subjects in law, paid their own taxes, and decided their own affairs. Over the following century and a half, however, in a gradual process of evolving relations, discrete government measures and judicial decisions, and without any general enabling legislation, serfs became tied also to the person of their master, subject to his will in almost all respects. Serfdom took on its severest forms in Russia, evolving ultimately, in the eighteenth century, almost into chattel slavery. Full slavery already existed in Muscovy, as in Kiev Rus: prisoners of war were often enslaved, and forms of debt and indenture ('limited contract') slavery were common – selling oneself into slavery could be a means of finding support or protection. Now traditional attitudes towards slaves helped to mould the emerging severe forms of peasants' dependence upon their masters. Peter I abolished slavery (slaves do not pay taxes!), conflating the status of slave and serf. In the end landlords' peasants were left with no effective rights of their own: they could be bought and sold, and the only major difference between them and real slaves was that they remained liable to state taxation and service in the armed forces.

Ivan IV's immediate legacy was a society shattered by terror, and the burdens of warfare and natural disaster. To this was added his destruction of the dynasty. His numerous marriages had produced few male heirs; and in 1581, in a fit of rage, he struck and fatally wounded his eldest and only capable son. The only other remaining prince of suitable capacity and descent, Vladimir of Staritsa, had been destroyed in the oprichnina. It was an irony that the success of the Daniilovich rulers in replacing collateral with vertical succession finally left them with no viable heir at all to the throne. On Ivan IV's death in 1584, he was succeeded by his son Fëdor Ivanovich (r. 1584–98), a pious, passive ruler, more interested in Church ritual than state affairs: the succession was legitimated by an Assembly of the Land. Fëdor's government was directed for practical purposes by his brother-in-law Boris Godunov, a boyar of prestigious Tatar descent and considerable abilities. The only other surviving son, Dmitrii Ivanovich, was a child, and technically illegitimate since he was the product of Ivan's seventh marriage, uncanonical in Church eyes. In 1591 Dmitrii died, under uncertain circumstances, of a stab wound. On the death of Fëdor in 1598, childless and intestate, the Riurikid dynasty was extinguished.

3

1600–1760
Moscow and St Petersburg: the Genesis of the Imperial State

The end of the Riurikid line presaged a collapse of state authority and social order only remedied by the establishment of the Romanov dynasty in 1613. During the following century, Muscovy became increasingly integrated into European affairs and had to make painful changes to meet the realities of international military, political and economic relations: a process which brought schism in the Church and the final establishment of serfdom, and culminated in the military successes and sweeping 'reforms' of Peter I, the Great, bringing Russia into the European mainstream. The Russian Empire proclaimed after the defeat of Sweden in the Great Northern War (1721) was consolidated during the following decades, and the powerful Russian performance in the Seven Years' War (1756–63) led to the brink of premier international status; the new elite culture followed a similar course of development.

CRISIS, RECOVERY AND CHANGE

The 'Time of Troubles'

The opening years of the seventeenth century have gone down in Russian history as the 'Time of Troubles'. With the extinction of the dynasty, the country was gripped by increasing crisis. At its heart lay the absence of legitimate political authority, exacerbated by economic disaster, social tensions and foreign invasion.

In the power struggle following the death of Fëdor, his brother-in-law, Boris Godunov, emerged as the new ruler. Godunov was not without virtues and talents. As chief minister under Fëdor, he had shown statesmanship. He had followed a successful foreign policy, conducting a five-year war with the formidable Swedes to an acceptable conclusion, largely keeping peace on the volatile southern frontier, and encouraging settlement further south and east. He had cultivated Muscovy's profitable relations with England. Godunov watched over the successful negotiations with the Patriarch of Constantinople in 1589 for a Moscow Patriarchate, an event of outstanding importance for Muscovy. He had also shown himself adept at the faction-fighting which was endemic in Moscow. On Fëdor's death in 1598 these skills continued to serve him well. Backed by the Patriarch, Godunov organised popular and military support and had a rudimentary Assembly of the Land offer him the throne. Two years later, to consolidate his position, he moved against his main rivals, the Romanovs, family of Ivan IV's first wife Anastasia. The senior Romanov, boyar Fëdor Nikitich, was forced to become a monk and thereby give up worldly political ambition: under the name of Filaret he soon became a senior figure in the Church.

However, the new Tsar's government never enjoyed the charisma and legitimacy of his Riurikid predecessors, and soon faced widespread discontent. Disgruntled aristocratic factions disliked Godunov as a parvenu, and his lack of dynastic authority allowed a resurgence of elite in-fighting. Rumour also persistently linked him to the death of Dmitrii Ivanovich. In 1591 Godunov as chief minister had instituted a commission of enquiry under boyar Vasilii Shuiskii, which had refuted allegations of murder and concluded that the epileptic Tsarevich had fallen on his own knife; but Shuiskii later changed his story, more than once, and the allegations would not die down. In 1601–3 the impoverished peasants were stricken by harvest failures, the result of a European-wide 'little ice age' which produced large-scale distress, starvation and death, exacerbated in Russia by the new prohibition on peasant movement. Brigandage became rife, and strenuous government efforts to find sufficient food supplies for the starving who converged on urban centres were unsuccessful.

In 1604 came a new challenge to the regime. A pretender appeared on the southern border, supported by Polish adventurers and claiming to be Tsarevich Dmitrii, escaped from his alleged assassins. Whereas the 'divinely appointed' Riurikid Ivan IV had committed his atrocities with personal impunity and his rule had never been seriously challenged, the new non-Riurikid monarch was vulnerable to accusations of murder and to military insurrection. 'Dmitrii' was the first of many pretenders in Russia in the seventeenth and eighteenth centuries, most of them low-born: all claimed to be the true tsar who had escaped death and was returning to save his people from a usurper. The southern frontier was a cauldron of simmering discontents, insecurities and factional interests, and 'Dmitrii' attracted widespread local support. His insurgency turned into what was effectively a civil war, drawing in all levels of society, with Cossacks playing a significant role. The story of Boris Godunov and the False Dmitrii (or Dmitrii the Pretender) is one of the great national tales of Russian history, immortalised in the nineteenth-century play by Aleksandr Pushkin and the opera of Modést Musorgskii. The Boris of history may possibly have been guilty of murder, as his opponents and Pushkin suggested. The government's claim that the pretender was in fact a renegade monk, one Grigorii Otrepev, has been widely credited, but is equally unproven – Dmitrii's true identity remains unclear. As far as the sparse evidence goes, the pretender seems to have possessed superior talents, and to have believed in his own princely status.

Initially government forces contained the insurgents in the south; but in 1605 Godunov died suddenly, and the way was opened to 'Dmitrii' to enter Moscow and be crowned tsar – Godunov's young son and possible successor was assassinated. However, the new ruler lasted only one year: his pro-Polish attitudes, Polish Catholic wife and Polish entourage offended Muscovite sensibilities, and he was soon murdered in a plot hatched by the ambitious and opportunistic Shuiskii – his ashes were fired from a Kremlin cannon in the direction of Poland. Shuiskii, candidate of the aristocratic party in Moscow, replaced him. As part of a compact with his supporters, Shuiskii swore an oath to rule equitably, not repeating the depredations of Ivan IV against the elite. But this 'boyar Tsar' was equally unable to impose himself: his accession antagonised elite rivals, as well as disgruntled lower-class elements. Civil war flared once more (1606–7), the opposing forces led initially by a former military slave, Ivan Bolotnikov, and a second, cruder False Dmitrii emerged (the 'Felon of Tushino', 1608–10). The war and social confusion were exacerbated by Polish and then Swedish intervention, with Polish

Figure 4 Memorial to Minin and Pozharskii, Red Square, Moscow (nineteenth century)

From the personal collection of the author.

troops occupying Moscow from 1610 after Shuiskii's fall. Muscovy was in imminent danger of collapse, subjugation or dismemberment. However, following an appeal by the Patriarch, Hermogen, who died in Polish captivity shortly afterwards, and one abortive attempt to retake Moscow, an effective militia army gathered at Yaroslavl in the north-east of the country, the area least affected by the Troubles and most able to meet the costs of a new military campaign. It was organised by a town elder, Kozma Minin, a butcher by profession, and led by a Prince, Dmitrii Pozharskii (Figure 4). Orthodoxy, under threat from Polish Catholicism, provided a crucial focus for national unity. In 1612 the Polish invaders were driven out. In 1613, with the Poles gone, an Assembly of the Land, socially the most representative ever held, attended – most unusually – by Cossacks and free peasants, gathered to elect a new tsar. Rejecting royal Polish and Swedish candidates, the delegates chose Mikhail Romanov, the 17-year-old son of Godunov's unsuccessful rival Fëdor Romanov/Filaret and great-nephew of Ivan IV. Mikhail was a native Russian with (distant) Riurikid connections; youthfully innocent and malleable; and favoured by the Cossacks because his father had supported the second, Tushino pretender against Shuiskii. The election re-established a nationally acceptable ruling house, and also the principle of autocracy: despite rumours of secret promises made by Mikhail (like Shuiskii) under oath, there is no evidence that his power was circumscribed in any formal way. Thereafter the Romanov dynasty reigned for three centuries as unlimited autocrats.

Table 3   The Romanov Rulers

Mikhail	1613–45	Ivan VI	1740–41
Aleksei	1645–76	Anna Leopoldovna	
Fëdor III	1676–82	of Brunswick-	
Sophia, regent	1682–89	Lüneburg, regent	1740–41
Natalia Naryshkina,		Elizabeth	1741–61
regent	1689–94	Peter III	1761–62
Ivan V, co-tsar	1682–96	Catherine II	1762–96
Peter I, co-tsar 1682–96	1682–1725	Paul I	1796–1801
Catherine I	1725–27	Alexander I	1801–25
Peter II	1727–30	Nicholas II	1825–55
Anna	1730–40	Alexander II	1855–81
		Alexander III	1881–94
		Nicholas II	1894–1917

*The Consolidation of Autocratic Power and the Question of
National Security (1613–1700)*

The election of Mikhail resolved the political crisis of legitimacy in
Muscovy and marked the end of the Troubles, although full stability
took longer to re-establish. Relations with Muscovy's neighbours
were resolved, first by the unfavourable treaty of Stolbovo (1617)
with Sweden: territorial concessions cut Muscovy off from the Baltic
for a century, although reciprocal commercial access was preserved.
Further fighting with Poland ended in stalemate and the Truce of
Deulino (1618). An exchange of prisoners brought home Mikhail's
father, Filaret, held captive while negotiating with the Poles.
Mikhail's rule (1613–45), initially fragile, received strong support
from the Assembly of the Land during the young Tsar's first years;
but on his return in 1619 Filaret, a powerful personality, assumed the
vacant office of Patriarch and the principal role in government. He
received the title of 'Great Lord', usually reserved to the monarch,
and until his death in 1633 was the power behind the throne.

After the Time of Troubles, government and elite faced problems
and challenges which shaped the development of Muscovy for the
rest of the century. In internal affairs, the first requirement was social
cohesion and political stability: this involved both the formulation of
an acceptable version of monarchy after the terrifying excesses of the
oprichnina and Godunov's and Shuiskii's failed rule, and the further
development of the central administrative system, as territory and
population continued to grow. Social grievances had to be addressed
and, since the Troubles seemed to many a divine judgment, the
Church also faced, and led, calls for spiritual and moral regeneration.
In the military sphere, Ivan IV's failure in the Livonian War had
shown that his upgrading of the armed forces was insufficient for
success against the military machines of European neighbours: a
more effective army was essential, as were the resources to fund it.
Measures were required to restore the economy, make it more
productive, and gather revenue more effectively – Muscovy had lost
almost half its population during the Troubles. These issues were the
more critical because the country was being drawn steadily into
closer relations with states to the west which possessed or were
developing superior military and economic capacities: European
economic growth was increasing as trade expanded, driven by new
tools such as extended banking and credit networks. International

demand for cereals was making Poland the granary of Europe, and as English and Dutch financial and maritime power fuelled commercial turnover, the Baltic as well as the White Sea became major commercial highways, arenas of increasing economic and therefore political competition. Muscovy was tied into this commercial nexus because traditional commodities – tar, hemp, timber, potash – acquired new international value as naval stores. Its military success during the century also faced it with a powerful competitor in the south, the Ottoman Empire. These developments and pressures posed problems whose resolution would call in question the society's structures and self-image and present it over the century with a crisis less urgent but no less fundamental than the crisis of the Troubles.

The society over which the new dynasty ruled was highly stratified. Population totals have been estimated, roughly, at around 6.5 million c.1550, 7.0 million c.1600, the same c.1650 after recovery from the losses of the Troubles, 9.6 million c.1680 including Left-Bank Ukraine, and 12.7 million at the time of the 1719 tax-census: a remarkable feature of early modern Russian history is the huge growth in population, which started in the sixteenth century and continued into the twentieth, easily outstripping growth rates elsewhere in Europe. The population can be divided crudely into servicemen and taxpayers. At the social apex were the great families around the Court, the wealthy elite and upper service class, whose members were eligible for the 'duma ranks' (membership of the Boyar Council), and lesser high nobles holding the state offices immediately beneath, the so-called Moscow ranks. In 1630 they numbered together 2642 men (actual holders of the four duma ranks numbered 29 in 1613, 57 in 1650, and 153 in 1690). These were the families who owned votchina estates and were inscribed in the 'precedence books' controlling the mestnichestvo system. It was they who followed the increasingly common practice of secluding their womenfolk: elite women occupied their own separate domestic quarters, the *terem*. Below the elite families came the 'middle service class'. This consisted of provincial gentry making up the traditional cavalry levy, servicemen who were the main beneficiaries of the pomest'e system and the numerically largest group of serf-owners. The middle service class numbered 20,000–25,000 in the mid-seventeenth century, with their families 70,000–80,000 people, owning on average 5–6 peasant households. As their numbers in the army declined during the century, they increasingly joined the expanding pool of provincial chancellery officials. They predominated in the centre, west and south: the traditional areas of pomest'e grants were those where land was available and fertile, and where the presence of military forces was needed or useful. Chancellery officials were also allowed to own land and serfs, as were the tiny number of *gosti*, the wealthy elite merchants who engaged in large-scale commerce. Senior clergy (the so-called 'black', monastic, churchmen who manned the ecclesiastical hierarchy) and monasteries (some 25,000 persons were in monastic orders in 1700) likewise controlled peasants living on Church estates, though their rights over them were less complete. The next layer were 'lower service class' personnel, a socially varied stratum drawn up into the lower ranks of the Muscovite army as these expanded and became more differentiated. They were not eligible for pomest'e grants or serf-ownership, and served 'by contract' for cash payment: mostly tax-paying town-dwellers, when not in service they lived by farming or smallholding, crafts or petty trade. By the 1680s this group made up the majority of Moscow's armed forces.

The permanent, registered townsfolk (members of the urban community, *posad*) had some degree of self-government, owed taxes and local services to the Crown, and after 1649 were bound to their community. Around 1680 the registered urban population may have totalled some 3 per cent of the whole, mostly engaged in artisanal crafts or petty trade; they also tended to have secondary agricultural occupations, since Muscovite towns were poorly differentiated from their rural environment. Parish priests, the married 'white' clergy, lived in their parishes, where they received land as well as payments for services; they were not much better off than the peasants to whom they ministered. At this time entry into the parish clergy was open to outsiders, and congregations had a say in the selection of priests, although priestly families were increasingly interrelated. In the eighteenth century the white clergy became effectively a closed hereditary cast.

The vast majority of the population, 80–90 per cent or even more, were peasants. In 1719 peasants numbered probably 11.45 million (up from 8.6m. in 1678). Of these, 6.39 million (55.8 per cent) were landlords' peasants, the group properly called serfs; 1.58 million (13.8 per cent) were monastery peasants, and 1.01 million (8.9 per cent). Court peasants, living on estates which serviced the imperial family. Almost all the remaining peasantry (2.46m., 21.6 per cent) were tax-liable ('black-ploughing') peasants who lived on state land and paid direct taxes to the government; they were renamed 'state' peasants under Peter I. (Over the next two centuries proportions changed: in 1857 state peasants made up 47 per cent and serfs and other dependent peasants 53 per cent of the total.) The lowest social level was occupied by slaves (*kholopy*), about 2 per cent of the population in 1678, who were dependent on their masters but could be found in a variety of occupations.

These social categories were, however, never exact: the stratified, stable society envisioned by tsarist legislation was belied by fluid reality. Occupation by no means always matched official status. Social boundaries were porous. Sometimes they dissolved: 'strolling people' of no fixed abode wandered the roads – beggars and vagabonds, runaway serfs, itinerant religious, pilgrims and peddlars, minstrels and popular players (*skomorokhi*). The frontiers, especially in the south, were social melting-pots, where distinctions between different 'conditions' or 'estates' were often ignored or distorted. While the major Cossack hosts occupied distinct lands of their own, many Cossacks also served in the border defences, where urgent military needs and lack of close control meant that persons from almost any social category could find a living. And as the Empire grew, the Great Russian heartland was surrounded by a patchwork of other ethnic groups, in the far north and Siberian east, and down the Volga into the steppes and the north Caucasus, with a mixture of other Europeans in the lands absorbed to the west. Religion was equally mixed – Orthodoxy was interspersed with Islam, Buddhism, animism, and in the west Judaism, Lutheranism and Catholicism. This complexity increased as Muscovy expanded further during the seventeenth century.

Apart from an unsuccessful revenge attack on Poland in the Smolensk War (1633–5), Moscow initially remained at peace. It took no part in the international Thirty Years' War (1618–48), from which Sweden emerged as the dominant regional power; and it avoided entanglements in the south with the Ottomans and their Crimean vassals. In 1635 the government returned to a successful traditional policy, and began construction of a major new southern defence system, the Belgorod Line: an 800-km.-long series of palisades and ditches, studded with fortified points, manned by a variety of minor servitors and hired Cossacks as well as regular forces sent from the centre. The Belgorod Line was extremely effective, finally protecting the heartland from Tatar attack, thus freeing the army for other needs, and forming an excellent base for further advance into the steppe.

Ukrainian affairs, however, led to confrontation with Poland in 1654. The Orthodox Zaporozhian Cossacks of the Left-Bank Ukraine (east of the Dnepr) had long sought to defend their independence against the pretensions of their overlords, the mainly Catholic Poles. In 1648 the Hetman (elected leader), Bogdan Khmel'nyt'skyi, raised a rebellion and, rather than submit to superior Polish power, sought the protection of Orthodox Muscovy. An agreement was struck at Pereiaslavl in northern Ukraine. The Cossacks viewed the arrangement as a reciprocal pact between protector and client which might be varied in the future. The Muscovite side viewed it as an absolute act of submission to the autocratic Tsar. This fundamental difference of perception has had far-reaching consequences for Ukrainian–Russian relations and for accounts of the history of the region. The Pereiaslavl Accord of 1654 effectively marked Muscovite annexation of the Left-Bank Ukraine: a critical development which gave northerly Muscovy extensive new territory and resources east of the Dnepr and extended its boundaries southwards to closer contact with Poles and Turks. It also brought Moscow the vibrant culture of Kiev and Ukrainian Orthodoxy and closer acquaintance with Polish culture, as well as the difficult legacy of the Ukrainian Greek Catholic (Uniate) Church.

It was clear that Muscovite acceptance of the Cossack overtures would entail war with Poland. Supported by an Assembly of the Land, the new Tsar, Aleksei Mikhailovich (1645–76), ratified the Accord and embarked on the Thirteen Years' War (1654–67); for a time he had to face Swedish intervention, too, in the First Northern War (1656–61). Aleksei led his forces in person, the first tsar to leave his country and fight abroad. The war devastated Poland; Muscovy was also stretched to the limit. The great frontier jacquerie led by the Cossack-cum-brigand Stenka Razin along the Volga in 1670 can be seen as a reaction to the hardships suffered by the lower sections of Muscovite society. Moscow emerged the stronger in the confrontation with the Poles: the Armistice of Andrusovo (1667) secured Muscovite gains in the Left Bank and also control for two years of Kiev on the Right. The 'Mother of Russian Cities' was a major prize; Moscow never gave it back. In 1686, when Poland needed

Muscovite support against the Ottoman Empire, Moscow's price was border concessions and the cession of Kiev in perpetuity: in desperation the Polish King Jan Sobieski signed a treaty of 'permanent' peace and alliance. The bilateral 1686 Treaty of Moscow between Muscovy and Poland brought Moscow as a junior partner into the Holy League, formed in 1684 by the Holy Roman Empire, Poland and Venice, with Papal support, after the failed 1683 Ottoman siege of Vienna: the first European alliance of the Muscovite state in modern times and a considerable success for Muscovite diplomacy. Moscow had already fought one war with the Ottomans, 1678–81, and now had to break the Treaty of Bakhchisarai (1681) with which that had concluded. Muscovy's role in the League was to divert Ottoman strength by attacking again in the east. Unsuccessful campaigns followed across the hostile steppe against the Crimean Tatars (1687 and 1689), and Peter I's river-borne campaigns against the Ottoman fortress on the Sea of Azov, finally successful, of 1695–6. The Peace of Karlowitz (1698) which ended the war between the Porte and the Holy League nevertheless excluded Muscovy: Moscow had to make a separate peace in 1700, a sign of its continuing subordinate status in European affairs.

During the seventeenth century, Muscovy spent 42 years at war. Accordingly, successive regimes worked, rather fitfully, to optimise the country's armed forces, responding to international innovation across what has been termed the 'Euro-Ottoman common zone' of contemporary military interaction, of which Muscovy became part. While now more engaged with enemies in the west (Poland and Sweden), Moscow still faced steppe warfare against the Crimeans and the Ottomans. The techniques and requirements of steppe warfare were considerably different from those in Central Europe, and could themselves become innovations if applied elsewhere: Eugene of Savoy achieved notable success by applying Eastern methods to Western theatres. However, for the conditions of the Smolensk War on its western border, the Muscovite government created new 'regiments of foreign formation', peasant musketeer infantry and heavily armed dragoons, based on European models and organised and led by foreign mercenaries. At first the new 'foreign' regiments were formed and disbanded *ad hoc*. Later they became permanent features of the Muscovite army, increasingly replacing the obsolescent cavalry levy. In the unsuccessful Crimean campaigns of the 1680s the new-style infantry made up 44 per cent, new types of cavalry 23 per cent, and the old middle-service-class cavalry only 7 per cent of an army of some 113, 000. At the same time, changes were made in other areas. A Dutch engineer built the first specialised munitions plant, at Tula in 1632; Western military manuals were translated. The command system was modified. The precedence rules had frequently been suspended on military campaigns for the sake of efficiency, and in 1682, under Fëdor, they were finally abolished, for the sake of 'the common good' – the first time this phrase appeared in Muscovite legislation. Freedom of appointment strengthened the power of the Crown. The total number of troops used also increased (with fluctuations): to 100,000 in 1650 and 200,000 in the 1680s – recruitment levies were introduced to maintain strength. At the same time Moscow maintained large irregular cavalry forces drawn from Cossacks and steppe peoples of the south-east. These developments looked forward to the reforms and the military successes of Peter I.

Military advances were paralleled by those in central administration. The chancellery (prikaz) network continued to grow, becoming by 1700 a developed early-modern state administrative apparatus, providing Mikhail and his successors with increasing ability to manage and control Muscovite society. The underlying function of this system was the realisation of revenue for military purposes: the armed forces increased by two and a half times between 1631 and 1681, and their cost threefold. A few of the 60 or so seventeenth-century chancelleries had geographical jurisdictions, but most were functionally defined. The *pomestnyi prikaz* dealt with service lands, the Ambassadors' Chancellery dealt with foreign affairs, and the Treasury Chancellery oversaw state finance. The personal affairs of the Patriarch, and of the Tsar, were also managed by dedicated chancelleries: for the latter the government created in 1654 the Secret Chancellery, which also operated as a police and control unit. The Boyar Council was now able to function more effectively with increased administrative support, although inflation of its membership later in the century diminished its power and prestige. The Assembly of the Land faded out – the last one properly so-called appears to have been that of 1653, though later smaller councils sometimes fulfilled similar functions. Both these institutions disappeared under Peter I, who ignored them.

Law Code, Church Reform and Schism

Bureaucratic procedures were basically at odds with the prevailing social culture: in the words of Geoffrey Hosking, the chancelleries' operations 'entailed an increasingly impersonal and rule-bound method of transacting official business, one which always risked affronting a people used to seeing monarchical power as personal and exercised according to traditional or divinely ordained moral norms.' A similar clash of cultures led to dramatic events in the early years of Aleksei, who succeeded his father Mikhail in 1645. Although the succession was uncontested, he soon faced popular discontent over taxation, corruption and terms of service. This was expressed in a mass petition offered him in 1648 by the population of Moscow: in accordance with the personalised, patriarchal nature of the traditional political culture, grievance was addressed directly to the ruler. However, the young and inexperienced Tsar initially refused the petition, thereby breaching the unspoken understanding between humble petitioner and merciful ruler and provoking the townsmen to riot. Groups of middle-service-class pomeshchiki, worried over the flight of their peasants and their own declining military status, took advantage of the situation to renew previous insistent petitions to the Crown. Aleksei defused the threatening situation only by sacrificing unpopular advisers and promising a revision of the offending laws under the aegis of an Assembly of the Land. The result was the 'Assembly' (or 'Conciliar') Law Code of 1649.

The Assembly Code is one of the great legal monuments of Russia. It was the first set of laws to apply to all areas of the country, and remained the basic law code until 1830. It represented a marked advance over the 1550 Code, providing substantive statements of law in many areas of public and social life, as well as clearly defined legal and judicial procedures. It was also the first secular work printed in Muscovy, produced in 2400 copies (a huge print-run for the time), by the new Moscow printing office, for distribution to government offices across the country. The Code was informed by Aleksei's personal concern for 'good order' in his realm. Its preamble expressed the idea succinctly with the formulation that 'the administration of justice . . . be equal for all ranks of people'. This meant not that all levels of society should be equally favoured, but that justice should be administered fairly and incorruptly, in the interest of society itself and of the sovereign. It reflected a consensual view emerging among the elite, traceable particularly in the frequent Muscovite litigation concerning personal honour and insult and which saw society as a rightly ordered 'godly community' which must be sustained: as Nancy Kollmann puts it, 'the state as composed of pious individuals, grouped in orderly families and arranged in a hierarchy of service to landlord and tsar'. The idea that right order should and could be achieved within the state, and was attainable through law, fostered social cohesion and integration.

The Code's provisions addressed both the insecurities of the Tsar, and the most immediate popular grievances. The early chapters specify in detail the prerogatives and protection of the Tsar and the Patriarch, with severe penalties for infringements. Among other things, direct petitioning was banned: petitions must now be presented to the appropriate government office (in fact the humble petition remained an essential form of political communication into Soviet times). The Code consolidated middle-service-class support behind the crown by unifying forms of land tenure and (as we have seen) abolishing the time-limit for reclamation of fugitive peasants. This had the effect of completing enserfment: now even illegal flight could not bring permanent freedom – once a serf, always a serf. Other provisions strengthened the institution of slavery. The townsmen's concerns were met by new penalties for corruption – a constant and insoluble problem – and exclusion of non-taxpayers from city land and privileges, although the Code also bound the townsfolk, like the peasants, to their communities. While many of its provisions were poorly enforced, or later neglected, the Code effectively enhanced government control and authority. Besides offering more systematic procedures for administering justice, its provisions gave less emphasis to rights than to obligations and service, and also stiffened the estate distinctions of Muscovite society. The simultaneous creation of a Monastery Chancellery which could intervene in ecclesiastical administration also weakened the institutional power of the Church.

The aftermath of the Troubles, and increasing engagement with Christian powers (Catholic and Protestant) to the west, posed serious questions for the Church as well as the government. In the decades after the Troubles a renewal movement emerged led by 'Zealots of Piety', a group of churchmen and laity preaching a renewal of spiritual values and Church life. The Zealots' concerns went to the heart of Moscow's cultural and national identity. They were worried not only about morals, but also about purity of faith and the faithfulness of the Church: over the years, through copying and other errors, changes had crept into the Orthodox liturgy. These concerns led to radically differing conclusions.

With Ivan IV's triumph over the Tatars and the establishment of the Moscow Patriarchate, Muscovy had emerged as an increasingly powerful political force in the Orthodox and Eastern European worlds. This pre-eminence was supported by the Greek Patriarchs, who looked to Muscovy for financial and political support and leadership. The Patriarchs encouraged Moscow to patronise Orthodox learning and to introduce educational institutions into the country, and some monastic schools were established. Consequently the variant readings of the Russian liturgy and sacred books became evermore conspicuous, and as early as 1616 steps were taken to revise corrupted texts. The young Aleksei was closely associated with members of the Zealots, especially the archimandrite Nikon, initially a close friend and mentor. Aleksei summoned a Church Council in 1650 which discussed questions of reform; in 1652, with his support, Nikon, a man of peasant stock, unbending character and great ambition, became Patriarch. The reform discussions continued apace; Nikon imperiously revised Church books and liturgical ritual, over the protests of conservatives, who came together at the Solovki monastery on the White Sea in 1657 to proclaim their devotion to the custom-hallowed unrevised texts and liturgy. They became known as Old Believers or Old Ritualists. The Old Believers identified form with substance, and believed (in the formulation of Gabrielle Scheidegger) that 'each and every change, even . . . the deletion of a single letter, had a hidden significance: . . . to pervert the accepted teachings of God and to deliver believers into the arms of Satan.' When Aleksei went to war with Poland in 1654, Nikon was placed in charge of government affairs and, like Filaret, accorded the title of 'Great Lord'. But without Filaret's blood tie to the Tsar, Nikon was highly vulnerable. His arrogance and pretensions alienated Court circles and when Aleksei returned, more experienced and self-assured, Tsar and Patriarch fell out. The estrangement culminated in the deposition of Nikon at a Church Council in 1667 and the unambiguous assertion of the temporal over the spiritual power: an abandonment of the traditional Byzantine 'symphony' between Emperor and Patriarch, and a negation of the view of Moscow as a universal Orthodox empire.

However, the Council simultaneously confirmed Nikon's liturgical reforms and anathematised the Old Believers. The decision precipitated a schism which alienated millions of people from the state and its official 'Nikonian' Church; the split also reflected the Church's incomplete authority over its believers and the tense relations, especially in the countryside, between higher churchmen and grass-roots believers who had grievances and aspirations of their own. While politically impotent, in time the schismatics constituted an alternative society within the Russian polity, with important consequences. They saw the use of alien foreign learning to change hallowed Muscovite forms and practices as a betrayal of true Muscovite Orthodox spirituality, sanctified by the Church Fathers and handed down intact through generations – a betrayal which led straight to apostasy and damnation, and clearly presaged the coming of Antichrist. Such was the view of Archpriest Avvakum, another 'Zealot of Piety'and later the Old Believers' most famous voice, if not at the time an important leader. Avvakum's magnificent autobiography was one of the first major writings in the Russian vernacular. While Nikon, deposed, ended his days as a monk in 1681, Avvakum was burnt at the stake the following year. Nevertheless the Old Belief survived, despite persecution. Some dissenters sought to escape Antichrist by self-immolation; many more sought refuge in remote places, contributing to the settlement of outlying areas. They developed their own culture, with a relatively high degree of literacy and specialisation in the manuscript reproduction of Old Believer texts: as recently as the 1960s a secret Old Believer writing-house was discovered in a hidden Siberian valley. Old Believer traditions of self-help and solidarity led to economic success: some of the leading nineteenth-century Russian entrepreneurs were adherents of the Old Belief, whch still exists today.

Nikon's liturgical reforms, aimed at correcting obvious errors, represented paradoxically a conservative attempt to return to 'pristine' Russian Orthodoxy, by aligning Muscovite usage with Greek texts. Moreover, lacking the necessary expertise for this, Moscow had to bring in monks trained abroad, from Mount Athos and Ukraine. Kiev was more sophisticated in these skills, since Orthodoxy there had long faced the ideological threat of Catholicism. In 1634 the Metropolitan of Kiev, Pëtr Mohyla, had set up an Orthodox Academy, modelled on the Jesuit schools which he sought to resist. The Mohyla Academy became a powerful centre of systematic learning at a time when Muscovy had nothing similar. The first comparable secular school in Moscow, the Slavonic-Greek-Latin Academy, was not opened until 1686. After the deposition of Nikon, Ukrainian clerics filled many senior positions in the Muscovite hierarchy.

Cultural Change

The conservatism of the official Church in the seventeenth century also found expression in the broader cultural sphere, leading to a rearguard action against the gradual spread of alien cultural influences in Muscovite society. Such contagions were brought in principally by outsiders required for state purposes. Nikon, while imperiously altering the liturgy, publicly destroyed icons painted in realistic, non-traditional style. The use of tobacco was spreading, an abomination in Church eyes, and some individuals were even desecrating Man's divine image by shaving their beards. Tsar Aleksei issued a decree in 1675 forbidding the wearing of foreign dress and the cutting of hair. In 1652 the growing colony of Western foreigners resident in Moscow (soldiers, merchants, craftsmen) was segregated in a separate settlement on the city's outskirts, replacing that destroyed by Ivan IV. (The Tsar, aghast at the recent sacrilegious beheading of Charles I of England, had banished the English community temporarily to Archangel.) The New Foreign or German Suburb flourished: unity was strength.

At Court the cultural atmosphere was also changing. Aleksei was famous for his devotion to Church observance: he gained the nickname 'most quiet one' for his religiosity. Nevertheless, while supporting liturgical reform, he tolerated neither the caesaro-papism of Nikon nor the obscurantist xenophobia of Avvakum: the deposition of the Patriarch and the excommunication of the Old Belief were further markers of the growing authority of the Crown. Nor did his public condemnation of foreign fashions accord with his private practice. Aleksei's forays into Poland during the Thirteen Years' War had been a seminal experience: although he was familiar from childhood with imported Western objects and the ways of visiting foreigners, Poland and its palaces revealed to him a new world of culture and intellectual opportunity. On his return, as his English physician Samuel Collins recorded, 'his thoughts advanced and he began to model his Court and Edifices more stately'. Without challenging

Church rulings on matters of morality and cultural practice, in private Aleksei, his family and entourage interested themselves in novel ideas, activities and artefacts. European instruments and baubles were acquired systematically through commission agents. New furnishings within their quarters matched new architectural ideas without: the so-called Moscow or Naryshkin Baroque architecture of the late seventeenth century (Figure 5) shows clear Italian influence, and Aleksei's Kolomenskoe Palace was decorated in novel style. Court theatricals were arranged, in strict privacy, and Aleksei appointed a Belorussian cleric and poet, Semën Polotskii, as tutor for his children, some of whom learned Latin and Polish. A few Western artists found employment in Moscow – portraits in the Polish *parsuna* style became fashionable among the elite; the brilliant Semën Ushakov spearheaded an innovative representational trend in icon painting; in 1683 a workshop for secular art was added to the official icon-painting studios. A few members of the Court elite also adopted a different lifestyle: the best-known is Prince Vasilii Golitsyn, chief minister under the regency of Aleksei's daughter Sophia, noted for his grand house, liking for foreigners, and command of foreign languages. Cultural change was gradual and unofficial, confined to narrow circles, but percolating through the elite.

Similar innovations could be observed in the economy and economic thought. Mercantilist doctrines, current in Eastern as well as Western Europe, slipped into Muscovy with foreign merchants and makers of grand projects. The government sought to strengthen the economy and its own revenues by encouraging foreigners to set up industrial enterprises – the foundry at Tula (1632) was one of many – but also tried to protect Russian merchants from foreign competition. It imposed heavy duties on imports and monopolised export commodities. The outstanding proponent of mercantilist policies was the minister Afanasii Ordyn-Nashchokin, who took advantage of the Thirteen Years' War to pursue Russian trading interests on the Baltic and authored the landmark 1667 New Commercial Code at the war's end. Although Moscow had no naval tradition, dreams of Eastern commerce led Aleksei to construct a flotilla on the Caspian, under Dutch supervision: but his ships were burnt by Stenka Razin in 1670. The development of mercantilist policies, which were designed to further state-building and the strengthening of state power, prefigured the aggressive cameralism of Peter I which derived from European mercantilist doctrine.

Figure 5 Moscow Baroque: Church of the Transfiguration (1687–8), Novodevichyi Convent, Moscow

From the personal collection of Professor Lindsey Hughes.

During the seventeenth century the new Romanov dynasty developed a system of government and an economic and military capacity which enabled it to dominate society, support its wars, and prevail over its old enemy, Poland. It consolidated its power by increasing its administrative reach and ensuring the support of the service elite, while tightening its grip over the peasantry, the towns, and the dangerous and volatile southern frontier. There were no countervailing institutional restraints: Aleksei's reign marks the full establishment of an absolute regime, and scholars speak of the 'hypertrophic development of state power' (Richard Hellie) in Muscovy. But this process itself called into question the traditional Muscovite worldview and culture and Muscovites' self-image, developed since the fifteenth century; it caused a 'crisis of traditionalism', undermining Muscovite confidence through closer contacts with alien societies, the search for survival amid the imperatives of international competition. The gradual spread of unorthodox cultural attitudes also reflected a growth of individualism and secularism within the elite. The clash of cultures was vividly summed up in Peter I's reign, both in the person and behaviour of the Tsar himself and in his confrontations with society, which he encouraged by police methods to adopt new values.

PETRINE RUSSIA

The Apprenticeship of Peter I

Aleksei died relatively young in 1676, and his successor, Fëdor Alekseevich, his son by his first wife, did not live long. Fëdor's death, childless, in 1682 provoked a succession crisis and power struggle between the two wives' families, only resolved by the creation of joint young tsars under a regency: Fëdor's brother Ivan, sickly and retarded, and his bright younger half-brother Peter, 9 years old, son of Aleksei's second wife. The regent was Sophia, Ivan's sister. Peter (Pëtr, Peter I, the Great, 1682–1725) spent the following years (1682–9) away from most official affairs and the traditional life of the Court. This time was crucial for the boy's development: he received a patchy formal education but was free to live as he pleased. He soon abandoned Muscovite clothing in favour of foreign dress, and from an early date went clean-shaven. His penchant for things military was gratified by the 'toy' or 'play' regiments, with real foreign officers, into which he dragooned his playmates, and which later grew into the elite Preobrazhenskii and Semënovskii Guards regiments. In an estate barn he discovered a small English boat, and was enchanted when a Dutch sailor taught him how to sail it. It sparked Peter's lifelong infatuation with things nautical, later expressed in his creation of a powerful navy. The practical utility of foreigners brought Peter into growing contact with residents of the Foreign Suburb, especially after the death of the intimidatingly xenophobic Patriarch Ioachim in 1690. He developed a taste for coarse carousing. From this period too dates the curious 'All-Mad, All-Drunken, All-Jesting Assembly', comparable to the Hellfire clubs of contemporary England, a vehicle for riotous parties and carnivalesque inversion of authority, which he maintained assiduously throughout his life. In the Foreign Suburb Peter also discovered dancing; fencing; his only foreign language, Dutch; the toleration of religious diversity which became a hallmark of his dealings with foreigners; and – more elusively – an entrepreneurial mind-set, rationalistic, pluralist, open to new horizons. He also studied the arts of love, with Anna Mons, daughter of a foreign wine-merchant, despite his very conventional marriage in 1689 to Yevdokia Lopukhina, traditionally educated daughter of a lesser noble clan. She bore him two sons, but he found no common ground with her, and eventually forced her to take the veil.

In 1689 a confrontation between Peter and Sophia ended the latter's rule. Sophia's regency was a remarkable fact in the history of the Russian monarchy, almost the first time a woman had overtly controlled power in the lands of the Eastern Slavs since Olga in tenth-century Kiev. Moreover, Sophia inaugurated a unique 'female century' for Russia's ruling house. Between 1682 and 1796 the state had 12 monarchs or regents, of whom seven were female; these women held power for 79 of the 114 years.

In 1695, a year before Ivan's death made him sole ruler, Peter was confronted with the hard demands of real life, in the form of serious military action, once more in the cause of the Holy League, and directed this time not at the impregnable Crimea, but at the Turkish coastal fortress guarding the Sea of Azov. The outcome was a fiasco like those of 1687 and 1689: the Muscovites lacked siege techniques and naval capacity. Peter's response was radical: he returned the following year with new Dutch-designed galleys and Austrian gunnery experts, paid for with extraordinary taxes. The Turkish fleet was driven off, the fortress walls breached, and Azov surrendered. Peter celebrated with a secular triumph more reminiscent of Classical Rome than Muscovite Orthodoxy; he also began to plan a new city and port on the Azov site, to be called Petropolis – a project overtaken by the creation of St Petersburg, and the later loss of Azov to the Turks. But the episode made clear the need both to revitalise the anti-Turkish alliance and to improve military and naval know-how: Peter set off to Western Europe.

Like Poland for Aleksei, the Great Embassy of 1697–8 – primarily to Holland and England – was seminal for Peter's reign. He was well received, for reasons of commercial policy; the outlandish and somewhat uncouth young Tsar, six feet seven inches tall, trying to pass incognito, was as much a curiosity to London crowds as England was to him. However, his experiences showed Peter that the anti-Ottoman campaign was dead – the great powers were engrossed in Spanish affairs. And he now saw at first hand the knowledge and technology, the wealth and diversity of which he had heard in the Foreign Suburb. He studied naval architecture and administration, sailed with the British fleet, hired English and Dutch technical specialists, and purchased everything which might help him along the same path at home. On his return to Moscow, in a famous gesture, he signalled a radical programme of cultural change by personally cutting off the beards of the courtiers who came to greet him. Meanwhile, active hostilities with the Ottomans were in abeyance, and Peter started to reorganise the army, recruiting 27 new regiments to be trained in European methods. He also laid the foundations of a new metallurgical industry in the Urals, where large ore deposits provided an indigenous supply: hitherto Sweden had furnished most Russian metallurgical requirements.

These were essential precautions, because on his way home in 1698 Peter had met Frederick Augustus, Elector of Saxony and King of Poland, and hatched an alliance against Sweden and its new boy-king, Charles XII: Frederick wanted Livonia, and Peter was eager to regain access to the sea and the wider world through the Baltic, lost at Stolbovo a century before. An existing alliance with Brandenburg (1697) was now supplemented by treaties with Poland and Denmark and, as soon as the Peace of Constantinople with the Ottomans was secure in 1700, Peter committed his untried army to war, unprovoked, against the Swedes.

The Great Northern War, 1700–21

The Great Northern War filled most of Peter's later reign. Initially, together with the War of the Spanish Succession (1701–14), it made warfare pan-European. The beginning was disastrous. Charles XII proved to be the outstanding soldier of his age, and commanded the best army in Europe. Swiftly knocking Denmark out of the coalition, he crushed the Muscovite army at Narva on the Gulf of Finland (1700), and chased Frederick Augustus's Polish-Saxon forces south through Poland. The years after Narva were a struggle for Russian survival. As internal tensions rose under the pressure of war and social change, uprisings occurred in Astrakhan (1705) and on the Don (1708–9): it seemed likely that if Peter lost a major battle, he would face catastrophic revolt. Peter desperately shored up the Saxon resistance to Charles, introduced internal changes to strengthen his own military capacity, developed his army and a new Baltic navy, and gradually advanced against the Swedish forces left in Livonia while Charles pursued the Saxons. The fortress of Saints Peter and Paul was founded in 1703 on land near the Gulf of Finland taken from the Swedes. The fortress formed the nucleus of St Petersburg, built, contrary to legend, not on empty marshes but near a small town attached to the captured Swedish fortress of Nienskans; the tsar began to call the new city his 'paradise'.

Despite Peter's far-reaching mobilisation of Muscovite resources, his forces could not face the superb Swedish army on even terms. The Tsar therefore turned the vast land itself into a weapon against the invader, withdrawing before him, using scorched earth tactics, attacking his supply routes and cutting off his allies. When the final confrontation came, at Poltava in the Ukraine in summer 1709, the Russian army hugely outnumbered the Swedish forces in men and artillery; the Swedes, weakened by a bitter winter with inadequate supplies, were underequipped, and Charles himself immobilised by a wound in the foot. The Swedish army was annihilated. However, Charles escaped to Turkish territory: a consequent Russian expedition against the Ottomans in 1711 led to near-catastrophe for Peter on the river Prut, and loss of Azov at the subsequent Treaty of Adrianople (1713). But the rout of the Swedes destroyed their army and permanently broke Swedish power. Peter, satisfied with his territorial gains and after 1717 dominant not only in Livonia but in Poland too, soon wished to make peace. But only in 1721 could he finally compel agreement at the negotiating table. By then Russia had replaced Sweden as the dominant naval as well as military power of the region. The Treaty of Nystadt gave Peter not only St Petersburg, but all of Livonia: Livland and Estland with their great port cities of Riga and Reval (Tallinn). The Baltic was open to Russian commerce, and the Baltic German nobilities of Livonia would henceforth provide notable servitors for both the Imperial army and the civilian administration. At his death four years later Peter left a standing army of some 200,000 men, acknowledged as formidable by the best European standards. In 1725 the new navy counted 27,000 men, 34 ships of the line, some 40 smaller ships and several hundred galleys, a force which seriously alarmed the mighty British naval establishment – though after Peter's death it soon fell into decay.

Peter's successes in the Great Northern War thrust Muscovy brusquely into prominence as a new power in Europe. Moreover, the wide-ranging and rapid internal changes which he introduced confronted the Muscovite elites with new ways of thinking and behaving. This process was symbolised above all by the creation of St Petersburg – a completely new city, built in European styles, and which soon became the new capital – and by the redefinition of Muscovy as the Russian Empire in 1721, after the Treaty of Nystadt had confirmed Russia's victory. The new Senate declared Peter 'the Great, Father of the Fatherland' and 'Emperor of All the Russias'.[†] The next two centuries of Russian history, to 1917, are conventionally known as the Imperial or St Petersburg period.

Petrine Reforms and the Petrine State

In order to achieve victory over the opponent he had so underestimated, Peter restructured the entire military machine and its support systems. The army was largely reformed on European lines by 1705, and a new military establishment took shape over the next two decades. The old Muscovite service classes were all gathered into a single new category of 'nobility' (*dvorianstvo*), with equal rights and obligations. All nobles were liable for service at the tsar's pleasure,

---

† *Imperator Vserossiiskii*. The adjective designating ethnic Great Russians is *russkii*. The Latin form for Russia, *Rossiia*, gave the adjectival form *rossiiskii*, which is applied to the totality of lands (and peoples) under Russian rule. The distinction is not made in English, which uses 'Russian' for both.

for life, starting in the lowest rank, and were compelled to acquire education – onerous obligations which many tried hard to evade. A law of 1714 conflated pomest'e with votchina lands, giving security of property rights; but it also abolished the established elite tradition of partible inheritance – now only one son was to inherit, at the father's discretion, the others being required to find some useful occupation away from home. The new law was uniformly detested, caused great strife in noble families, and was honoured as much in the breach as the observance. Peter's restructuring also affected all areas of military life. The training and supply of officers – initally foreign, then increasingly Russian; the creation of a new career structure to replace mestnichestvo, a problem finally solved by the Table of Ranks (1722); the new recruiting system which made all tax-paying (lower-class) males liable to service in the ranks for life, and also supplied the new navy – 53 levies raised 300,000 men during the reign; the working out of new military regulations, completed in the Military Statute of 1716; heroic efforts to solve the intractable issues of logistics and supply, particularly difficult in sparsely populated Eastern Europe; the development of indigenous sources of equipment, weaponry and munitions; the marvellous expedients used to raise funding for this colossal undertaking, until the introduction of the Soul Tax (1719–22), specifically designed to cover military expenditure – all these measures and processes were worked out and successively put in place during the reign.

Major reorganisation in the middle of a desperate war was inevitably difficult: Peter's military reform, Lindsey Hughes tells us, was 'a process of trial and error, a hotch-potch of orders issued from various campaign headquarters, adaptation and resourcefulness underpinned by a set of gut-feeling convictions about Russia's humiliation as a result of military backwardness'. But it worked, both in defeating Charles XII and in laying lasting foundations: after 1700 the Russian state enjoyed a century and a half of extraordinary military success (some individual defeats notwithstanding), until the Crimean War, and radical military reform was next undertaken only in the 1870s. However, many of Peter's measures only came to full fruition later; things were often chaotic and decided *ad hoc* during the war itself, and Peter's skill in adapting east-European fighting techniques to wear down Charles XII did not save him from over-confidence and complete defeat against the powerful Ottomans in 1711.

At the same time, the Tsar and his advisers were fully aware of the broader dimensions of military power and international status. By this time in Europe's development, a great power needed not only an effective army, but also productive administration, sound legal, financial and economic systems staffed by competent, trained and knowledgeable personnel using rational criteria. Peter hastened to remake Russian society in the image of the best practice he could find, though always bearing in mind Russian specifics and interests. He was interested in Chinese as well as Dutch medicine, Venetian as well as English shipbuilding. He consulted about education with Protestant Germans, but allowed Jesuits to set up a school in Moscow. Russians were sent all over Europe, as far as Spain, to learn and train. Naturally, some models offered more than others: in particular the northern Protestant powers were influential. In the years before Poltava the main focus was on immediate practical concerns and war needs, but from 1710 larger issues were addressed – some of the major war-related reforms were only completed in the 1720s.

Peter's changes affected almost all areas of the life of the state: he wished both to re-order institutions and to mould and discipline his subjects – especially the noble elite. In this he was following the best traditions of the early Enlightenment and the so-called 'well-ordered police state', the theory of interventionist government and prosperous, regulated ('policed') society which had been elaborated in France and by cameralist administrators in the German lands. This all-encompassing, rationalistic, activist approach to government was new in Russia, as was the concept of 'progress' – the word now entered the Russian language – and the distinction between ruler and state which Peter articulated. However, almost all Peter's individual reform measures had seventeenth-century precedents (St Petersburg, his new city, was the exception). On one hand, his zeal for change, foreign forms, systematic thought and legislation, was offensive to Muscovite tradition. Even great families were frequently still illiterate, established custom was deep-rooted and cherished, erudition was monastic, secular knowledge distrusted – foreign learning was 'guile' and 'deception' leading Russians to humiliation or perdition. But on the other, the door to elite understanding and acceptance of his vision was opened by the early influence of mercantilism from which cameralism derived, by creeping cultural change, increasing secularism, the ideas of 'good order' and 'common good' which inspired Aleksei and Fëdor, the parameters of the elite's 'godly community', and Peter's continued upholding of elite status and privilege. The results were mixed. Peter met huge resistance from the traditionalist mass of the population – passive, but also erupting in uprisings, brutally suppressed: since in popular imagination no true Orthodox tsar could behave as he did, rumours circulated that he must be a German changeling, or Antichrist. There was also much dissent within the elite. Peter had to confront boyar rivalry and opposition even from people attuned to reform. More conservative opposition crystallised around Peter's heir-apparent, Yevdokia's hapless son Aleksei Petrovich; in 1718 father and son fell out completely, the Tsarevich was accused of treason, and died under torture in prison. As a result of this episode, the Tsar passed a decree placing the succession entirely at the monarch's discretion – a radical departure from all previous practice; and Peter's new secret police office, the Preobrazhenskii Chancellery, watched vigilantly for the slightest manifestations of sedition. But besides the opposition, there were also many in the elite who came to understand what Peter was doing, and became his devoted supporters, the 'fledgelings of Peter's nest'.

In the short span of 30 years Peter tried to remake Russian society, and especially the elite. He radically reorganised both central and local administration, largely along Swedish lines: the central chancelleries were replaced by 12 ministries known as Colleges, and in 1711 a Governing Senate was created which effectively filled the gap left by the Boyar Council. A legal commission was set up in 1700 to recodify the laws, though without success. Educational and scientific provision was introduced, beginning with technical schools for the armed forces (artillery in 1699, navigation in 1701), proceeding through a nation-wide network of provincial elementary 'cipher' schools and Church seminaries (1714–22), to the St Petersburg Academy of Sciences created in 1725–6 on the advice of Leibniz. The Academy uniquely combined the functions of research centre, government department and university. Staffed initially by foreigners, it nevertheless made Russia a part of the eighteenth-century European 'republic of scholars' in a way previously inconceivable. A first museum, the Kunstkammer in St Petersburg, exhibited Peter's own collection of scientific samples and instruments, and (in the taste of the day) monstrously deformed creatures.

Peter also reshaped Church administration, asserting state control. On the death of the Patriarch in 1700 the office was filled by a *locum tenens*; in 1721 the Patriarchate was abolished and replaced with a

'Most Holy Governing Synod', parallel to the Senate but structured like a College. The Church's revenues were curtailed, and it was expected to take on new educational and social tasks. The celebration of major Church festivals and religious events became more secular; the old Creation calendar had been replaced in 1700 by the counting of years from the birth of Christ (the Julian calendar). Peter encouraged the arts in European style – the Court patronised foreign painters, engravers and architects, and official building programmes fed a 'Petrine revolution' in architecture. The first public theatres opened. Printing was encouraged. After an abortive episode under Ivan IV, a Church press had been established under Mikhail – three operated in late Muscovy; now up to ten presses worked at the Senate, Academy of Sciences and elsewhere, and a new 'civil' script was introduced (1710) to simplify the ornate complexity of Church Slavonic. Newspapers appeared; book publishing began to grow, though production was minuscule by other nations' standards and still largely of religious texts. A whole new vocabulary was elaborated to express new military terms and alien concepts, initiating a century-long evolution of the Russian literary language. Peter radically transformed noble life-styles. Beginning with the beard-cutting of 1698, the government introduced new fashions of dress, hairstyles, address, deportment and socialising, enforcing them upon male and female nobles alike. These waves of social change swept across the upper classes like a whirlwind. Day-to-day living was transformed, particularly for those at Court.

However, not only did Peter's reformist activity rest firmly on seventeenth-century beginnings, but in crucial areas he changed nothing, and reinforced Muscovite structures. Relations between different social groups remained essentially the same. Nobles dominated society as before. The towns remained weak and subservient to government requirements – Peter's use of state monopolies largely destroyed the wealthiest townsmen, the *gosti*. Social reclassification produced some new social categories – the 'state' peasantry already mentioned, or the *raznochinets* ('person of other rank'), a catch-all category for anybody who did not fit into an existing social slot; but these had negligible effect upon the social hierarchy. The peasantry was untouched by the cultural changes, keeping beards and worldview intact, but it became more than ever the fundamental beast of burden, taxed and conscripted as never before. Peter received proposals for the abolition of serfdom, but strengthened it instead.

The society which emerged from his reign was essentially a sophis-ticated up-dating of the Muscovite service state, and he deployed to the full the authority and coercive power of the Muscovite autocrats. Nor did his institutional changes, and his liking for low-born 'new men' (and women), change the fundamental importance in Russian society of rank, kinship and patronage networks, and the power of persons. In these respects his reform was conservative. It was, however, adequate to the requirements of the day.

Many Petrine institutions and innovations remained incomplete, imperfect, or ineffective. But in almost all spheres Peter laid the foundations of an Imperial edifice of state and public life which, while requiring further adaptation in due course, successfully supported the country's great-power status and lasted well into the nineteenth century, in some cases to 1917. His legacy was a state increasingly powerful in military terms, staffed by a small privileged and increasingly cultured elite, but resting on the exploitation of its large peasant population, whose cooperation was assured by a mixture of ideology, force and minimal protection; it was a state whose economic and resource development and administrative reach, although expanding, were still barely sufficient for the tasks of government it faced, especially in the provinces and on the periph-ery. The vast Russian Empire was always under-governed.

Peter I's reign was pivotal in Russia's history, and he remains a touchstone of discussions about Russian destiny. His activities, in all their diversity, brutality, hasty imperfections and incompleteness, resolved the 'crisis of traditionalism' facing seventeenth-century Muscovy, and allowed Russia to develop as a major economic and military power. Peter is consequently revered as the creator of Russian greatness, a statesman of vision, resolve and tireless energy; but he is also reviled as despotic and cruel, a precursor of Stalin who reinforced social unfreedom and sought 'progress through coercion'. He is admired as the ruler who brought Russia into the European mainstream, and sometimes condemned as the creator of a cultural, social and spiritual divide between masses and elite which ultimately caused revolution. It is in connection with Peter's reign more than any other that historians have used the misleading and value-laden concepts of 'backwardness' and 'Westernisation'. Other interpreta-tive models are more fruitful. Peter's regime prefigured many features of 'Enlightened Absolutism' (discussed further below): he has been interpreted as introducing a 'statist', government-controlled variety of the early Enlightenment. Russia also fits the concept of the 'military-bureaucratic' or 'fiscal state' of early-modern Europe, which was organised to extract maximum resources from its population for military purposes: though Russia was less well endowed with fiscal techniques than the states of Western Europe on which the model is primarily based.

THE 'PEASANT STATE': THE PEASANTRY AND SERFDOM

Another approach to the same set of relationships is the concept of the 'peasant state', developed by the rural sociologist Gerd Spittler. It highlights aspects of interaction between peasantry and ruling authorities which pertained in Russia right up to the fall of the Soviet Union. The model applies to countries with relatively authoritarian governments, peasant populations, and poor market development. This is a state, governed in interventionist manner by non-peasants, in which peasants form the majority of the population and provide the fundamental sources of wealth, while relations between peasant society and government are mediated by peasant leaders, representatives or administrative organisations: in Imperial Russia the government dealt with the peasant commune or the pomeshchik landowner.

In a general history of Russia (or any pre-industrial, agrarian country) it is difficult to give due importance to the peasantry (Figure 6). They were not principal movers and shakers, and the slow rhythms of peasant life rarely coincided with the speed of national events. Peasant culture was not literate and has left few records. Sources are very limited before the modern period; Russian peasant society is reasonably well documented only from the nineteenth century, and even then little is known of life on small estates. Peasant society and its mind-sets are alien to later, educated, urban ways of thought. Yet throughout Russian history, until the mid-twentieth century, peasants made up the vast majority of the population. Court, nobility and servicemen constituted a vanishingly thin layer atop the mass of peasants. In the eighteenth century, townsfolk composed on average roughly 4 per cent and all tax-exempt categories together – nobles, civil servants, clergy, the army – some 6 per cent of the population: as before, c.90 per cent were peasants.

It is also difficult to generalise about peasant society, which shared fundamental traits but varied widely in different places. In the

Figure 6   Russian peasant. Drawn by J. A. Atkinson *c.*1800

J. A. Atkinson, *A Picturesque Representation of the Manners, Customs and Amusements of the Russians* . . . (London 1812).

north and central regions of poorer agriculture, outside the black-earth area, non-agricultural activities – crafts, trade, transportation, lumbering – loosened ties to the land and made peasants more mobile. Ukrainian peasant traditions differed from those of Great Russia. State peasants had greater autonomy than serfs, and there could be a great difference between economic regimes. Most Russian estate-owners in the Imperial period were absentee landlords (because they were in state service, or preferred town life, or because wealthy owners had more than one estate); the administration of a steward was usually less favourable to the peasantry. Flogging was a standard and common punishment. Peasants of servile villages who owed labour-rent (*barshchina*) to their lord stayed on the estate to work his fields; serf peasants who paid quit-rent (*obrok*) in cash or kind could largely run their own affairs provided their dues were paid, and were relatively free to come and go. Great houses kept large numbers of serf peasants as servants, and these 'courtyard people' lived more than any other category directly under the eye of their master or mistress: this could result at one end of the spectrum in gross physical or personal abuse, at the other in a happy life as long-term family retainer.The latter was particularly common for wet-nurses, who remained lovingly for years with their noble charges. Imaginative literature provides vivid portraits. Probably the best-known literary nanny is Tatiana's nurse in Pushkin's *Eugene Onegin* (1823–31). Ivan Turgenev's story *Mumu* (1852) tells of a big, gentle, speech-impaired peasant (symbol for the peasantry itself) who is subjected to heart-rending treatment by his thoughtless and selfish mistress. Chekhov's bleak picture of post-emancipation rural life in *Peasants* (1897) contrasts with Tolstoi's idealisations.

Some peasants – a small minority – moved about widely; and illegal flight was common throughout the early-modern period. Flight could have various causes – intolerable conditions at home, but also hope of better conditions elsewhere, rumours of free land, or escape from punishment for crime. After 1649 special investigators were appointed to track down illegals, backed if necessary by military force, and they continued to operate until their functions were absorbed into local government in the 1770s. In Kazan province alone, 13,188 male fugitives were caught in the years 1722–7. Gangs of runaways sometimes fought pitched battles with police or troops. Military expeditions crossed the Polish border to recover such people. On the other hand, on the southern border, and wherever extra hands were needed, the authorities were ambivalent about returning useful runaways to their masters. Peasant attitudes to fugitives were also ambivalent. Because the system of collective responsibility, rooted back in Kievan practice, still obtained, remaining peasants had to pay the taxes due from them. Substantial rewards were offered for the denunciation or capture of runaways.

The life of the majority of peasants who stayed in their appointed place centred on the village (Figure 7). Peasant identity was usually focused there; and in larger villages a village church also played a central role. Villages in the Imperial period were sometimes very small, especially in the north: hamlets averaging five or six households. Steppe villages were usually more populous. Within the village the basic unit of life was the family (Figure 8), and its farm. The peasant world was a non-literate, visual and spiritual universe, energised by animist belief and magic, peopled by saints and spirits, the year measured by the seasons, holy festivals and the agricultural cycle. Every peasant had an 'beautiful corner' with icons in his house, but also paid due reverence to the *domovoi* or house sprite.

Figure 7   Russian village

J. A. Atkinson, *A Picturesque Representation of the Manners, Customs and Amusements of the Russians . . .* (London 1812).

Figure 8   Izba: peasant interior. Note the sleepers on the stove and the suspended cradle

J. A. Atkinson, *A Picturesque Representation of the Manners, Customs and Amusements of the Russians . . .* (London 1812).

The received wisdom of Orthodoxy was authoritative, though often poorly understood, and the peasantry with few exceptions remained outside the secularising changes and imperial aspirations of Peter I's new elite culture. Peasant life had its own aesthetic norms, its own traditions of song, dance and material culture. The women wove fabrics and braids of striking design and colour. Men were extraordinarily skilful workers in wood: the peasant tool of choice was the axe rather than the saw. The peasant house, sometimes two-storied in the north, mostly a single-storied hut (*izba*) of rough-hewn logs with wood-shingled or thatched roof, could be decorated with fine wooden fretting. In the south, outside the forest zone, white-washed wattle and daub or clay construction was common. In forest Russia most architecture was wooden, a peasant building tradition with forms and history all its own: the pinnacle of its achievement was the glorious wooden Church of the Transfiguration (1714) at Kizhi on Lake Onega, now a World Heritage site (Figure 9). In the village, life was close to nature: the izba, built around the big stove, often with earth floor, sometimes no chimney, led through an outhouse straight on to the muddy yard, household plot and unpaved village street – Great Russian homesteads tended to be grouped ribbon-fashion along a roadway or water-course. Life was face-to-face, lacking privacy, either between or within extended families – large numbers of people crammed into small houses; it was stench-filled and bug-ridden – especially in the winter, when openings would be kept closed, mixing smoke with cooking smells, stale air and body odours. Disease was familiar: children constantly died. On the other hand, the steam-bathhouse was regularly used, and the basic peasant diet was well-balanced in normal times, averting the scurvy that could haunt townsmen and the armed forces.

Life was typically communal, the land held in common and divided ('repartitioned') between families, which gave rise both to cooperation and to quarrels and conflict. The commune (*mir*) and the communal meeting (*mirskoi skhod*) which regulated village affairs

Figure 9   Church of the Transfiguration, Kizhi, Lake Onega, 1714. Made entirely of wood, it is a 'summer' church, neither heated or draught-proofed; together with the smaller 'winter' (heatable) Church of the Intercession on the right, it served the Kizhi district

From the personal collection of the author.

gave all heads of household the right to voice their opinions, a noisy affair, after which the village elder or the weighty men declared decisions reached by binding majority consensus. Vodka and other undue influences played a significant role: villages had their own networks of kinship, patronage, economic and social relations, their own politics. Customary law, not state law, governed interpersonal relations through the commune, including such punishments as public shaming. Village elites emerged: particularly in the later eighteenth and nineteenth centuries a few serfs became wealthy entrepreneurs, and even owned serfs themselves. Since serfs could not own immovable or human property, these people had to hold property in the name of their lord, who was of course pleased to have such prosperous subjects, and also sometimes helped himself to this wealth registered in his name. There has been much discussion of social and economic differentiation and social mobility within the peasantry, especially since Soviet Marxists claimed to see in growing differentiation a development of capitalist relations in the countryside. Most scholars now view differences of wealth as more typically cyclical, reflecting the rise and fall of family size and labour potential.

Family life was highly patriarchal, and violence routine. Nineteenth- and twentieth-century records of village life show peasants' characteristic unsentimental self-interest in dealings with each other, within and outside the family, and the more so with outsiders. Resources were scarce, outside authority arrogant and brutal: peasants, submissive to irresistible power when they met it, behaved arrogantly and brutally when they had the chance to exert power themselves, even with their own kin. Compassion was usually aroused by religion: itinerant religious, pilgrims and beggars 'in the name of Christ' were rarely turned away (Figure 10) and helpless convicts marching in chains down the long road to Siberia could expect ready alms. Cooperation and reciprocity occurred where the interest of the village as a whole was involved – fire victims, for instance, were helped back on to their feet so that they could pay their share of taxes. The peasant head of household (*bolshak*) held unregulated despotic power, the greater because from the later seventeenth century the servile economy encouraged large, extended families of several generations – landowners liked the guarantee of an economically strong peasant unit. The bolshak's wife lorded it likewise over the women of the house,

Figure 10   Peasant wanderers (1913)

C. Obolensky, comp., *The Russian Empire: A Portrait in Photographs* (London 1980).

particularly daughters-in-law. Women in general were second-class beings: peasant proverbs, in which Russia is rich, are frequently misogynistic, ridiculing long hair and short brains, or suggesting that 'A crab is not a fish and a woman is not a person'. Women were especially subject, too, to physical violence, commonly from their husbands – 'The more you beat the old woman, the tastier the soup.' And they were liable to sexual abuse by both the head of household and philandering pomeshchiki – some eighteenth-century landowners kept harems of peasant girls. But a man could not fully be a peasant without a wife (and a horse); and women upheld and contributed vitally to the well-being and culture of the village, not only as child-bearers and equal workers with the men, but as repositories of lore, tellers of fortunes and folktales, and transmitters of tradition.

Labour was constant in village life, less pressing in the long, snow-bound winters and hardest in the short summer harvest season, the 'time of suffering' when the harvest had to be got in at all costs. By the seventeenth century the communal three-field system, with strip farming, was dominant in agricultural production; the main consumption crop was rye. The seventeenth and eighteenth centuries are the period when trade, especially in grain, began to develop from local into regional markets, and from the 1760s onwards exports of grain expanded. Prices rose towards higher European levels as Russia became integrated into bigger markets (a 'price revolution'). Peasants were beneficiaries of these developments, but more so the noble estate-owners. Peasant surpluses were not large in most cases, though some peasant grain was traded, and they could be destroyed completely by natural calamities: harvest failures occurred on average once or twice a decade. In normal times Russian peasants lived reasonably comfortably, but famine was never too far away. Peasants were therefore conservative in their practices, averse to resource-expensive and risky, untried 'new-fangled invention', especially if it ran counter to their understanding of the world, though they were rational in adopting innovations whose effectiveness they understood. When potatoes, first introduced in the late seventeenth century, were pressed upon peasants in the 1840s by reformist officials, they were rejected as infernal 'devil's apples' because, evidently, they grow upside down; the new crop took many decades to find general acceptance.

It was possible, though difficult, to leave the village permanently. In the Imperial period considerable numbers of peasants settled and registered themselves in towns, but this was a complex and expensive process, and after 1722 serfs needed their lord's permission. Peasants who went away to work usually did so on a temporary basis; they tended to team up in a group with fellow villagers or locals (*zemliachestvo*), and to form labour cooperatives (*artel*) which mirrored the commune at home, and gave vital mutual support. Peasant seasonal labour migration became a large-scale practice only in the nineteenth century, but already in the eighteenth one observer compared it to the seasonal movements of flocks of birds. For the average village dweller, however, the world outside the village was a hostile place: outsiders were rarely well-disposed, be they other peasants who made contested land claims, dishonest traders, or robbers, and policing arrangements were rudimentary. Intervention in village affairs by higher authority, whether policemen, officials, army officers, or the pomeshchik or his steward, always brought demands and impositions, and often, beatings. In general outsiders were to be mistrusted.

Peasant serfdom was one of the defining institutions of Russia, from the seventeenth century to the nineteenth: even after its abolition in 1861 its residual influence was profound. By Peter's time the serf was fully under the control of his landlord: the Tsar published a decree in 1721 proscribing the sale of peasants 'like cattle, which is not done anywhere else in the world,' and 'all the more when a serf-owner sells a daughter or a son apart from their family, which causes much distress'. It was a clear statement of the existing state of affairs; the prohibition remained a dead letter. Peter deliberately took steps which extended and reinforced serfdom, as part of his effort to bend society more productively to his overall vision. He conflated slaves with the tax-paying servile peasantry. He created industrial forms of serfdom, to provide unfree labour for state and private enterprises: 'ascribed' and 'possessionary' peasants respectively. His new recruiting system freed recruits *de jure* from their master, but re-enserfed them *de facto* under military discipline, until death or debility. The Soul or Poll Tax, payable by all lower civilian classes, became a major indicator of servile status and a means of enserfment, since the census registers taken to indicate liability for the tax were also used to demonstrate landlord serf-ownership. The introduction of internal passports (1724) for travelling peasants made movement easier to control. The serf was thus completely at his master's beck or call; the remaining peasantry, most of them 'state' peasants, are called state serfs by some historians since they were subject to similar control by state agencies, but this ignores the fundamental difference that they had no personal lord and could not be sold. When they had opportunity, landlord peasants frequently expressed their aspirations in terms of transfer to the state peasantry.

Mature Russian serfdom has been equated with chattel slavery, and its deleterious effects on the character of some serfs – ignorance, apathy, laziness, drunkenness, deviousness, thieving – were rehearsed many times by later sympathetic observers who rightly saw in these traits both forms of resistance to landlord authority, and the effects of hopelessness and lack of any incentive to self-improvement; whereas supporters of serfdom held that such vices justified tight control. It should be stressed that until the later eighteenth century, majority public opinion throughout Europe was quite comfortable both with white serfdom and black slavery – only abuses caused concern. The desirability or otherwise of serfdom was not a significant issue in Petrine Russia. In general landowners

treated serfs harshly by modern standards (as early British industrialists treated their workforce), but there was an accepted range of
relationships, a 'moral economy' within which both sides could
behave without dire retaliation from the other. Killing serfs was
forbidden, though if they died after a beating the lord was not held
culpable; but such cases, though sometimes notorious, were probably exceptional. Peasants sometimes murdered landlords, but almost
always under extreme provocation or in times of social upheaval.
Some peasant disturbances became violent, were put down with
troops, and very occasionally involved serious bloodshed. Peasants
also made shrewd use of complaint and petition, despite the restrictions on petitioning. But most peasant resistance took passive forms,
foot-dragging, poor work, malingering, pilfering. In general, it is
surprising that there was not more conflict and confrontation.
However, serfdom also offered protection and guaranteed access to
land: the serf-owner was obliged by law in 1734 to feed his peasants
in times of harvest failure, estates provided defence against robbers,
and it was customary that peasants received a share of demesne land
for their own use. In the Imperial period (as noted) some successful
peasant entrepreneurs emerged, and most of them were of serf origin:
a lord's protection was necessary to build up capital. Moreover, as
we have seen, serfs could live very varied lives. Within the village,
steward, peasant elder and heads of household all had positions of
power to defend, and therefore had an interest in the *status quo*. For
many villagers, especially those on quit-rent, the servile regime gave
considerable flexibility and autonomy, while the internal politics of
the village sometimes outweighed the intentions of the landowner.

    This brings us back to Spittler's model of the 'peasant state',
which dwells upon the relationship between peasant village autarchy,
with its own internal hierarchies and dynamics, and the outsider
demands upon it of the resource-mobilising state. Government was
able to impose coercive resource mobilisation on the village: for
instance taxation, labour and military levies, production of particular
crops. But attempts to co-opt, communicate with or influence the
population were dependent upon the cooperation and the interests
both of the peasants' representatives – the village elder or commune
– and the peasants themselves, who had their own values and agenda.
Efforts to modernise peasant agricultural practices – Peter I's
prescription of scythes rather than sickles, for instance – foundered
on traditional village culture. Village politics were also often at odds

with outsider designs: success for a villager in his community depended not on government decree or the will of the landowner, nor even on the justice of his cause, but on his influence or protection within the village, and the decision of the commune. Village elders derived power less from carrying out orders *per se*, than by carrying them out (or ignoring them) to the benefit of themselves, their friends, the village as a whole. Government, and usually landlord too, stood outside this interface. Information flows were also a major issue. Despite occasional previous cadasters, the eighteenth century in Russia inaugurated the age of serious statistics: governments increasingly wanted to count what they were administering. They also wanted the administered to understand and accept what they were doing. Peter I's decrees are full of explanatory clauses: do this not just on pain of punishment, but for the following good reason. But urban officials, who in any case usually brought ignorance, prejudice and arrogance (not to mention bribe-taking and corruption) to their dealings with rural peasants, often failed either to understand or to persuade them. Seeking rational interpretations, officials readily created their own version of the countryside and its relationships which diverged from peasant wishes or reality. When Catherine II, personally, from the best of motives, tried to improve her own estates by reorganising the peasants' landholding on a rational basis, she was met with violent resistance (which she promptly countered with force and deportation). Moreover, it could be hard for paper-based officials, or landlords, to know accurately what was happening in the village. Peasants told the truth to outsiders only when it suited them. Bureaucratic written culture confronted peasant oral culture; the autarchy of peasants in an incompletely marketised economy resisted external efforts to measure and control production.

This pattern of relationships became real in Russia with the newly activist cameralist government of Peter I. Previously, little attempt had been made to influence peasant culture or production methods. The rulers henceforth assumed the obligation and right to direct peasant affairs on their own terms and without consulting those involved; and they largely failed either to achieve any meeting of minds with peasant society or to reach their own major goals. Initially this was consistent with social relations in general, and did not have serious effects, since eighteenth-century government's reach into the countryside was still relatively weak, and Peter was primarily concerned with commerce and industry: agriculture became a fashionable object of policy only after 1750. But it set a precedent reflected in all future major state initiatives in rural affairs, right to the end of the Soviet period. Most obviously, perhaps, Soviet refusal from 1929 to understand or treat peasant society in any except Stalinist terms led not only to the disasters of collectivisation, dekulakisation and mass famine, but contributed to terror and the permanent hobbling of Soviet agriculture. This approach also had wider implications for social relations and social integration throughout the revolutionary period. And it goes to the heart of a fundamental and enduring dilemma which has shaped the whole of modern Russian history up to the present: the impossibility of integrating city with countryside. In the Petrine and post-Petrine decades, nevertheless, serfdom, for all its defects, served a purpose useful to the state: it underpinned and enhanced the state's ability to mobilise and direct its resources, and to compete in the contemporary world. As yet the structural disadvantages of an unfree society did not affect the projection of state power. The servile Russian Empire grew richer internally and strong internationally.

PETER'S SUCCESSORS, 1725–62: THE AGE OF PALACE REVOLUTIONS

Peter I died in 1725, aged 52, of disease of the bladder, gangrene and his doctors' indecision. Despite decreeing that the monarch should nominate his successor, he failed to do so before weakness overtook him. He was succeeded by his second wife, Catherine. A servant-girl captured in the war in Livonia, Catherine (her baptismal name) had slept her way to the top, as mistress first of the Tsar's favourite Aleksandr Menshikov, then of the Tsar himself. She became the mother of his children, his wife, and finally his crowned consort in 1724. Her accession, against the claims of younger Romanov males, was due to the prompt action of Menshikov, who had her proclaimed by the Guards. This set the pattern of succession for the next century: until 1801 not only were most well-established rulers female, but half came to power through *coups d'état*, 'palace revolutions' backed by Guards' support. The influence of Peter's succession decree, which is frequently held responsible for this state of affairs, was negligible: the *coups* reflected both the absence of convincing male candidates, and the fluidity of contemporary Court politics. To help her rule, Catherine created a small Supreme Privy Council of senior statesmen. She died in 1727, and was duly followed by her nominated heir, Peter I's grandson, as Peter II. However, the young prince died suddenly of smallpox on the eve of his coronation in 1730, leaving no nominated heir-apparent.

The members of the Supreme Privy Council thereupon decided to offer the crown to Peter I's niece Anna Ioannovna (Ivanovna), dowager Duchess of Courland, on condition that she accept limitations upon her authority. Effectively the 'conditions' offered transferred sovereign power to the Privy Council. Anna, living an impecunious and isolated life between her Baltic-German duchy and Russian estates, readily accepted. Meanwhile news of the deal leaked out to the nobles gathered for Peter II's coronation and the Council had to confide in them; but they were wary of its obvious oligarchical pretensions. When Anna arrived, she was forewarned of the situation. Immediately she breached the 'conditions' by declaring herself colonel of one of the Guards' regiments and, backed by them, faced down the councillors, personally tore up the 'conditions', and assumed absolute power. The sole eighteenth-century attempt to place constitutional limits on the power of the ruler thus failed miserably. To conciliate and reward the nobility, Anna lightened conditions of service, repealed Peter's hated 1714 inheritance law, and created a special Noble Land Cadet Corps (1730) to provide exclusive noble education. She also abolished the Supreme Privy Council, making the Senate once more the supreme office of government.

Anna brought with her a retinue of Baltic-German courtiers, including her favourite, Ernst Bühren (Biron). Her reign (1730–40) subsequently became notorious as a time of foreign tyranny, the *bironovshchina* ('evil reign of Biron'), but in fact, apart from a few highly visible German individuals, Anna's administration was neither particularly German nor exceptionally tyrannical. The evil reputation was constructed after the event by publicists of Anna's successor, Peter's pleasure-loving and unmarried daughter Elizabeth (Elizaveta Petrovna, 1741–61), who mounted her own *coup* in 1741. Denigrating one's predecessor was part and parcel of a *coup d'état*. Overthrowing and imprisoning Anna's great-nephew and legitimate nominee, the baby Ivan VI, and his German mother and regent, Elizabeth assumed power with French and Swedish support, but in the name of a 'national', 'Petrine' cause against the 'foreigners'.

Childless, the new Empress shortly summoned her nephew Karl Peter Ulrich to St Petersburg as her heir. He was the son of her sister Anna Petrovna, Duchess of Holstein. When Elizabeth died late in 1761, Karl Peter duly succeeded her as Peter III; but he squandered his political support and was overthrown within six months by his wife, Princess Sophie Auguste Friederike of Anhalt-Zerbst, better known as Empress Catherine II (1762–96). The deposed monarch died shortly afterwards of a 'haemorrhoidal colic': in fact by violence during a brawl with his keepers.

Peter I's measures had desacralised the monarchy in the eyes of the elite, and legitimate monarchs could now be overthrown, on flimsy pretexts, by better organised and more skilful rivals. The new Guards regiments functioned as praetorians or janissaries. Faction-fighting at Court made individual rulers' tenure fragile unless they could rapidly establish themselves politically – it is appropriate to speak of the politics of the autocratic court. But this in no way affected the stability of autocracy as an institution: as the events of 1730 showed, in the Imperial period the elite saw no desirable alternative to its compact with the Crown, whereby its social privilege was guaranteed in return for acknowledgement of the sole right of an autocratic ruler.

International Relations 1725–63

The post-Petrine turbulence around the throne had very little effect on Russia's international position, and its continuing rise towards great-power status. It was now fully locked into the power-play of European international relations, in which it had previously been only marginally involved. It was soon equally fully locked into European diplomatic networks: whereas Muscovite rulers had had almost no permanent envoys abroad, Peter and his successors developed an extensive range of permanent diplomatic missions and consulates, and foreign powers likewise established missions in St Petersburg. If Peter made Russia the pre-eminent regional power in the north, under his successors it continued its rise, through the successes of the Seven Years' War, to become one of the leading European land powers in the decades before the French Revolution.

The 'upstart' status of Russia in the concert of powers in Peter I's time can be gauged by its Court's marriage policies. It was uncommon for Muscovite rulers to seek brides abroad, and the daughters of the ruling house did not marry. Peter returned to the standard international practice of foreign marriage alliances. During his visit in 1717 to France, the leading great power, he proposed the marriage of his daughter Elizabeth to the French dauphin, an offer renewed by Catherine I in 1725: Russia would replace France's ally Sweden in the French scheme of European relations. In fact Louis XV married Maria Lesczynska, daughter of the Swedish-backed candidate for the Polish throne. For Peter's son Aleksei, and for his other daughters and nieces, the best that could be obtained were German princelings – Aleksei married (1711) a princess of Wolfenbüttel, who was not required to convert to Orthodoxy, and the ladies became Duchesses: Anna Ioannovna of Courland, Yekaterina Ioannovna of Mecklenburg and Anna Petrovna of Holstein, with the purpose of extending Russian influence along the southern Baltic coast. Elizabeth remained single. Another indicator of relative prestige was the new Imperial title: it took decades to achieve universal diplomatic acceptance, and squabbles over titular details with the French in particular soured Russo-French relations.

In 1726 Russia acceded to the Austro-Spanish Treaty of Vienna, which guaranteed it assistance against the Ottomans. Despite further negotiations with France, it fought against the French in the War of Polish Succession (1733–5), which was followed by a war together with Austria against the Ottomans (1736–9): by the Treaty of Belgrade, Russia regained Azov. Under Elizabeth, Russia repulsed a Swedish attempt at revenge (1741–3), gaining Finnish territory as a result, and dealt extensively with Austria and Britain regarding alliance and subsidies, even sending an expeditionary force to the Rhine in 1748. Russia's Austrian orientation made relations with France difficult, but after the 'diplomatic revolution' which ushered in the Seven Years' War (1756–63) it found itself fighting with Austria and France against Prussia, which was supported by Britain. It was the weight of Russian power more than anything else which finally wore down the brilliant Frederick II of Prussia, as well as Elizabeth's personal determination to pursue him to the end. News of her illness made her commanders cautious in 1760, and her death in 1761 saved Frederick from destruction. As Frederick knew, Elizabeth's successor, Peter III, was his ardent disciple; Peter at once withdrew from the war, restoring conquered lands and framing an alliance with Prussia. On her accession, Catherine II repudiated Peter's actions, but – with the country exhausted and her own position fragile – did not resume hostilities: the war was formally ended by the treaty of Hubertusberg in 1763.

Russia's dramatic rise in the European league tables after its destruction of Sweden reflected not only its projection of military strength, but also changes in the long-term balance among the powers. Russia advanced to the extent that other states failed to prevent it. The French were frequently distracted by other issues; the Habsburgs found Russia a useful ally. The brilliance of Charles XII had masked the fact that Sweden was over-extended and lacked the resources to maintain its regionally dominant position. Poland had been steadily losing ground internationally, and dissension between Crown and nobility in the aftermath of Frederick Augustus's defeats allowed Russia to obtain a stranglehold on Polish affairs in 1717. Ottoman power had peaked in 1683; as Peter found to his cost in 1711 it was still formidable, but it gradually declined thereafter as the Ottomans, like their Tatar vassals, failed to adapt adequately to military change. Prussia and Britain, the other rising powers, found it generally in their interests (geopolitical and commercial respectively) to maintain good relations with the new northern giant. Post-Petrine Russia had become fully engaged in European politics, but its wars of the 1730s and 1740s, while not unsuccessful, had had none of the impact of the Great Northern War. The Seven Years' War by contrast, despite its muted outcome for Russia, demonstrated once again beyond doubt the military capacity of the new Empire.

Crown and Nobility

By 1763 Russia had an ample supply of home-grown officers, the result of Peter I's restructurings. Peter had bound the newly constituted nobility tightly to his new, onerous service system. Elite life was cast in state service terms. Since Ivan IV service had been universal, but episodic: servitors came when summoned – war had normally consisted of a succession of short summer campaigns. Now service became comprehensive, full-time and permanent. Service careers were defined through the Table of Ranks, an enduring innovation which lasted till 1917. Prestige was still conferred by lineage, but more so throughout the Imperial period by rank on the Table. The latter consisted of three columns (armed forces, civil service and court) each listing 14 parallel ranks; all service posts in the state were assigned to one or another rank. The Table also tied service and noble status inexorably together: non-nobles who progressed far enough were automatically ennobled. The lowest commissioned army rank (Ensign) conferred the bottom rank, 14, in the military table, and with it, noble status for non-nobles; the equivalent in the civilian scale was rank 8, Collegiate Assessor. General-officer status carried one of the top four ranks, which on the civilian side were reserved for the Chancellor (head of foreign affairs) and privy councillors. While promotion was to be by merit and length of service, the provisions of the Table specifically recognised claims of birth. But because the Petrine state needed exceptionally large numbers of servitors for its forces and administration, non-nobles could also get a footing on the service ladder. Even so, nobles were advantaged; and in the decades after 1722 the top ranks were colonised very much by descendants of the great Muscovite families.

Immediately on Peter's death, the rigour of his system was relaxed. In 1725, not only was Russia at peace after Peter's last war against Persia (1723–4), but the country was exhausted. The new government was sensitive both to the plight of the tax-paying peasantry, and to servicemen's pressing need for time to attend to private affairs: a leave system was quickly introduced. This marked the beginning of a gradual but steady lessening of the noble service burden. Besides abolishing the 1714 inheritance law and unifying votchina and pomest'e rights, Anna limited the length of noble service to 25 years. The question of how nobles should serve remained at the forefront of elite interests throughout the first half of the century, however: as service burdens lessened, and the economy flourished, nobles increasingly thought in terms of other activities. It was also the case that Peter I's overwhelmingly urgent need to mobilise every last man had passed: the system was now producing sufficient civil servants and officers. Illegal refusal of service was common under Elizabeth, and the issue exercised the Law Commission which met from 1754–66 to recodify state law. A proposal to abolish compulsory service was included in the Commission's draft code, which however was never enacted. Finally in 1762, as the Seven Years' War came to an end, the provisions of the draft were embodied in a manifesto published by Peter III, shortly before his overthrow, which abolished obligatory service altogether. It was a momentous point in Russian social history. Henceforward nobles were obliged to serve when summoned in emergency, and to ensure that their children were capable of service, on pain of social disgrace and exclusion from the Court. But in normal times all nobles could now serve or not as they chose. Many chose service: while the small number of magnates enjoyed great wealth, the majority of nobles were poor, owning few serfs and in some cases no land at all, and such people valued their service salary. Service was seen, too, as a noble prerogative, also the ladder to favour and influence. In principle, however, the nobility now became a landed leisure class, able to devote itself if it chose to its estates, and to pursuits opened to it by the new post-Petrine Europeanised culture of the elite.

The New Culture

The pre-Petrine nobility had shared the traditional culture of Muscovite society based in Orthodoxy. As we have seen, cultural change began to creep in during the seventeenth century. In the last decades novel literary forms began to appear, 'school dramas' and popular secular tales, and there is evidence of further secular tendencies among the elite – for instance a declining belief in miracles. But the elite world-view was still largely religious; it was a culture shared with all strata of society. Peter's measures stimulated further change and the development of a new, European-style culture which grew initially around the Court and in noble circles. Besides the noble's new service requirements, government intervened comprehensively in his daily life too, with prescriptions regarding personal culture and appearance, official titles and public dignities. This approach found most complete expression in the new capital, St Petersburg. Peter compelled magnates, nobles and merchants to move to his half-built 'paradise', and to construct themselves houses of prescribed design. Mannequins set up in public places in the town demonstrated the new compulsory fashions. The Tsar, although himself of frugal tastes, expected his principal courtiers to engage in conspicuous consumption. Himself still addicted to gross drunken carousing, in 1718 he instituted special social gatherings for the nobility, *assamblei* (from the French), in private houses, where the guests would practice *politesse*, the social arts of conversation, card-playing, dancing and consorting with ladies, who were brought out from their seclusion in the terem and required to join the men in polite conviviality. Foreign instrumental music was played, a break with centuries-old Orthodox disapproval of such devilish pastimes. (This politesse, like so much else, was compulsory: guards were posted on the doors to ensure that nobody left early, and guests – male and female – who failed to attend or 'misbehaved' could be punished.) In 1706 the first manual on the niceties of letter-writing appeared, in 1717 a conduct manual, the *Honourable Mirror of Youth.*

The role of noble women underwent considerable change in this process. The old practices had been generally very restrictive: one foreign observer wrote of provincial life in the 1660s: 'You keep your women locked up like slaves and make them work all day long. No man is allowed to look them in the face, and you marry off your daughters without even showing them their fiancés from a distance.' In 1700 women living in towns were compelled to adopt the new European dress. Over the course of the reign, and especially in St Petersburg and at Court, some also took on the other manners of polite European society: as another foreign observer noted in 1724, of Court life: 'The Russian woman, until recently coarse and uneducated, has changed for the better to such a degree that now she concedes little to German or French ladies in subtlety of manners and good breeding and in some respects is even superior to them.' Away from the eyes of the Tsar, change occurred of course more gradually and patchily (and far more slowly in non-noble urban households), and externals were adopted more easily than new attitudes of mind; but the foundations were laid. Other measures also gave women more control over their lives: for instance, forced and early marriage was officially forbidden, and women had exceptional control over their own property compared to contemporaries elsewhere in Europe.

Peter's measures transformed the creeping, unofficial changes in seventeenth-century culture into an officially ordained flood. The compulsory new fashions and modes of behaviour effectively required nobles to act as foreigners in their own country. However, the new regime, while discrediting old values, did not encompass all aspects of personal and private life, and especially the later part of the century saw searchings within the elite for new moral and philosphical values to justify its new status. The new fashions in dress and behaviour also provoked considerable resistance: nobles often slipped back into Muscovite dress at home. Most nobles did not entirely lose contact with popular culture, since it surrounded them in their peasant servants and the life of the landed estate. Orthodox religious observance remained an important part of life.

Nevertheless, within a generation education and familiarity had largely accustomed nobles to their new roles and appearance; they had internalised the public norms and manners derived, at second hand, from the culture of European contemporaries.

As a result, Russian eighteenth-century elite culture and mentalities underwent a rapid evolution. One hundred years after Peter's beard-cutting was born Aleksandr Pushkin (1799–1837), who would become Russia's national poet: essentially European, a cultured writer of cosmopolitan talent, dandy, man of the world in the fullest sense. In the first stages, to the middle of the century, the foundations were laid. The role of Court patronage and cultural consumption in this acculturation process was critically important, although strangely little is known about the Imperial Court as an institution. Peter's patronage of painting and architecture encouraged first foreign, then domestic talent, including the portraitist Ivan Nikitin. The first public theatres were patronised by Peter and his sister Natalia; a Russian state troupe was created later, in 1757. Foreign opera and ballet troupes, supported by orchestras, became fully established at Court (at huge expense) in the 1730s; at the same time (1738) Anna founded a special school for native singers, to maintain indigenous choral musical traditions. Great debates took place on the use of language and the most appropriate literary forms in which to couch poetry and plays, largely intended for Court occasions: in 1731 the Academy of Sciences published a first dictionary, and a 'Russian Assembly' (1735–41) was formed at the Academy to improve the language of translations. These proliferated. Aleksandr Sumarokov, the self-styled 'Russian Racine', translated Boileau's *Art poétique* and wrote verse and neo-classical drama to exemplify it. Educational institutions were expanded, and the practice of hiring foreign private tutors (notoriously of very variable quality) spread among the higher nobility. Scientific and engineering knowledge was occasionally taken to the provinces by state functionaries such as mining director Vasilii Tatishchev (d. 1750), who administered the state Urals iron industry and lived in Yekaterinburg: graduate of Uppsala in Sweden, he was a geographer, statistician, naturalist and historian, and maintained good contacts with the Academy of Sciences.

The Academy's University did not flourish, but a new one, founded in Moscow in 1755, became (and has remained) Russia's leading higher-education institution. Its creators were the urbane courtier Ivan Shuvalov, a favourite of the Empress Elizabeth much concerned with education and things of the mind, and the exceptional genius Mikhail Lomonosov, Russia's 'universal man'. Son of a prosperous White Sea fisherman and fish merchant, by formal status a peasant, Lomonosov learnt to read from relatives and a local priest, disguised his origins in order to gain secondary education in Moscow, studied in St Petersburg and was sent to university in Germany. He was one of the first Russian members of the Academy of Sciences, which began to add native scholars to its hitherto foreign staff in the middle of the century, and did serious and pioneering work in a wide range of fields – chemistry, physics, history, grammar, court poetry, glass-making and mosaic – as well as involving himself in academic administration. Lomonosov climbed the Table of Ranks, ending as State Councillor (rank 5), ennobled and a serf-owner. His career was unique, but symptomatic of the rapid evolution taking place.

Besides *belles lettres*, first works on Russian history appeared, part of an expanding but still tiny book trade which also included the first literary journals. In 1757 an Academy of Arts was founded. Foreign languages came into fashion: primarily of course French, the language of elegance, diplomacy and Versailles. (Latin was confined to Church seminaries.) Most of these developments affected the capitals and the higher nobility and aristocracy. Rank-and-file nobles were still far from fully at home in their new element: the provincial nobleman Andrei Bolotov, later a noted agronomist and memoirist, recorded his delighted youthful amazement when he first saw a bookshop, filled with a treasure-trove of books, in Königsberg during the Seven Years' War.

Among the most cultured noble households a few women, too, were learning languages and reading books, even trying their hand at writing. The earliest poems published under the name of a woman, Yekaterina Sumarokova, appeared in the journal of her playwright father Aleksandr Sumarokov, *The Industrious Bee*, in 1759. This presaged the accession to the throne in 1762 of the century's most prolific woman author, a 'crowned intellectual': Catherine II.

4

1760–1860
Russia and Europe: Apogee and Decline of the Autocratic State

Under Catherine II the Russian Empire became a first-class power, and continued to expand at the expense of traditional adversaries. The French Revolution and the beginnings of industrialisation presented challenges which the Petrine system was still able to surmount, and the Russian defeat of the 1812 Napoleonic invasion made Russia the dominant European land power. However, the autocracy was not well equipped to deal with the developments of the nineteenth century, ideological, economic and international. Growing internal disaffection culminated in the abortive noble 'Decembrist' revolt of 1825, and despite Russia's relative insulation from the nationalist and revolutionary trends of the post-Napoleonic decades, the shortcomings of the system were exposed in the debacle of the Crimean War.

THE SERVILE-ABSOLUTE SYSTEM: DOMESTIC CONSOLIDATION AND DECAY

The century from the Seven Years' to the Crimean War marks the apogee and end of the Petrine socio-political system. Successive governments grappled with the same basic tasks which had faced Peter I: achieving effective administration and mobilising military strength in the vast peasant state. The differing styles and political priorities of each monarch underline the significance of the individual ruler in the autocratic system, and the course of their reigns demonstrates, too, the corrosive effects of age on absolute rulers who stay long in office. The maturity of the system coincided with the French Revolution and Napoleonic wars, which posed fundamental challenges, ideological, political and military. Until this point change had been government led: Peter I and Catherine II were significantly more radical than their elites. But after 1789 monarchs stood increasingly on guard of legitimacy and the *status quo*, while a minority of the elite espoused more radical values. This process culminated in the abortive 'Decembrist' revolt of 1825, the last 'palace revolution' but simultaneously the first revolutionary attempt to overthrow the regime. After the Decembrists' failure, Nicholas I reasserted autocratic control, driving dissent underground and abroad until the 1860s. However, his regime bore the seeds of its own downfall.

Catherine II

Catherine II, the Great (1762–96) came to power in a *coup* mounted by her lover, Guards officer Grigorii Orlov, and his brothers. Her husband Peter III, a man of most unkingly character, had succeeded within six months in alienating many among the elite, lay and ecclesiastical, by his treatment of Church, army and Senate and his unpopular foreign policy. Peter promulgated some important measures which addressed major issues. But his treatment of his ambitious and clever wife made her fear (she claimed) that she would be immured in a convent; and when her supporters raised the army and Guards on her behalf, Peter's position crumbled. As Frederick II acidly put it, he was deposed like a child sent off to bed. Catherine was proclaimed Empress, pre-empting her 8-year-old son Paul, the logical heir apparent, and his supporters. She had no dynastic right to the throne, but claimed that she had taken power at the wish of the people to save Orthodoxy from the unworthy Peter III. Herself not deeply religious, throughout her reign she was ostentatiously punctilious, like the more superstitious Elizabeth, in Orthodox observance and public devotion. She began the reign with the death of her husband on her hands, compounded by the murder of Ivan VI: kept in prison ever since his deposition as a baby in 1741, he was dispatched by his guards during an attempted *putsch* in 1764.

Nevertheless, Catherine's reign was a period of prosperity and power. She ascended the throne at a critical juncture in European affairs. The Seven Years' War had exhausted the combatants, and peace gave opportunity for governments to restore and strengthen societies and economies. This was the time of the so-called 'Enlightened Despots', of 'Enlightened Absolutism': a label applied by historians to the absolute monarchs of this period, from Catherine II in the east to Charles III of Spain in the west, who between 1760 and the French Revolution undertook significant reform, drawing upon the thought of the Enlightenment to further their systematic state-building. The primary goal was state power; Enlightenment ideas and values were influential only insofar as they furthered that goal. Enlightened humanitarianism could also play some role, but governments' concern with good administration and law, public health, education, population growth and the state of the peasantry had a strong utilitarian motive: welfare and warfare were closely connected. Most such policies reflected in any case the cameralism still dominant at the time. Late cameralist authors combined it with the French Physiocrats' new emphasis on agriculture, which became a major European preoccupation in the mid-century.

Catherine's concerns were fundamentally those of her eighteenth-century predecessors, to strengthen the state both internally and externally; consequently she continued many previous trends. Her first years were busy with state affairs, but also exploratory, with a steep learning curve. From 1774 she found her direction, and began a decade of personal legislative initiatives, indulging what she called her 'legislomania'; the impetus for innovation only slackened after the 1780s. After the relative personal indifference to state affairs of Anna and Elizabeth, Catherine was a hands-on activist in the Petrine mould; her papers are more voluminous than those of the rest of the Romanovs put together. Russia's military forces were reviewed and reinforced after the strains of the war. The latter had equally emptied the Treasury; initially the Senate could not even give Catherine an exact picture of national income. Finances were successfully stabilised and economic growth fostered, especially through trade; soon, however, further wars compelled foreign loans and the introduction of the first paper money ('assignats') in 1769, and expenditure became excessive later in the reign. Catherine paid particular attention to administration. Following piecemeal measures in the 1760s, her provincial statute of 1775 and legislation of the 1780s (especially the Welfare or Police Statute of 1782 and the Charters to the Towns and Nobility of 1785) sought to streamline central offices and release national potential by addressing a chronic problem of Russian government, the imbalance between centre and provinces: she devolved administrative power (but not political control) to towns and provincial localities, giving greater autonomy to local communities and seeking to involve non-serving nobles in local affairs. The new 1775 administrative structure was implemented gradually, over the following two decades, and also applied to provinces with previously different traditions, such as Ukraine and Livonia. The populations and administrative arrangements of these areas were now brought into greater conformity with the Great Russian centre. Catherine's devolved system seems to have worked better in its time than most historians have given it credit for. Nevertheless, provincial government remained weak, with landowners' estate authority largely replacing effective local government; and by the end of the century the system was creaking.

Catherine took a close interest in social policy. A central concern was population growth, a fundamental pillar of cameralist theory with obvious military and financial implications. Although European populations were in fact growing, giving sense to the dire predictions of Thomas Malthus in his *Essay on Population* (1798), most eighteenth-century governments perceived their populations as too small. Population growth could also be assisted by public health, welfare and philanthropy, concerns both practical, economic and moral; it also related to the status of the peasantry and serfdom, discussed below. Further concerns were education, and the problem of law and order which touched not only administration, but peace and productivity in town and countryside. The new government addressed all these issues actively during the reign. To increase population, colonies of returned native fugitives and German immigrants were created on the Volga and the Black Sea. Foundling Houses were established. A new Medical College oversaw the building of hospitals, while in 1768, in a dramatic 'Enlightened' gesture confronting popular ignorance and epidemic death, Catherine had herself and Paul inoculated against smallpox (the AIDS of the eighteenth century). The Police Statute of 1782 established Boards of Social Welfare with wide-ranging local responsibilities. In education, the major achievement was a national school system, established in the 1780s following Prussian and Austrian models, fully adequate to contemporary educational thought if not to the needs of the population as a whole. The system had insufficient funding and teachers, however; and despite much discussion no new universities were created.

The area in which Catherine made herself the greatest reputation was law: the title 'Great' was offered to her by her 1767 Legislative Commission – she declined it, but it stuck. Every principal regime since Peter I had addressed the confused state of Russian law and its codification; the abortive Elizabethan Law Commission worked from 1754 to 1766. In 1765 Catherine decided to convene a commission of her own, elective and widely representative, for which she personally wrote a set of guiding principles, deliberately culled straight from the best authorities (principally Montesquieu): her *Instruction* (*Nakaz*, 1767). The 1767 'Commission For the Drafting of the Plan of a New Code' was a very serious undertaking. It has been unjustly criticised, both at the time, and later, since it did not result in a new code, and its active life was short. In 1768 its main assembly was suspended on the outbreak of war with the Turks; its specialist sub-commissions ceased work *c*.1774. Contrary to common belief, however, the commission was a genuine (if over-optimistic) approach to codification; the reason for the assembly's suspension was real, and the institution's clerical infrastructure was maintained until 1796, and subsumed into the codification commissions of subsequent reigns. Only in 1830 did the government of Nicholas I succeed in producing a *Complete Collection of Russian Laws*, in 44 fat volumes, while a new *Digest* finally codified existing legislation and provided a consolidated, up-to-date legal source. Catherine's commission did nevertheless have significant results. For the Empress it was a crucial mechanism both for consolidating her political position, by forging a national consensus around the law of the realm with her at its head, and also for understanding the views and aspirations of the commission's constituent social groups. The proceedings showed most of the majority urban and noble deputies to be ignorant, self-seeking and conservative: the Empress discovered that neither understanding nor support would be forthcoming for radical policies. But the papers and drafts, which in fact more or less add up to a coherent whole, provided a mass of information about local circumstances and national needs, which she drew upon extensively in her subsequent legislation.

A woman in a man's role and world, Catherine has had a mixed press. Her vivid private life has often overshadowed the real achievements of her reign; her treatment of peasants and nobles has been anachronistically condemned, her personal friendships with Voltaire and Diderot viewed, simplistically, as a cynical public relations exercise. In fact Catherine was relatively well-educated, and unusually attuned to the contemporary intellectual life of Enlightenment Europe; but like other contemporaries, Frederick of Prussia for example, she was a skilled politician and above all a pragmatist, concerned to maximise the power, prestige and influence of Russia, and with it her own. Both domestic and foreign policy was bent to that end. She was, moreover, essentially a ruler of the *Ancien Régime*, divided from the modern world by the French Revolution, of which she became an implacable enemy in her last years, when new ideas challenged the absolute monarchy which she represented. Catherine was an effective ruler, and fortunate or skilful in her choice of collaborators, whether the outstanding military men Grigorii Potëmkin (probably her secret husband), Pëtr Rumiantsev and Aleksandr Suvorov, or the linchpin of her government for most of the reign, the Procurator-General (prime and finance ministers in one), Aleksandr Viazemskii. She also performed the role of empress in accordance with European tradition. She largely ran her own foreign policy, which in its own terms of *real-politik* was extremely successful. The brilliant and civilised Catherinian Court presided over the efflorescence of the culture inaugurated by Peter I. This has traditionally been seen as the 'Golden Age' of the now-'emancipated' nobility in Russia, when Court and elite were most at one and aristocratic culture most splendid: although at the other end of the scale there were nobles so poor that they tilled their land themselves like peasants. Female rule contrasted with the militarised manners of the male Imperial Romanovs; and the savage mores of Peter I's time became increasingly less acceptable in high society. Catherine, allegedly tone-deaf to music and indifferent to cuisine, patronised other arts: theatre, opera and literature, in which she was herself a prolific practitioner, and architecture and painting – she was a great builder and an avid collector, founding the present Hermitage collections in St Petersburg.

Paul I, Alexander I, Nicholas I

Catherine was succeeded by her son Paul I (1796–1801). Kept resentful in the shadows throughout his mother's reign, Paul, like his putative father Peter III, was of unbalanced temperament and lacked judgment.

His first act was to pass a new law of succession (1797), prescribing primogeniture. His reign re-established central government control over the now rather strained devolved system of his mother. Paul, with his love of uniforms and parades, inaugurated the militarisation of official life prevalent in the nineteenth century. However, his excessively rigorous treatment of the army and civilian elites and the wild swings of his foreign policy aroused great discontent: he was consequently deposed in a *coup*, with the consent of his own son and heir, Grand Duke Aleksandr. In a scuffle, the Tsar was accidentally strangled: Aleksandr, distraught, came to the throne a parricide.

Alexander I (1801–25) combined military preoccupations with an idealistic education – his tutor was a Swiss republican. High personal culture and a capacity for informal and diplomatic charm made him one of the most personally engaging of the Romanovs. After Paul, change seemed undoubtedly to be in the air in what Pushkin called 'the wonderful beginning of Alexander's days'. Moreover, his rule marked the full coming of age of the new culture. Alexander faced the same perennial problems of governance which had exercised his predecessors, now exacerbated by the ideological legacy of the French Revolution, the changing face of Napoleonic Europe, and the growing industrial revolution. The Tsar proclaimed himself a lover of constitutions, but found neither the political confidence nor the social partners which would have enabled him to change the autocratic system; moreover his conception of constitutions focused more on streamlined administrative order than checks and balances. He gave constitutions to peripheral areas of the Empire and its dependencies – Poland, Finland, the Ionian Islands. But despite several commissioned projects, he kept his powers at home intact, taking measures only like those of his predecessors to enhance national administration and efficiency, and military strength: the introduction of central ministries to replace the Petrine colleges, strict educational requirements for civil servants, a new education system centred around six new universities. In the increasingly prominent question of serfdom, over which he agonised throughout his reign, Alexander similarly sought change in the peripheries (the Baltic provinces and Ukraine) but took only limited measures at the centre; and the notorious military colonies which were created to limit army costs under the martinet administration of his chief minister, Aleksei Arakcheev, effectively combined army structures with the servile village. Set up in 1810, they lasted until 1858.

Alexander was in any case much distracted by war: the Napoleonic years led up to the catastrophe and triumph of 1812–15. The Russian defeat of Napoleon testified to the endurance and the strengths of the Russian army (especially its artillery), and to the prosperity of the newly developed south which provided the army's supply base; but it represented also the success of Muscovite steppe warfare tactics – withdrawal and harassment, deployment of popular and irregular forces, use of space and famine – over west-European military organisation, and over genius thinking in Western-theatre terms. On the eve of the French invasion Alexander underwent a religious awakening, and was converted to an ecumenical mystical evangelicalism, which found its clearest political expression in the Holy Alliance (1815). His initial enthusiastic support for the Protestant-inspired Russian Bible Society established in 1813, which sought to make Holy Scripture available to all, was tempered when he reverted in 1819 to a more conservative Orthodoxy, consistent with the politics of his later reign. The war also left a devastated economy: stabilisation of the inflated currency became a major on-going issue. Government specialists were fully alert to the industrialisation which was developing elsewhere in Europe, but had gained a relatively slight foothold in Russia. After the Congress of Vienna (1815), which set the stage of post-Napoleonic Europe, and especially after 1820, the government was increasingly wary of dissent, and primarily concerned to maintain stability at home and combat unrest and revolution in Europe. This it hoped to achieve through the Holy and Quadruple Alliances, and the 'Congress System' of international collaboration between the great powers which guaranteed the European *status quo*. Alexander's later stance so alienated the more idealistic wing of the nobility that the reign ended in revolt. Young nobles, mainly military men, attempted a *coup* in order to change the regime. The 'Northern Society' staged a rising in St Petersburg on 14 December 1825; their officer colleagues of the 'Southern Society', based at an army base in Ukraine, and assisted by lower-ranking members of a 'Society of United Slavs', tried a week later to march on Kiev. However, the 'first Russian revolution' was a shambles, easily suppressed: the Decembrists are remembered as heroic martyrs rather than effective revolutionaries.

Alexander's younger brother Nicholas I (1825–55) came to the throne through the blood of the Decembrist mutineers: believing God had justified him in the confrontation, he devoted his life to combatting the hydra of revolution, and to the maintenance of autocratic power, good order at home and Russian international status. In the wake of 1825 he created a new police force, the public 'Gendarmerie' and the secret 'Third Section' [of His Majesty's Own Chancellery], which set out not just to control, but also to mould public opinion, as well as to keep an eye on government. Direct intervention in social and official life was facilitated by new institutions and methods – the Chancellery itself, increasing numbers of censorship bodies, the deployment of adjutants as personal representatives. Nicholas's ideal was one of service to the autocratic state: 'all human life is service', he once remarked. A conservative reformer, he worked earnestly at the better governance of the realm; but he construed his autocratic power very personally. Serfdom was as yet too dangerous to be touched, but a major state-peasant reorganisation could become a pattern for action in the future. The education system was further fine-tuned to state requirements, with a new statute in 1835. Nicholas was also concerned with law as a tool of effective autocratic government: besides completing codification, he established an Imperial School of Jurisprudence, which greatly expanded legal training, while at the same time a new generation of competent high-flying young 'enlightened bureaucrats' were training in the Ministries, juniors now, but future executives of the 'Great Reforms' of the 1860s. The civil service was greatly – excessively – expanded: bureaucracy flourished. The uniformed minor civil servant now became a recognisable social type, a hero or anti-hero of the new realist novel. The military system was extensively reorganised in the 1830s, but change did not go deep. It proved impractical to organise a reserve system; senior commanders were increasingly conservative armchair officers; and budgetary constraints prevented Russia from keeping up with accelerating change in weaponry and technology. Similarly, both financial constraint and ideological aversion hindered serious state encouragement of industry or railway-building: the latter, in the view of the Finance Minister, Count Yegor Kankrin, encouraged vagabondage and the 'unquiet spirit of the age'. The mercantilist Petrine tradition followed by later monarchs had favoured protective support of private enterprise, and state creation of industries necessary for national purposes, principally military. But ever since Peter's times, industrial development had produced side-effects seen as increasingly undesirable, even while its necessity was appreciated. Elizabeth had passed decrees limiting industry in cities, to avoid shortages of fuel and food, and riotous worker behaviour; and by the 1840s that European phenomenon, the 'proletariat', was a well-recognised social danger. Industrialisation, while not restricted, was not promoted, and left largely to private enterprise. Even military technology was not given government priority: in the Crimean War, the Russian navy under sail faced Allied screw-driven steam-ships, while peasant carts across the steppe stood in for non-existent strategic railways.

Nicholas's exalted view of his God-given role was increasingly out of keeping with both European and Russian society, in which change was encouraging new ideas and signs of social mobility. In Russia the Alexandrine education system was producing educated minds outside of, as well as within, the government apparatus; the copyright law of 1828 stimulated print culture; and new French and German philosophical ideas were finding increasing resonance within cultured circles. Besides the bureaucrat, this age formed the intelligentsia (discussed below), and the foundations of civil society. This was also the age of nationalism in Europe, emerging out of confrontation with Napoleonic universalism: it affected both government thinking, and sentiment in the peripheries. The Polish rising of 1830–1 reflected continuing resistance to Russian domination since the eighteenth-century partitions. In Kiev in 1846–7 the Society of Saints Cyril and Methodius, one of whose founders was the Ukrainian national poet Taras Shevchenko, aimed to promote Slav unity and federation, and Ukrainian culture and independence; its programme looked back in part to the Decembrist Society of United Slavs. But the army quickly dealt with the Poles, and the Third Section with the Ukrainians. Meanwhile Count Sergei Uvarov, polyglot orientalist, urbane President of the Academy of Sciences, and long-time Minister of Education, responded to these trends by formulating in 1833 a mission statement for his ministry which became in effect a public ideology and glorification of Nicholaevan absolutism. Uvarov's doctrine of 'Official Nationality' summarised Russian grandeur and uniqueness under the tsar in the trinity of Autocracy, Orthodoxy and Nationality. The latter rather vague concept (*narodnost*, the quality embodied by or associated with the people) was widely equated simply with serfdom, which Uvarov supported on the grounds that the serf-owning landlords were the bedrock of autocracy. But after 1848 government attempts to control society became so extreme that even Uvarov was forced to resign, and the conservative government supporter Mikhail Pogodin accused the regime of imposing 'the quiet of a graveyard, rotting and stinking, both physically and morally'.

In foreign affairs Official Nationality was expressed in the pursuit of stability and legitimacy in Europe: the Orthodox Greek revolutionaries received only grudging help against the Turkish Sultan, and in 1849 Nicholas sent military aid to the Austrians against Hungarian insurgents. However, Russian treatment of the Poles, the perceived threat of Russian expansion in the East, and Nicholas's apparent designs on Constantinople, generated strong reactions and Russophobia in Britain and France. Between 1815 and 1853 Russia faced no major wars; Nicholas's government enjoyed considerable domestic support and was very successful in holding its own against the European tide of change and revolution, which scarcely touched Russia, even in the upheavals of 1848. But in the process it created a society of appearances, in which the veneer of strict autocratic order covered disorder, corruption, and the increasing variety and complexity of mid-nineteenth-century grass-roots life: a society vividly reflected in Nikolai Gogol's classics *The Government Inspector* (1836) and *Dead Souls* (1842). Finally, the Crimean War (1853–6) demonstrated that Russia had critically lost pre-eminence in the one field on which its European status rested: military capacity. Military and diplomatic failure was intimately linked to personalised autocratic rule and the hypertrophic power with which state authorities had stifled criticism, transparency and independence in their search for government-defined order. As the liberal censor A. Nikitenko confided to his diary: 'the problem with the reign of Nicholas I was that it was all a mistake.' P. Valuev, one of the new 'enlightened bureaucrats', a clever and acute civil servant and qualified supporter of autocracy, summed up elite disenchantment in the dying days of the war with his *Thoughts of a Russian*, which circulated in manuscript: he castigated the 'universal official lie' which had led to 'brilliance [when viewed] from above, but rot underneath'.

Nicholas died at the same time as his government system, in 1855. It was left to his son Alexander II (1855–81) to salvage the situation. The new Emperor was rightly persuaded by his advisers that the military-diplomatic situation was hopeless, and signed the humiliating Peace of Paris in 1856: Russia lost territory, and its navy was excluded from the Black Sea. Although a conservative, Alexander became convinced that major domestic reform was inevitable.

RUSSIA AND THE BORDERS OF THE EUROPEANS' WORLD

International Relations, Internal Consolidation, Self-Discovery

'Russia is a European state', declared Catherine II in her *Instruction* of 1767. But Muscovy had appeared to many Europeans as an alien country, a 'rude and barbarous kingdom' or at best – in the words of John Milton's *Brief History of Moscovia* (1682) – 'the most northern Region of Europe reputed civil'. Peter I had projected it into the European mainstream both culturally, diplomatically and physically, and despite the persistence of hostile and condescending foreign views, the process was largely completed by his successors over the next two centuries. After 1763 Catherine built on the military successes of the Seven Years' War by humiliating the Ottomans in two wars, 1768–74 and 1787–92, and dismembering Poland in the successive partitions of 1772, 1793 and 1795. These events confirmed Russia's status as a first-class European power. By her prestigious joint mediation with France of the Treaty of Teschen (1779), ending the War of the Bavarian Succession, Catherine acquired a powerful voice in the internal dispositions of Central Europe, and her Armed Neutrality (1780) dictated the law of the sea to the mighty British navy. Her huge territorial acquisitions also moved her borders further west, and south.

The annexation of the southern Ukraine, Crimea and eastern Poland gave Catherine a vast and hugely fertile tract of territory and the bases for a southern navy. The strategic implications of these acquisitions made themselves fully felt only in the nineteenth century. Russia's southern border now followed the northern shores of the Black Sea, and by the Treaty of Kuchuk-Kainardji (1774) the Turks conceded unarmed Russian passage through the Straits to the Mediterranean. Where previously Austria and Russia had faced the common Ottoman danger largely as allies, now Russia's growing domination threatened Austria's southern Danubian interests; and as a naval Mediterranean power it confronted France and Britain. The 'Eastern Question', the problem of great-power rivalry at the Straits, dates from Kuchuk-Kainardji. Moreover, the Polish partitions gave Russia common borders with two other major powers, Prussia and Austria. It was now possible that it could face great-power opponents simultaneously all along its south-western, western and north-western (Baltic) boundaries: an unbearable military position. Although Alexander I sought to maintain an army after 1815 equal to

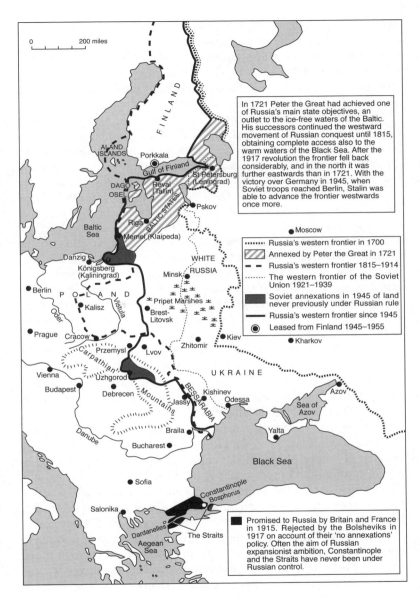

In 1721 Peter the Great had achieved one of Russia's main state objectives, an outlet to the ice-free waters of the Baltic. His successors continued the westward movement of Russian conquest until 1815, obtaining complete access also to the warm waters of the Black Sea. After the 1917 revolution the frontier fell back considerably, and in the north it was further eastwards than in 1721. With the victory over Germany in 1945, when Soviet troops reached Berlin, Stalin was able to advance the frontier westwards once more.

0   200 miles

- Moscow

··········· Russia's western frontier in 1700
▨ Annexed by Peter the Great in 1721
- - - Russia's western frontier 1815–1914
·········· The western frontier of the Soviet Union 1921–1939
■ Soviet annexations in 1945 of land never previously under Russian rule
━━━ Russia's western frontier since 1945
◉ Leased from Finland 1945–1955

- Kharkov

■ Promised to Russia by Britain and France in 1915. Rejected by the Bolsheviks in 1917 on account of their 'no annexations' policy. Often the aim of Russian expansionist ambition, Constantinople and the Straits have never been under Russian control.

Map 7 Russia's Western Frontier, 1700–1945

© Sir Martin Gilbert, *The Routledge Atlas of Russian History* (London and New York, 2002), no. 145.

twice those of Austria and Prussia combined, Russia needed an alliance system that would not leave it exposed. Initially the Congress System of consultation established after Vienna ensured this security. But Nicholas I's failed diplomacy created just such a situation in the 1850s, with the dire results of the Crimean War. The Treaty of Paris marked the final dissolution of the Congress System.

Catherine's acquisitions had moved Russia's southern border finally to its natural geographical limit: the Ukrainian borderlands were secure and could now be acculturated. As the Tatar-Turkish threat diminished, waves of settlement spread down the Volga and towards the Caucasus in the 1720s–40s and 1750s–70s, and after the two Turkish wars the new Black Sea territories, renamed 'New Russia', became the focus of intensive development. The great Cossack-peasant rising led by Yemelian Pugachëv on the Volga in 1773–74 (discussed further below) was in part a reaction to the increasing state presence and to pressures by colonisers on the local populations, as well as to burdens created by the Turkish war. After initial panic, Pugachëv was destroyed, and the government quickly reined in the Cossacks, integrating them into the regular army structure: a major move towards control of the steppe and transformation of the Cossacks into an arm of the state.

After 1775 the now-pacified south and south-east came under the rule of Catherine's new favourite Potëmkin, Governor-General of the provinces of New Russia, Azov and Astrakhan, and largely responsible for Caucasian and Transcaucasian affairs. Potëmkin remained in overall charge until his death in 1791, and used his vision and his unique access to resources to drive on development at a furious pace. The notorious stories of 'Potëmkin villages' – supposed mock village façades in empty places, theatrical stage-sets allegedly erected to please and fool the Empress during her visit of 1787 – were false, a slander devised by the Prince's detractors: they persisted possibly because they matched Potëmkin's theatrical and outsize personality. Potëmkin's most ambitious project was the city of Yekaterinoslav ('Catherine's Glory' – now Dnepropetrovsk), designed as a southern counterpart to St Petersburg, a focus of European civilisation in the steppe, with plans for a huge Italianate cathedral, university and music college. After Potëmkin's death Yekaterinoslav languished: it had none of Petersburg's commercial or capital-city potential. At least the cathedral was completed, years later. The true southern counterpart of Petersburg was Odessa, founded in 1794 under

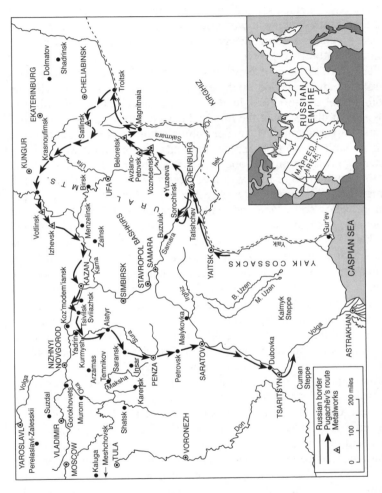

Map 8 The Pugachëv Revolt

J. Alexander, *Autocratic Politics in a National Crisis*, Bloomington, IN, and London, 1969.

Potëmkin's successor as favourite, Platon Zubov, at an outstanding natural harbour. Odessa mushroomed and within a few years became an international port-city, second in the Empire only to the capital, channelling the produce of the south to the Mediterranean: shipped by Greek skippers, Ukrainian grain fed Europe in the first decades of the nineteenth century. It was also shipped north up the rivers to the Russian centre, feeding the growing population and the increasing non-agricultural workforce.

The development of New Russia and the Black Sea littoral was paralleled and preceded by the exploration of Siberia. Following on from initial explorations in the seventeenth century, the Siberian voyages of discovery of the Imperial period rank with those of James Cook, Lapérouse and Alexander von Humboldt as feats of endurance and research. Scientific exploration and categorisation were part of Peter I's project from the outset: it was he who sent the Dane Vitus Bering on the first of his two expeditions (1724, 1733) into the Strait which bears his name, between Siberia and America. Further expeditions followed by land and sea, most organised by the Academy of Sciences, such as the 'Great Northern Expedition' (1733–43) and Gerhard Friedrich Müller's Siberian journeys in the 1750s. Russia was engaged in the Europe-wide project to observe the transits of Venus in 1761 and 1769, critical recordings in contemporary science's search for the solar parallax – while the newly appointed James Cook took British measurements at Tahiti. The last Russian naval expedition of the century, 1786–94, under the Englishman Joseph Billings, set out to the Aleutian Islands and Bering Strait in order, a contemporary noted, 'to complete the geographical knowledge of the most distant possessions of that Empire, and of such northern parts of [America] as Captain Cook could not possibly ascertain'. In the last third of the century Academy land explorers, Russian, German, Swedish, criss-crossed the newly occupied southern territories and older eastern borderlands, gathering mineral and botanical specimens, charting topography, altitude, latitude and longitude, recording weather conditions and the lives of the peoples among whom they passed. The published accounts of these explorations are irreplaceable records of lands and societies about to be irreversibly changed. Stepan Krasheninnikov's *Description of Kamchatka* (1755), Johann Georg Gmelin's *Flora Sibirica* (4 vols, 1747–69) and Peter Simon Pallas's unfinished *Flora Rossica* (2 parts, 1784–8) rank among the scientific masterpieces of the century.

The Provinces of Russia in 1750

Territory annexed by Russia 1762–1796, giving Russia an outlet on the Black Sea, and a common frontier with Prussia and Austria

Map 9   Russian Expansion under Catherine II, 1762–1796

© Sir Martin Gilbert, *The Routledge Atlas of Russian History* (London and New York, 2002), no. 41.

Just as much as Potëmkin's assertion of control and construction in New Russia, they exemplified the Enlightenment's desire to know, record and penetrate the borderlands of its world.

In the south-east, Potëmkin also drove forward Russian penetration of the Caucasus. Having made a compact with the independent Transcaucasian Christian kingdom of Georgia in 1769, Russia steadily advanced in a 100-year military campaign against the patchwork of warlike mountain peoples, largely Muslim, who were worn slowly down by superior Russian resources and sometimes brutal terror methods. Successive viceroys of the Caucasus faced bitter tribal and religious resistance, notably the long jihad (1834–59) of the Islamic leader Shamil. The Caucasus was finally pacified in 1866, leaving Russia in control of the mountains, and of Transcaucasian Georgia, Eastern Armenia and what is now Azerbaijan. As with the Tatar Crimea, the mountain wars, in spectacular scenery against fierce and exotic highlanders, captured the romantic imagination of Russia's now Europeanised literary elite: Caucasus and Crimea are the settings for Pushkin's narrative poems 'The Prisoner of the Caucasus' (1821) and 'The Fountain of Bakhchisarai' (1822), as for the Byronic Mikhail Lermontov's masterpiece *A Hero of Our Time* (1840).

The southern and western borderlands also offered Catherine II a solution to her incipient Jewish problem. Historically there were few Jews in Muscovy, and the bigotedly devout Elizabeth had specifically expelled the 'enemies of Christ'. At the beginning of Catherine's reign, the tolerant Empress sought to avoid offending Orthodox fervour by ordering Jews to be admitted clandestinely to the western fringe of the Empire, Riga and New Russia. Only in 1772, with the first Polish partition, did the authorities have to concern themselves with a large Jewish population, which was living on the annexed territories; 1783 brought them the Karaite Jews of the Crimea. Initial policies of deliberate toleration and equality gradually gave way to more restrictive practices, and legislation of the 1790s and 1804 confined Jews largely to a 'pale of settlement' in the south-western lands of New Russia, former Poland and White Russia. Odessa developed a vibrant Jewish culture.

In the nineteenth century, the task of recording the vast Russian hinterland and its peripheries continued. In 1829 the government sponsored the expedition to Siberia of Alexander von Humboldt, the outstanding scientific explorer of his day. The travels of Nikolai

Przhevalskii, perhaps the greatest Russian explorer, formed part of the 'Great Game' of colonial eastern expansion played by great powers in the second half of the century: from 1867 until his death in 1883 he ranged across Eastern Siberia, Mongolia, Tibet and Turkestan on several extremely productive expeditions. Back in European Russia, other less high-profile Academy and Ministry of Finance expeditions charted and increasingly sought to open up the country's resources. Thus in 1840 the young Baltic-German geologist Alexander von Keyserling made a trip which brought back, as well as scientific research observations, industrially valuable information on new coal deposits.

Keyserling noted in a private letter: 'We have lived in such amazing contrasts, now in the most wretched peasant huts, with meagre food, surrounded by people staring famine in the face, now in palaces, at over-opulent tables, and drawn by state carriages.' Previous travellers had also drawn contrasting anthropologies of Russian society. However, Keyserling's observation reflected growing government and social concern at home over social conditions. It also coincided in time with two other famous accounts of journeys of discovery, sociological rather than natural scientific, European works which deeply influenced European perceptions of Russia, and Russians' perceptions of themselves – the Marquis Astolphe de Custine's *Russia in 1839* (Paris, 1843, in French), and Baron August von Haxthausen's *Studies on the Interior of Russia* (Hannover, 1847–52, in German). Custine, a French aristocrat and disillusioned supporter of autocracy, depicted Russia emotively as a closed police state. His famous book further fuelled growing European antipathy. In outraged response, Nicholas's government invited the conservative agrarian expert Haxthausen to tour European Russia and report his findings. Haxthausen was primarily concerned with social and economic issues, but his descriptions and his social taxonomy were as epoch-making as those of the eighteenth-century botanists. The Russian countryside, old centre and far new south, was dispassionately and sympathetically laid bare, in its mid-nineteenth-century shape, for European inspection. For the first time Haxthausen described to the world – and the Russians – the Russian peasant commune, as an indigenous and singular institution which he pictured as economically restrictive but socially invaluable. Here the Russian intelligentsia, as well as Haxthausen's European audience, saw the Russian peasant masses in a German mirror.

THE PEASANT QUESTION

The Coming of Abolitionism

The state and status of the peasantry became a significant issue of debate in Russian elite and government circles under Catherine II. By the middle of the eighteenth century the influential ideas of the French Physiocrat economists, reflecting the contemporary 'agricultural revolution', had made clear to pre-industrial Europe the economic primacy of land and agriculture, and of the peasant as primary producer. Enlightenment social theory also stressed the value of free subjects in developing urbanisation and commerce. And around 1750 a sea-change took place in European attitudes to black slavery: harbinger of the abolitionist movement. The new Empress brought to the throne a moral aversion to the enslavement of free people, as well as her concerns for the economy, demographic and fiscal growth, and law and order – she inherited major peasant unrest in the Urals from Peter III. In addition to the future role of the newly emancipated noble landowners, she thus had to consider the question of the peasantry and serfdom. She at once issued a manifesto demanding peasant obedience, and sent a military expedition against the peasant insurgents, but also ordered its commander to enquire into and satisfy their grievances. During the 1760s she then personally posed the question of peasant status and how (if at all) it should be changed, in a series of careful measures designed to promote public discussion without exposing her fledgeling rule to hostile dissent or danger. The issue was discussed at the *Landtag* (provincial diet) of the Baltic German nobility in 1765, in the Free Economic Society newly founded the same year, in a much-trumpeted Economic Society essay competition, and in the first drafts of Catherine's own *Instruction* – though her advisers radically revised that section. It came up for discussion in the Legislative Commission, sparking a sharp exchange of abolitionist and conservative opinions. However, the upshot of all these focus-group investigations was a surprise to the new ruler: public opinion, such as it was, remained overwhelmingly favourable to the *status quo* and serfdom, and wished if anything to extend it.

Pugachëv the Pretender

The Turkish war (1768–74) distracted the government from such delicate internal matters; and before its end the Pugachëv revolt broke out on the Yaik river. Yemelian Pugachëv, a renegade Don Cossack, the greatest eighteenth-century Russian pretender, proclaimed himself in 1773 to be Peter III, allegedly escaped from his usurping wife's assassins. Pugachëv rapidly attracted huge popular support. Peasant attitudes to authority were traditionally ambivalent, and have been summed up in the term 'naive monarchism'. Whilst peasants usually perceived real, immediate outside authority as undesirable or threatening, the tsar's was not: the tsar was God's appointed, by definition holy and good, a 'little father' who wishes the welfare of the people. Grievances, if brought to his attention, would therefore be remedied (hence the popularity of petitions). If evil happened and was not remedied, this was because the tsar did not know, or was kept in ignorance by bad advisers, officials, landlords. If the tsar knew but took no action, or knowingly did evil, he – and even more so, she – must be a false tsar (thus Peter I was a changeling, or Antichrist). Pretenders could validate their claims by appearing princely and meeting popular desires – Pugachëv showed alleged 'royal marks' on his body, created an ersatz court among his aides, and his manifestos offered Cossack freedoms to all who followed him. Peasants followed a pretender either out of real conviction, or because they hoped to use his authority to achieve change: many of Pugachëv's lieutenants knew that he was in fact a Cossack.

Pugachëv's initial following was among the disgruntled Yaik Cossack host – his own people, the Don Cossacks, stayed aloof; but his rebellion gathered together the grievances of local communities from Astrakhan to the Urals, as well as the Old Belief. It was less a class war, as portrayed by Soviet Marxist historians, than a great frontier jacquerie, attacking symbols of central authority – increasingly intrusive in the borderlands but still weak enough to be assailed. The movement never threatened the centre. Discontent was sharpened by the burdens of the war. Dozens of nobles were lynched or executed, the city of Kazan stormed; government and elite were seriously alarmed, and the insurrection was only put down by regular troops once peace had been signed with the Turks. Together with the (rather different) Bohemian peasant disorders of the same period, this was one of the largest pre-revolutionary popular movements in Europe in the eighteenth century. It showed the dangers of weak control and of raising expectations, and was ruthlessly suppressed;

Pugachëv was executed publicly in Moscow in 1775, beheaded and quartered.

The Peasant Question, 1774–1860

After the lessons of the 1760s and of Pugachëv, the Empress changed tack. There was no further public talk of peasant status. Catherine's concern remained the development of society and the economy. Initially she had thought to achieve this by freeing the potential of the enserfed peasantry. Now she moved to give autonomy to the 'free' sections of society, the nobility, towns and state peasantry, if necessary at the serfs' expense. The 1785 Charters to Towns and Nobles were to have been accompanied by a State Peasant Charter, but it was never promulgated. In 1783 the extension of the 1775 statute and the poll tax to Ukraine harmonised legal structures and improved fiscal administration there; in the process Ukrainian peasants finally lost the right to move. As before, serfdom retained its value for state purposes. Nevertheless, the 'peasant question', once raised, remained current. Cameralist and Physiocratic economics both presupposed a free population, as did the *laissez-faire* doctrines associated with Adam Smith's *Wealth of Nations* (1776), which became influential in the Empire; and the moral issue became no less acute. Serf unrest and flight was endemic, a constant problem of law and order; serf discontent posed a constant possible threat. During the French Revolution many owners imagined a peasant 'sans-culotte' under every bed, although there is no evidence that Russian peasants were influenced by French events. Productivity in servile agriculture was in general low, but sufficient: despite accelerating population growth in the Imperial period, in normal years few people starved. But it was also technically primitive and inflexible: peasant practices and inventory usually determined estate farming methods.

From Catherine's reign onwards, successive governments (with the exception of Paul) examined ways to improve the situation and to dismantle serfdom. First limited steps were taken in the reign of Alexander I. The 'Free Agriculturalists' law of 1803 established for the first time a legal framework through which serfs could be emancipated with land, by agreement with their masters, and become small landowners; but few lords made use of it. In 1816–19 the Latvian and Estonian peasants of the Baltic-German nobility were set free, in a landless emancipation. This proved socially and

economically problematic, and the Baltic experience became a negative example for the reformers of the 1860s. In the same years
Alexander commissioned projects for emancipation in Ukraine and
Russia from individual advisers; but he did nothing with them, and
in the last reactionary years of his reign no change was possible.

As the revolutionary post-Napoleonic decades unrolled in Europe,
the Russian authorities became increasingly sensitive to signs of
social unrest, which seemed to be on the increase. Under Nicholas I
the Third Section kept detailed records of peasant disturbances, and
its annual report to the Tsar gave them a prominent place. In 1839 it
declared that Russia was a powder-keg of dissatisfaction. In a noted
speech to the State Council of 1842 Nicholas declared serfdom 'an
evil, palpable to all', but quickly added that it was too dangerous to
be tampered with: Pugachëv had demonstrated the fury and unpre-
dictability of the masses. Instead, the former general and diplomat P.
Kiselev, named by Nicholas as his 'chief-of-staff in the peasant question', carried out a major reorganisation of state-peasant administration in the 1840s which was also intended to provide a model for
future emancipation. His reorganisation was a comprehensive
measure, well-informed and well-intentioned, but also paternalistic,
compulsory and bureaucratic; in keeping with the times, and the
traditions of the 'peasant state', no peasant was consulted.

The peasant question now also became part of the wider issue of
economic efficiency. In the century between 1762 and the 1861 emancipation, former noble servitors did not, with few exceptions, transform themselves into effective farmers. Larger estates were more
efficient in this respect than the more numerous smaller ones, and in
the first half of the nineteenth century some successful commercially-
run estates emerged in the fertile south, producing such commodities
as sugar-beet and merino wool. In the rather infertile centre and north,
as the nineteenth-century growth of internal markets encouraged
economic specialisation, craft-based cottage industry became a more
profitable peasant occupation than agriculture, and *obrok* (quitrent)
the normal form of peasant dues; but with one or two notable exceptions, such as the Sheremetev estates of Ivanovo in Vladimir
province, and Pavlovo near Nizhnii Novgorod, which became manu-
facturing towns, crafts rarely grew into industrial enterprises. Cottage
industry remained strong throughout the nineteenth century, and
complemented rather than competed with larger industrial production
as that developed. Peasant labour migration continued to grow

through the period. Moreover, the average landowner possessed few serfs, little capital, and less agronomic or business know-how. But the new noble lifestyle inaugurated by Peter I and encouraged by his successors in the Imperial period required ever-greater income. The more entrepreneurial landowners met this need by diversifying estate production: nobles were prominent in new industrial branches based on local rural resources – especially distilling spirit, a noble monopoly from 1754 to 1863. The majority however put pressure on their peasants, or borrowed: a Nobles' Land Bank created in 1754 lent on generous terms against serfs (not land). By 1842 one-half of all serfs were mortgaged to the Bank and other institutions. Debt can be a creative way of funding economic growth, and there is some doubt as to the relative burden of landlord debt at this time; but it is clear, at the very least, that much money was spent in unproductive ways.

Many nobles, moreover, took little account of profit and loss, thinking of their labour costs as nil; in fact serfs were always present and their living costs formed part of the estate budget, while unfree labour was less productive than contract labour. The agrarian economy remained profitable throughout the first part of the nineteenth century, contrary to claims that emancipation was triggered by economic crisis; but overall it was not dynamic, and the average estate was not a lucrative enterprise. While extensive growth of agriculture in the south and east allowed the growing population to be fed, and southern grain growers to make some profit, intensive growth was rare, markets grew only slowly in the pre-railway age, and the primitive technical level of most agriculture prevented the accumulation of capital which could have been invested in industry. Grain yields were fairly static until the second half of the nineteenth century. Towns remained underdeveloped. Larger-scale industry did develop, but from a small base, slowly, and unevenly across the economy. The few serf entrepreneurs who had made good through their own initiative and the protection of their lord, as in the Sheremetev cases, became major merchants and industrialists in the nineteenth century; and a significant proportion of industrial innovation came from foreign capital and foreign entrepreneurs. Overall, therefore, the still predominantly agrarian, servile economy was not well structured to support strong industrialisation and expansion, while the majority of noble estate-owners remained deeply attached to their now traditional way of life.

The Petrine model of economic growth, resource distribution and tax- and tribute-taking based on an unfree population was adequate in both productivity and flexibility to support and fund the Empire in the pre-industrial period. But as the needs of the economy and the military grew, and change and industrialisation accelerated in Europe in the nineteenth century, it no longer provided the economic backing for an internationally competitive great power. Kankrin's attempts to stabilise the currency under Nicholas were frustrated by military expenditure, while the state even so could neither produce nor afford to buy sufficient new rifles to replace all the muskets of its huge, expensive standing army.

There were few serious peasant outbreaks under Nicholas I, although peasant discontent was widespread. During the Crimean War rumours circulated that peasants joining militias could gain military exemption or emancipation, which caused turmoil; and once the forthcoming emancipation had been officially announced in 1857, a growing number of peasant disturbances indicated peasant impatience for change and suspicion of cheating by landlords or authorities.

The preparation of the emancipation generated tension within government and among the peasantry, but also polarised noble opinion. While the silent majority of petty and provincial estate-owners, and many aristocratic conservatives, bowed to the Tsar's will but remained unpersuaded, more liberal and cultured nobles were strongly in favour. From the late eighteenth century onwards, elite attitudes to the peasantry had been changing. Across Europe the ideas of Rousseau and Herder led at the turn of the century to a 'discovery of the people', a new appreciation of folk culture and peasant humanity. While peasants had appeared in some previous eighteenth-century tales and comic operas, the epoch-making sentimental story by Nikolai Karamzin, 'Poor Liza' (1792), portrayed a pure peasant girl who drowns herself when betrayed by an unworthy nobleman. The more radical literary travelogue of Aleksandr Radishchev, *Journey from St Petersburg to Moscow* (1790), presented dignified, highly moral and intelligent peasants subject to a litany of abuses. Collections of folk-songs were published from the later eighteenth century onwards; the agreeably idealised peasant images of the artist Aleksei Venetsianov brought peasant life to painting for the first time in the early nineteenth. The peasant theme in pre-emancipation imaginative literature culminated in Ivan Turgenev's hugely influential *A Sportsman's Sketches* (1847–52): its skilfully crafted and vividly simple vignettes presented serfs as dignified and attractive human beings, and made the book the equivalent of Harriet Beecher Stowe's contemporary American abolitionist classic *Uncle Tom's Cabin* (1850–2). *Sportsman's Sketches* greatly impressed Grand Duke Aleksandr Nikolaevich, the future Alexander II, and is credited with influencing his decision to end the servile system.

THE COMING OF AGE OF RUSSIAN CULTURE

Literature

From the middle of the eighteenth century, especially under the patronage of Catherine II, *belles lettres* developed rapidly. Catherine herself wrote plays, tales and historical works. In the early years of her reign she set up a society of translators, and in 1769 herself edited the first of a new literary breed in Russia, the 'moral weeklies' modelled on Addison and Steele's English *Spectator* which satirised social foibles and addressed issues of the day. The main editor of such journals was Nikolai Novikov, initially Catherine's protégé, a journalist, publisher, and later noted Freemason. In 1783 the Russian Academy (*Rossiiskaia Akademiia*) was founded, 'to outshine the glory of France in Russia'; it worked as an independent entity until amalgamated with the Academy of Sciences in 1841. Its first President (1783–96) was Yekaterina Dashkova, a literary intellectual of aristocratic family. Almost as remarkable, and atypical, in cultural terms as her good friend Catherine II herself, Dashkova was simultaneously President of the Academy of Sciences. In 1789 the Russian Academy published the first fundamental dictionary of the Russian language.

In 1783, Catherine passed a seminal decree allowing the establishment of private printing presses, a crucial step in the development of literary production and the literary market (rescinded, however, in 1796 under the impact of the French Revolution). Censorship was in general light and rather unsystematic under Catherine, whereas Paul introduced stringent restrictions. The first comprehensive statute on censorship was promulgated in 1804, and thereafter censorship remained a major, if varying, constraint.

In the second half of the eighteenth century major original literary talents emerged, though writing remained principally an amateur pursuit for nobles . The poet Gavriila Derzhavin's individuality and intimacy contrasted with the heavy solemnity of Lomonosov's ceremonial odes. The first novelists appeared. The fabulist Ivan Krylov also published literary journals. The plays of Vladimir Lukin and Denis Fonvizin marked the turn from Classical drama to comedy of manners. Fonvizin's very successful *The Brigadier* (1768), an attack on gallomania, was modelled on the Dane Holberg's *Jean de France*; his masterpiece *The Minor* (1782) can be compared in content and style with Oliver Goldsmith's *She Stoops to Conquer*, and is still in the Russian repertoire. Theatre flourished under Catherine; public and Court theatres were now also complemented by the private enthusiasms of many wealthy nobles, who kept their own theatres, staffed by serf artistes. (A famous, and tragic, case was that of the immensely wealthy and aristocratic Count Nikolai Sheremetev, who fell in love with and finally secretly married the leading actress of his theatre, the talented and cultured serf Parasha [Praskovia] Zhemchugova: however the social difficulties of the match blighted their lives.) Literary culture also spread out to provincial centres. Derzhavin, Governor of Tambov, was not alone in organising amateur theatre and literary activities with his local nobility; presses and journals likewise appeared in the provinces.

At the turn of the century literature became increasingly political. Hitherto much (though not all) literature had existed under Court auspices, near the Court or in courtier society. Catherine subsidised Novikov's journals; Derzhavin won decisive favour by hymning the Empress; Fonvizin's plays were initially read and performed at Court. With the coming of the French Revolution Catherine became much less tolerant, while writers themselves were showing increasing independence. A classic example was Radishchev, already mentioned. Educated at the elite Corps of Pages, he was sent to study at Leipzig, where he encountered the political and social thought of the Enlightenment, and experienced oppression at first hand in the person of the group's despotic mentor. On his return he made a career in military and civilian law, ending as deputy director of Customs at St Petersburg. His *Journey* excoriated abuse of power in all its forms, including that of officials and rulers. Catherine thought the anonymous author 'infected with the French madness', though Radishchev rather warned against than celebrated popular revolution. Radishchev, the 'father of Russian radicalism', paid for his rashness with a sentence of ten years' (not uncomfortable) Siberian exile. It should be added that he was a client of the Vorontsov family, at the time not in favour at Court, and part of his attack was directed against Potëmkin and his policies; also that he was able to publish such a pamphlet by using his own private press, and slipping the book past a careless censor. Radishchev, who was amnestied by Paul and rehabilitated by Alexander I, marks the beginning of a parting of ways between the establishment and the liberal nobility.

The on-going debate on the literary language was finally resolved in a confrontation in the first years of the new century between the literary schools of Karamzin, ground-breaking prosaist, journal editor and later Russia's first modern historian, and Aleksandr Shishkov, admiral, later Minister of Education, and President of the Russian Academy 1813–41: a debate which provoked furious satire and controversy. The day was won by the Karamzinists, who advocated a register based upon vernacular speech and French models, against Shishkov's appeal to Church Slavonic. Pushkin followed Karamzin, and his language later became the benchmark of modern literary Russian. The literary 'Golden Age' of the first three decades of the nineteenth century was dominated by poetry, which became for some a way of life: the poem was private letter, political pamphlet, social epigram, entry ticket to one of the growing number of literary salons. Pushkin was the centre of a 'pléiade' of talented but lesser practitioners, while there were also many poets, and close friends of Pushkin, among the Decembrists.

Pushkin's generation was often at odds with the establishment, Byronic and libertine: the young Pushkin wrote provocatively libertarian verses which got him exiled. Kondratii Ryleev, known for the impassioned civic patriotism of his verse, was the civilian leader of the northern Decembrists in Petersburg in 1825. In 1826 Nicholas I passed a new draconian censorship law. But a decree establishing copyright in 1828 made writing as a profession much more viable, and under Nicholas, despite censorship and frequent Third Section intervention, the literary audience and publications for it grew steadily, while literature became less aristocratic, as educated plebeian writers, particularly journalists, began to earn a living. The 'thick journal', the large literary-cultural periodical, now came into its own, carrying new writing, reviews and comment on current affairs. The pioneer was Karamzin's *Messenger of Europe* (1802–30). The most famous was *The Contemporary*, founded by Pushkin in 1836 and despite initial difficulty a leading voice until its suppression in 1866. Ivan Turgenev and Lev Tolstoi both made their debuts here. While a number of serious poets continued writing in the 1830s and 1840s, the poetic Golden Age was replaced by what later nineteenth-century critics called the Age of Gogol and realism – fantastic realism in Gogol's *Dead Souls* and 'Petersburg stories', romantic in Lermontov's *Hero of Our Time*, narrative in Sergei Aksakov's absorbingly innocent descriptions of his country family life, *Family Chronicle* (1856) and *Years of Childhood* (1858). Gogol initially seemed to his contemporaries to be a critic of social reality, offering 'laughter through tears' in his portrayal of a dysfunctional society. But *Dead Souls* was never completed, and his *Selected Passages from a Correspondence with Friends* (1847) revealed on the contrary a preachy religious justification of the existing social order and autocratic power; it met with general rejection, and a stinging denunciation from his friend Vissarion Belinskii, the leading literary critic of his day. Belinskii, a raznochinets, hugely influential, favoured civic awareness and social relevance.

The 1840s and 1850s mark the beginnings of the great age of the Russian novel. Part of Turgenev's *Sportsman's Sketches* appeared in *The Contemporary* in 1847, the complete work in book form in 1852. Turgenev's major novels, which were prized both for their style and their acute sensitivity to social currents, followed in the years 1856–62. The social engagement of Fëdor Dostoevskii's first work, *Poor Folk* (1846) evoked Belinskii's critical rapture. But Dostoevskii only found his quite different, characteristic later voice after his traumatic arrest and exile in Siberia (1848–59). During his imprisonment he underwent a deep religious crisis, which led to an intensely felt identification with the spiritual life and suffering of common people. He came, too, to a powerful awareness of the evil in human nature, and returned to St Petersburg a supporter of the *status quo* and the Church.

Childhood, the first work of Tolstoi – usually considered Russia's greatest novelist – appeared in *The Contemporary* in 1852. Tolstoi fought in the Crimean War, and *The Contemporary* published his *Sevastopol Tales* while the war was still on; he also spent time in the Caucasus. More autobiographical writing followed, but the major novels came later, in the post-emancipation decades. Meanwhile the critical role left vacant by Belinskii's death in 1848 was filled by a younger generation of largely raznochinets radicals centred once again on *The Contemporary*, the so-called 'men of the 60s' (the liberal '1860s', when censorship was somewhat relaxed, lasted from 1855 to 1865). The two main figures, Nikolai Dobroliubov and Nikolai Chernyshevskii, took literature as a text for radical comment, and developed an 'Aesopian' language to make political points under censorship. Chernyshevskii, son of a priest, was a journalist, economist, novelist, philosopher and critic, and contributed actively to the debate on emancipation.

Art, Architecture and Music

The foundation of the Academy of Arts in 1757 was critical for the further development of the visual arts. The most notable Russian portraitists of the eighteenth century, Vladimir Borovikovskii, Dmitrii Levitskii and Fëdor Rokotov, were all Academy graduates. They followed Classical styles, somewhat more formal than the later 'romantic' Classicism of their nineteenth-century fellow Orest Kiprenskii. The next generation of Russian artists achieved international recognition, particularly Karl Briullov and Aleksandr Ivanov. Both trained and worked in Italy, and owe a clear debt to Western prototypes and Romanticism. The advent of realist painting of Russian subjects in the 1860s was prefigured by the outstanding seascapes of Ivan Aivazovskii (who continued working throughout the century), the rather Hogarthian social genre paintings of Pavel Fedotov and the naturalistic but idealised rural images of Venetsianov, previously mentioned as the first painter of peasant life.

Sculpture was relatively little practised in the eighteenth century – the most famous piece, the 'Bronze Horseman' statue of Peter the Great (1782), was the work of the Frenchman Etienne Falconet. In the years 1800–30, however, sculpture came of age, with a number of talented practitioners: many of the familiar statuary groups which grace Moscow and St Petersburg date from this period. The eighteenth and early nineteenth centuries were the heyday of the construction of St Petersburg and the surrounding Imperial estates, also of neo-Classicism in Moscow, and of aristocrats' palaces around the two capitals. The work of Bartolomeo Rastrelli, 'master of the Baroque', included the final version of the Winter Palace (1754–64), and enlargements to the palaces of Peterhof (1746–52) and Tsarskoe Selo (1748–56) (Figure 11). Under Catherine II the neo-Classical style was dominant, but Gothic buildings also appeared. Catherine employed a number of significant architects, including the Scottish

Figure 11 The Age of Neo-Classicism: The Catherine Palace, Tsarskoe Selo/Pushkin (mid-eighteenth century, restored after World War II)

From the personal collection of the author.

Palladian Charles Cameron, who worked especially at Tsarskoe Selo and Pavlovsk, and Georg Veldten, who developed the quays along the Neva. In nineteenth-century St Petersburg, Roman and Greek models inspired Andrei Voronikhin's Cathedral of the Kazan Mother of God (1801–11) and Thomas de Thomon's Stock Exchange building (1805–10). The latter formed part of a great reordering of the northern areas of the city by Carlo Rossi under Alexander I and Nicholas I, which concluded with Alexandre Montferrand's stylistically eclectic St Isaac's Cathedral (1818–58). After the destruction of 1812, Moscow was rebuilt. A major commemorative work was Konstantin Ton's Church of Christ the Redeemer (1839–83), in the so-called Russo–Byzantine style; demolished by Stalin in the 1930s and replaced with a swimming pool, it was reconstructed in 1990–2000.

After decades of Italian dominance, music in European styles began to develop a native tradition in Imperial Russia about 1780. Early Russian operas – 'folk-tune plays' – appeared, notably by M. Sokolovskii and the Italian-trained Ye Fomin, using both Russian folk melodies and Italianate elements. The first Russian orchestras

appeared in the late eighteenth century. The St Petersburg
Philharmonic Society, founded in 1802, promoted contemporary
European music through major concert series, including perfor-
mances by European celebrities such as Berlioz and Liszt; in the
same period a permanent Italian opera company in the capital popularised Rossini, Bellini and Verdi. In Moscow the Bolshoi ('Big')
Theatre was founded in 1776, but from 1825, after reconstruction,
played Russian opera and ballet. Music became a popular part of
elite culture, and many wealthy nobles kept their own orchestras,
some composed of serfs. One specifically Russian phenomenon
which originated about 1750 and persisted until the 1830s was the
serf horn band, 36 horns of different lengths, each playing only one
note: the players were trained to perfect synchrony and harmony.
Despite the initial nineteenth-century fashion for Western Romantic
opera, Mikhail Glinka, the first major Russian composer, used
Russian folk themes in his operas *A Life for the Tsar* (1836, alternatively titled *Ivan Susanin*, after its hero) and *Ruslan and Liudmila*
(1842). The composers Aleksandr Dargomyzhskii and Aleksandr
Serov wrote in similar vein; Glinka's principal successor, Milyi
Balakirev, and the best-known classic Russian composers, worked in
the later decades of the century. Sacred music was developed in the
eighteenth century by the outstanding Ukrainian composer Dmitrii
Bortnianskii, who initially studied and wrote secular opera in Italy,
before becoming director of the Court chapel choir in 1777. A similar role was performed in the nineteenth century (1837–61) by
Aleksei L'vov, who also composed secular music, and in 1833 the
Imperial national anthem, 'God Save the Tsar'.

Natural Sciences

In the eighteenth century, the natural sciences were the preserve of
very few. They were focused in the Academy of Sciences, where they
did not always flourish. The Academy gave a home to notable scholars both native and foreign, but for much of the century top-heavy
administration hindered scientific enquiry; disputes and turf wars
simmered between German and Russian scholars, and between
proponents of pure and of applied research, both part of the
Academy's brief. Nevertheless the Academy maintained contacts
with the European scientific and scholarly community, by correspondence, by election of foreign and corresponding members, and

through its own Latin-language *Proceedings*, although the diffusion of its work was not always successful. A few aristocratic amateurs also maintained international contacts, like Prince Dmitrii A. Golitsyn, ambassador to several European Courts, who acted as an international conduit for information and ideas, undertook practical experimental work, and published well-received books which brought him election as President of the Jena Mineralogical Society.

The Academy developed a particularly strong tradition in mathematics. The Swiss Leonhard Euler, one of the leading mathematicians of his day, divided his career between St Petersburg and Berlin and acknowledged the uniquely favourable conditions afforded him in Russia, where he worked with another important Swiss Academician and mathematician, the Newtonian Daniel Bernoulli. Similarly eminent was the German botanist and zoologist Pallas, already mentioned as an explorer. By the end of the century, the majority of Academicians were Russian, many of them raznochintsy.

Other institutions crucial to the study of the sciences included Moscow University (1755), the Free Economic Society (1765), the Mining Institute (1774), the Medico-Chirurgical Academy (1798), the Moscow Society of Experimental Naturalists (1805). By 1800 an expanding number of Russian journals concerned themselves with scientific matters, both technical periodicals (*The Technological Journal*, 1800) and non-specialist publications which carried scientific materials, such as the Academy's *Monthly Publications*. Under Catherine II scientific culture also spread further into the provinces: the American traveller John Ledyard found a vibrant society in Irkutsk (Siberia) in 1787, where he came upon 'a circle as gay, rich, polite and scientific as if in St Petersburg', with 'disciples of Linneus' who joined him in his scientific explorations of the area. In 1789 the Irkutsk journal *Irtysh being Transformed into Hippocrene* published extracts from Newton's *Principia*. Comparable activities are reported of other Siberian centres, or port cities such as Archangel. Although scientific culture was certainly less well established in Russia than in, say, France or Great Britain, J. Scott Carver has argued that by 1800 'Russia had developed a sizeable, vital community of scientists and technical experts who directed the domestication of a modernizing scientific culture, who advised and served the state, and who contributed to the expansion of the scientific tradition.'

In the first half of the nineteenth century, the continuing growth of educational institutions, presses, and opportunities for international interchange brought further scientific development, despite constraints and increasingly obtuse censorship in the later years of both Alexander I and Nicholas I. Thus Nikolai Lobachevskii, founder of non-Euclidean geometry, and other distinguished mathematicians continued the Euler tradition. Medicine and pharmacy had been put on a firm foundation since Peter's time by Western physicians and foreign-trained Russians. The Crimean War brought to prominence the surgeon Nikolai Pirogov, subsequently founder of the modern Russian medical profession in the 1860s.

ENLIGHTENMENT, ROMANTICISM, REVOLUTION

The Enlightenment in Russia

Peter's *diktat* requiring his service class to adopt foreign cultural and behavioural norms led gradually to an openness to European values as well as fashions. Russians now joined the European cultural mainstream as consumers of philosophical as well as material culture, and their interests began to reflect major contemporary preoccupations. Voltaire enjoyed an increasing vogue in Russia, as elsewhere in Europe, from the 1730s onwards, and gave his name to a worldly scepticism, especially towards religious values, which became fashionable as *volterianstvo* ('Voltairianism'); since Peter's reforms, Church–State relations were not an issue in Russia. The universal European admiration for Versailles engendered the same gallomania, and then its opposite gallophobia, which could be found elsewhere in Europe: Fonvizin assailed the former both in *Brigadier* and his *Letters from France* (1777). With the coming of the French Revolution, adulation of things French tended to be replaced by anglomania, expressed, however, more in terms of admiration for English landscape-gardening, agronomy and material culture – beer, carriages, grooms – than for philosophy or politics.

Freemasonry came to Russia about 1740, and soon became as popular as elsewhere in Europe, especially under Catherine II; it offered anything from simple sociability to the answer to the mysteries of life. However, the Empress became increasingly sceptical and suspicious of the secretive organisation. Finally its most assiduous practitioners, the publisher Nikolai Novikov and his

Rosicrucian circle, fell victim to the growing European polemic about Masonry's purposes and the increasing doubts of the Russian authorities about their loyalty and Orthodoxy. In 1792, as the French Revolution intensified, the circle was dispersed, Novikov arrested and imprisoned. Freemasonry was banned, permitted once more at the start of Alexander's reign, but banned again in 1822.

In the 1770s Novikov had used his 'moral weekly' journals (1769–74) to satirise human foibles for his newly 'emancipated' noble readership: in practice the critique of vice presented a normative depiction of the qualities of the good man in society, as exemplified by the English gentleman or French *honnête homme*. The frequent condemnation here of people who maltreated their peasants was not (as often asserted) a condemnation of serfdom as such, but a statement that good men and proper gentlemen do not oppress dependents. This line of thinking led on to the moral ideas of true nobility expressed in the poetry of Derzhavin, and to the sentimental humanitarianism of Karamzin and Radishchev, who reached the same picture of the peasant masses from contrary political premises.

A few highly educated members of the elite were fully engaged with the theoretical thought of the Enlightenment, though they were rare, and Russia at this stage was a consumer, not a producer of ideas; it was also open to the heterodox religious currents abroad in Europe at this time. By the 1790s the Court was no longer at the forefront of new values, and Catherine's personal behaviour as well as her foreign policy elicited criticism from within the elite. Traditionally historians have suggested that malcontents in Catherine's reign were opposed to autocracy and serfdom, but before the French Revolution this was rarely the case: these issues became prominent only in the nineteenth century. The French Revolution caused more revulsion than enthusiasm in Russia, although over the next decades its philosophical challenges gradually changed the terms of social debate. In the 1780s and 1790s, however, principal fault lines of discontent ran through issues of just war, of aggressive territorial conquest versus domestic improvement, military expenditure on war or peaceful development at home. Paul initially declared peace to Europe, but soon changed his stance. Alexander I reprised Paul's initial pacifism, and seemed ready to address both serfdom and autocracy as well: but within a few years any such expectations were already disappointed.

The Decembrist Movement

The Decembrist 'movement' (1814–25), whose abortive revolt was discussed above, emerged partly in response to these disappointments; but it was also a cultural phenomenon, the product of a distinct and unique conjuncture in noble cultural development. It represented the liberal extreme of an increasingly polarised post-Napoleonic public opinion. It combined cosmopolitan European elegance and dandyism, Byronic libertinism and disregard for convention, youthful high spirits and excess, with education and intellectual culture, patriotic fervour, serious humanitarian concerns, and revolutionary enthusiasm for liberation movements such as Riego's in Spain and Bolivar's in South America. This was also the heyday of duelling in Russia, a means for dashing young men both to show their devil-may-care fearlessness and to circumvent the constraints of social hierarchy (any noble could challenge any other noble). The Decembrist rebels were very few in number – despite the best efforts of Nicholas and his police, only 121 people were convicted of criminal action. However, they represented the tip of a much larger iceberg: those who shared their general view but were not prepared to violate their oath to the Emperor or to take such thoughts to the ultimate conclusion of deeds. The Decembrists combined the Enlightenment's concern for just, rational and productive forms of society with the Romantic elevation of the individual, freedom and self-sacrifice. Their deeply felt patriotism was also part of the growing national consciousness which presaged the rise of nationalism. These nobles, mainly young, who had received a Europeanised education, now wished to discover and reclaim their Russian roots and to be able to take pride in their fatherland; while differing considerably as to method, they wished ultimately to bring about a free society in which all social strata would have a rightful place.

What is Russia?

The liberal post-Decembrist generation focused its intellectual pursuits in salons and private groups, above all the student 'circles' which grew up in Moscow University in the 1830s. Under the fashionable influence of German romantic idealist philosophy (primarily Fichte and Hegel), they tried to understand the country's present in the light of its past, and grasp its potential and its desirable future. The issue was posed critically by Pëtr Chaadaev in his sensational 'First Philosophical Letter' (1836), for which he was declared insane by the authorities. Two main lines of thought emerged to rival Official Nationality; they had much in common, including hostility to serfdom and Nicholaevan absolutism. That of the 'Slavophiles' declared Russia to be a unique civilisation based upon Orthodoxy and its essential quality of *sobornost*, the brotherly unity of all believers. Peter I's secularising imitation of European norms, in this view, had led the country into a fateful authoritarian cul-de-sac, degraded the Church and enabled the excessive power of contemporary autocracy. The way forward was a return to the alleged balance of the pre-Petrine past. The Slavophiles embraced the peasant commune, so persuasively described by Haxthausen, as a symptomatically Russian and Orthodox union of the unspoilt masses. The Slavophiles' friends and opponents, the 'Westernisers', believed on the contrary that Peter had been right, but had not gone far enough: in stopping short of embracing the full panoply of European law and institutions he had left the door open to the distortions of Nicholaevan despotism. What was needed was more, not less, assimilation of European norms. The principal Slavophiles were prosperous Moscow land- and serf-owners, intensely educated in the European manner, who rationalised their political impotence by criticism of the *status quo*. The Westerners tended towards socialistic ideas (Proudhon, Fourier) which were both theorised and realisable only outside Russia. Their outstanding and unusually activist representative, the wealthy Aleksandr Gerzen (Herzen), succeeded in emigrating in 1847, just in time to witness the European events of 1848. Herzen settled in London, founded the Free Russian Press, and devoted himself to propaganda against the autocratic regime. He was greatly disillusioned with the revolutionary failures of 1848 and the 'philistine' bourgeois culture he encountered in France, Switzerland and Britain, and at odds with his contemporary Karl Marx, whose personal dislike he heartily reciprocated. He came round to a view of the Russian peasantry not far different from the Slavophiles': Russia would be saved by the innate socialism of the communal peasant village. As his friend Turgenev jeeringly wrote: all his other gods had crumbled, so now he genuflected before the peasant sheepskin coat. Russian agrarian socialism was born.

The Intelligentsia

Under Nicholas I the 'parting of ways' between supporters and intellectual critics of the autocratic regime became complete. Activists of the post-Decembrist generation were either repressed (Herzen spent time in internal exile before emigrating) or went abroad (like Mikhail Bakunin, who was absorbed into European anarchism). Russia was little affected by revolution. Both the Decembrist revolt of 1825 and and the Polish rising of 1830 were traumatic for government, but easily put down. In 1848 Russia was quiescent: the only 'revolutionaries' uncovered were a discussion-circle hosted by the Fourierist civil servant M. Butashevich-Petrashevskii. The arrest and trial of his group, to which Dostoevskii also belonged, was a storm in a tea-cup. At the same time, a new social and cultural type was emerging, which in the 1860s would be named retrospectively the 'intelligentsia'. Its representatives were persons of education, capable of systematic thought, committed to a particular view of the social good, and motivated by moral conviction to act on his, and later her, principles, regardless of possible costs to themselves. Thinking members of the noble elite sought justification for their social role, and means to embody in their lives the moral standards insistently proposed by their tutors and the philosophical works which they studied; and those who could no longer find this in service to the state increasingly thought of service to the people – the *narod*, the mass of the population.

The term 'intelligentsia' is usually used in the context of authoritarian polities: intellectuals in democracies rarely suffer for their convictions, and usually find a place in pluralist society which allows them to make productive, even lucrative use of their knowledge and mental skills. In Russia, where nineteenth-century and later governments asserted a monopoly of the political truth, activist expression of alternative world-views and social theories provoked opposition and repression. As education became available to wider circles of Nicholaevan society, including non-nobles, enabling them to become writers, journalists or teachers, this type of mind-set became more widespread. The intelligentsia in such cases becomes cast, by itself and others, as the voice of national conscience. Where there is little freedom of expression, literature and art can become vehicles for presenting heterodox values. In Russia the intelligentsia, which in any case did not share one united viewpoint, was never a serious political force, unless it resorted to violence or could combine with other larger social groups. But its very political impotence, which also allowed it to avoid compromising its principles, together with its willingness to suffer for its beliefs, gave it great moral authority, as did the dignity, steadfastness and clarity of purpose of its representatives. The first generation of the left-radical intelligentsia, Herzen and his friends, 'men of the forties', were primarily nobles. Among the 'men of the sixties' social origins were more mixed. Herzen abroad, and Chernyshevskii at home, watched as the Tsar's government prepared the emancipation of the serfs. After 1860 both turned to clandestine revolutionism.

5

1860–1917
Europe and Russia: Stabilisation and Collapse of the Autocratic State

The Crimean defeat led to a period of far-reaching domestic reforms, of which the most important was the abolition of serfdom. Only the central political structures were exempt. The reforms changed the face of the country, giving new opportunities to its peoples and permitting the halting emergence of a civil society. However, social and cultural change, further accelerated by rapid industrial growth, increasingly conflicted with the rulers' attempts to maintain autocratic control. Russia expanded into Central Asia and the Far East, but German unification created a formidable new challenger to its position in Europe. Social divisions and clumsy repression, together with military defeat against Japan, unleashed revolutionary unrest in 1905, forcing constitutional concessions and a national assembly, the State Duma. However, the strains of World War I and the intransigence of the last Tsar finally provoked revolution in 1917.

FROM THE 'GREAT REFORMS' TO 1905

Domestic Reform: Revolution from Above

In 1856, after the Crimean debacle, Tsar and government recognised that Russia could not remain as it was. In this sense Alexander II emancipated to save his throne: serfdom was the knot which tied together all the evils within the state. Moreover, society of all political stripes acknowledged the inevitability of change. An officer visiting St Petersburg in 1857 reported 'an astonishing phenomenon: one and all are in the grip of an aspiration to reform'. The motives and concepts in the minds of those concerned were varied, and still remain to some extent a matter of argument. But the reform programme which took shape between 1857 and 1874 amounted to a thorough-going modernisation of government and social institutions. Initially the authorities reacted to the new situation with liberal measures, lightening censorship and allowing *glasnost*, 'openness', a limited freedom of press opinion on matters relevant to reform; in 1856 they also amnestied political prisoners. Reformist ministers had charge of government departments. In 1857 Alexander took the active first step, publicly inviting the Empire's nobility to join him in dismantling the servile system.

The preparation of emancipation lasted four years, 1857–61. It was essentially a government action, propelled by the Tsar himself, who showed tenacity and diplomatic skills in the face of difficulties and widespread noble disinclination, including among senior statesmen. Emancipation terms were hammered out in a succession of state commissions. Peasants were not consulted; provincial committees of nobles were allowed only limited representations, but had significant opportunity to shape implementation locally. Once personal freedom had been decreed, the major question was that of land. The negative consequences of the earlier Baltic landless emancipation were decisive in Alexander's decision for an emancipation with land. Peasants held that land belonged to God and those who tilled it: the lands they farmed on noble estates thus belonged to them. Landlords took for granted their Roman-law property rights over their entire estates. The final settlement, proclaimed on 19 February 1861 (in Lent, to encourage due deference), was inevitably a compromise. The landowners had to give up more land than they wished, with poor compensation; the peasants received less land, on more onerous terms, than they expected. Land was allocated not to individuals, but to the commune, newly redefined, which would control land distribution and tax collection under collective responsibility. This was a measure of social control, with the village commune replacing the lord's local authority, to keep the peasants orderly and attached to their land, and ensure continued payment of taxes and dues. In minor, daily matters the communes, grouped together into *volosts*, became largely self-governing, using their own customary village law rather than state law. This, and his continuing subjection to corporal punishment, set the peasant apart from other social groups. Personal freedom was immediate; but the land settlement took effect only after two years, or when contracts were signed thereafter between owner and peasant. The government, struggling after the draining war and a banking crisis in 1860, laid the costs of compensation on the peasants: they were to pay 'redemption dues', over 49 years, which would be used to compensate the landowners with interest-bearing state bonds. In 1857 peasants made up some 84 per cent of the Russian population; the emancipation legislation of 1861 applied only to the landlords' serfs, just under half (42 per cent of the peasantry). There were some variations, detailed statutes for different regions being announced successively. In 1866 similar terms, somewhat more generous, harmonised the position of the remaining state and Court peasantry.

Once emancipation was in place, a host of other reforms followed. In 1860 a new state bank had been created; further measures strengthened the budget, and regulated the formation of joint stock companies and commercial banks. In 1863 new statutes appeared governing university education (allowing greater autonomy), and the taxation of the sale of spirits – an extremely important measure, since the old vodka tax-farm brought in a large slice of state revenue, but was notoriously corrupt. In 1864 the *zemstvo* statute reformed local government in the central Great Russian provinces, creating elective all-estate (but noble-dominated) committees with local tax-raising powers, at district and provincial level; a parallel urban statute followed in 1870. Also in 1864 the old judiciary, secret, slow and corrupt, was radically reshaped along Anglo-French lines, with a jury system, irremovable judges, greater transparency and a new, independent, professional framework for lawyers. In 1865 censorship was loosened, to take effect post- rather than pre-publication. At the end of the war military reform was already under way. By the 1860s the navy was introducing steam and joining the Anglo-French race for ironclads. The army abolished most military colonies in 1858. Internal wrangles delayed army restructuring until 1874, but when it came it was radical, replacing the standing army with a reserve system of universal (though unequally applied) conscription for six years, and recasting the territorial infrastructure. All recruits were to be taught literacy and, it was hoped, civic consciousness: although literacy classes were later dropped. The Church was also drawn into the process of renewal; however, with no significant results.

The reform process was exceptionally wide-ranging. As subsequent experience showed, many measures were less than perfect; but change affected almost all areas of public life. There was, however, one major exception: the central political structure. The Tsar's authority was crucial not only in framing the emancipation, but during the in-fighting among different government and social interests over other measures. But while supporting reform elsewhere, the conservative Alexander II saw no grounds to alter his own prerogatives. Despite wide-ranging support in his entourage for a consultative national assembly, and calls by liberal nobles to crown the reform with a constitution, he refused. He confirmed a Council of Ministers, effectively a cabinet, initially established in 1857, but otherwise retained the full powers of autocracy. His refusal has been seen by some as a pivotal decision in Russia's modern history.

Responses and Consolidation, 1861–1905

Few of those directly affected by the process of emancipation were satisfied with its terms. While a few peasants rejoiced in a sense of *volia*, for most the land settlement violated their moral economy and their understanding of tsars' paternal justice. They responded with a wave of disturbances, many claiming that the landlords had hidden the 'true freedom' from them. The government had taken precautions, and troops were on hand; some blood was shed. With some liberal and public-spirited exceptions, landowners set out to salvage everything they could from their peasants. Liberal and conservative public opinion praised Alexander as the 'Tsar-Liberator', but the radicals were outraged that the serfs' reward for more than two centuries of slave labour should be what they saw as semi-freedom, a punitive land settlement and crippling 49-year debt. From the Tsar's and the government's point of view, however, this was the best compromise available. For them, peasant interests naturally ranked below those of the political nation, the state and nobility. The whole huge project of social engineering, directly affecting nearly 90 per cent of the population, was carried out within the existing economic framework of the country, and without major social or political upheaval. The contemporaneous American liberation of the slaves, 10 per cent of the population, was achieved only at the cost of civil war. Compensation of landowners was considered desirable both for social stability and as a matter of equity. After British abolition, the British too had compensated their slave-owners, handsomely, but not the slaves.

In effect, the 'great reforms' gave the monarchy an extra 50-year lease of life; but its continuing dominance validated the hierarchical social *status quo* and restricted further change, while its refusal to evolve contributed materially to the coming revolutionary breakdown. The political intransigence of Nicholas II (1894–1917) was a major factor in the revolutionary period 1905–17.

Already during the reform period, the government's stance began to alter. Disappointed by peasant and liberal responses to his reforms, Alexander was shocked by the ingratitude of the Poles, who reacted to changes in their provinces with renewed rebellion in 1863: Polish serfs (many of them ethnically White Russian or Ukrainian) were accordingly given especially favourable emancipation terms in 1864. He was even more outraged by Russian radical responses, as small numbers of activists set up clandestine revolutionary cells. In 1866 a student conspirator, Dmitrii Karakozov, tried to assassinate the Tsar. After that, the reform process continued, but glasnost was replaced by a heavier government hand. Most reforming ministers were replaced by conservatives, and the implementation of the reforms, as well as further change, became more problematic. In an attempt to focus loyalty upon the tsar as embodiment of a national identity, Russification policies among the Empire's ethnic minorities, dating back to Nicholas I, were now vigorously pursued in Poland, Ukraine, Finland and the Baltic provinces, and Russian control was asserted in the newly pacified or conquered territories in the east and south. At the end of his reign, again under pressure from liberals and from the revolutionaries of the 'People's Will' organisation in the aftermath of the 1870s Balkan crisis, Alexander did prepare a limited constitution, while simultaneously establishing wider police powers, replacing the Third Section with what became known as the *Okhrana* secret police. He was assassinated by a terrorist bomber on the eve of signature of his constitution. His son and heir Alexander III (1881–94), guided by his arch-conservative tutor Konstantin Pobedonostsev, later Over-Procurator of the Holy Synod, rejected it: another potential period of reform was aborted. The assassination was followed by stricter censorship, and the creation of reserve state emergency powers, which remained in force until 1917.

Paradoxically, while social autonomy expanded rapidly in the last Imperial decades, from 1881 until the revolution Russia lived under emergency police laws.

Although the next Finance Minister, Nikolai Bunge, attempted in the 1880s to improve the economic condition of the peasantry with some palliative measures, at the same time as introducing initial factory legislation in a gesture towards worker grievances, overall the government did little in practical terms to build on the potential for social development and prosperity offered by 1861. In particular, the regime did not seek to integrate the mass of the population into national society, preferring to rely upon its archaic vision of an alleged patriarchal love between peasant Russians and their 'little father' tsar and upon ethnic prejudices embodied in Russification and anti-Semitism – the last decades of the regime witnessed the rise of pogroms which the authorities did little to check. In the 1890s the new Tsar presided over a period of 'counter-reforms': the conservative government sought to remedy perceived defects in the reformed structures of the 1860s, and bolster the existing social order, by increasing state control over society. The zemstvo was seriously restricted, and a new local office of Land Captain created for the countryside, with almost dictatorial powers.

At the end of the century, Russia experienced a period of intense economic growth. The later 1890s were a period of further railway building and industrial expansion under Minister of Finance Sergei Witte, who took Russia on to the gold standard in 1897, triggering a rise in foreign investment. For a few years under the 'Witte system' Russian GDP grew faster than that of any other country, including the USA. However, this was still insufficient to provide the infrastructure for Russia's urgent geopolitical requirements – despite Witte's spectacular expansion of the railways, the network remained thinly stretched over Russia's vastness, a fatal weakness in the coming wars. Moreover, economic growth further accentuated social change, with consequent hardships and instabilities. Population and financial pressures brought land shortage and peasant disturbance. The growing industrial sector sucked huge numbers of culture-shocked peasants into its grim living and working conditions, creating a growing urban working class centred in concentrations of enterprise like St Petersburg, Moscow and Warsaw. Factories were often unusually large, which facilitated labour organisation and solidarity, bonding people from different parts and social groups of the

Empire. From 1880 onwards labour expressed its discontent in increasing waves of strikes. But it remained an industrial archipelago in the ocean of rural peasantry. Middle-class liberals were emboldened by government failures in the 1890s, and alienated by Nicholas II's dismissal of constitutional hopes as 'senseless dreams' at his accession in 1894. Student demands and demonstrations broke out at the end of the decade. Meanwhile revolutionaries, decimated by police action after 1881, began to re-emerge and form new, Marxist, groupings, though without much initial impact. In 1900–3 a world recession depressed wages, and threw many industrial workers out of their new jobs. Those who could do so returned, resentful, and hungry, to their villages; but the countryside was stricken with harvest failure in the same years. Professional and zemstvo bodies demanded reforms and civil liberties; revolutionary terrorists assassinated two successive, reactionary, Ministers of the Interior in 1902 and 1904, as well as Grand Duke Sergei, commander of the Moscow military region and the Tsar's brother, in 1905. The country was in a state of tension.

International Relations and Eastward Expansion

Meanwhile Russia sought to regain its place in the international community. Its Crimean defeat had finally broken up the European order established in 1815, and paved the way for Italian and German unification. After a brief *rapprochement* with Napoleon III, Russia watched as its former enemies Austria and France were successively crushed by Prussia in 1866 and 1870, and it took advantage of war and the Treaty of London (1871) to repudiate the neutralisation of the Black Sea. But Germany, industrialised and united, now posed an equal threat to Russia: throughout the rest of the century and until 1914, St Petersburg remained in a position of relative weakness – of which Russian military commanders were well aware – able to muster neither the economic strength and infrastructure, nor the military capacity, to guarantee great-power status and foreign policy interests securely in post-Crimean Europe. The war with Turkey during the Balkan crisis of the 1870s, which led to Bulgarian independence, showed up continuing Russian military weaknesses, and partial battlefield success was largely negated by diplomatic humiliation at the Treaty of Berlin (1878). The initial diplomatic strategy of reliance on Germany was replaced in the 1890s by entente with

France, and France's ally Britain. The power blocs of World War I took shape. As the international arms race of the pre-war decades accelerated, Russia's military expenditure soared, straining the budget, but doing no more than keep it in touch with the international leaders.

On the other hand, this was a period of new advance into Asia. Since the 1860s Russia had made steady advances into Central Asia, creating a Governor-Generalship of Turkestan, taking Chimkent, Tashkent, Samarkand, and imposing protectorates on Bukhara and Khiva. Russian advances into Afghanistan, potentially threatening India, led to crisis with Britain in 1885, resolved by an Anglo–Russian accord delimiting the Afghan frontier. The principal hero of this Central Asian advance was General Mikhail Cherniaev, a self-willed commander who continued local conquests despite official proclamations from St Petersburg that Russia had no policy of Central Asian expansion. He lost his command in 1866; but in 1883 Alexander III made him Governor-General of Turkestan.

In the Far East, China's weakness in the nineteenth century tipped the Sino-Russian balance of power in Russia's favour: 'unequal treaties' of 1858 and 1860 created a Russian Pacific 'Maritime Region' and permitted the foundation of Vladivostok. While Russia divested itself of its American territories, selling Alaska to the USA in 1867 for $7.2 million, it strengthened its Far-Eastern position by accommodation with the new Pacific power, Japan: the Treaty of St Petersburg (1875) clarified their relative spheres, Sakhalin for Russia, the Kurile islands for the Japanese. Twenty years later, at the end of the Sino–Japanese war, new Russian treaties with China (1896, 1898) brought the establishment of a Russo–Chinese Bank, important railway concessions, and a 25-year lease of the Liao-Tung peninsula and Port Arthur naval base; during the Boxer Rebellion (1900) Russia occupied Manchuria. The completion of the Trans-Siberian Railway in the same year, initially single-track, promised logistic security. Russian power seemed to be well established in the region. Simultaneously, Japanese interests in Korea were officially acknowledged. However, Imperial support for a Russian timber enterprise on the Yalu river, on Korean territory, and the establishment in 1903 of a Russian Far-Eastern Viceroyalty, brought the two expansionist powers into open conflict; and the Russo–Japanese War (1904–5) proved an unpleasant shock for St Petersburg. The unexpectedly able enemy defeated Russia on land and sea; Russian military ineptitude culminated in the destruction in May 1905 of the Baltic Fleet in the Strait of Tsushima off Japan, after an epic circumnavigation. Thus in international terms, in the later nineteenth century Russia remained relatively weak in Europe, while at the same time becoming increasingly well-established, but in fact also over-extended, in the East.

THE TRANSMUTATION OF THE COUNTRYSIDE AFTER 1861

The emancipation legislation of 1861 proved to be an imperfect instrument, and complete serf liberation was a long-drawn-out process. Potentially abolition made possible the integration of the majority peasant population into the Russian political nation, but the failure of the government to achieve this, and to consolidate peasant support for the existing social order, was a prime reason for its later collapse. The ambivalence of the regime towards its lowliest subjects was apparent in the ordering of their emancipation. While personal freedom took effect at once, the process of completing peasant–lord land agreements depended on negotiation and could be protracted – when agreement was made compulsory in 1885, some 20 per cent of serfs were still under so-called 'temporary obligation', the old pre-emancipation economic relationships. What Marxist historians have called 'feudal survivals' from the servile system proved very persistent. The peasant was firmly tied to the repartitional commune, and able in practice neither to leave the village permanently, nor to determine his own individual agrarian regime. The incidence and burden of the land settlement have traditionally been seen as very unfavourable to the peasantry: commentators of all persuasions have suggested that peasants broadly received less land under the emancipation settlements than they had farmed previously, and that landlords were able to manipulate allocations to their advantage. Recent research by the economic historian Steven Hoch, however, has shown gross deficiencies in the statistical basis for this received view, and suggests that peasant allocations were in general neither manipulated nor unfair. Nevertheless, many landlords held on to essential amenities and compelled peasants to pay rent for their use. Peasants now had the right to buy land, improve stock or inventory, but the government provided no credit: a Peasant Land Bank was established only in 1883, while land prices approximately doubled between 1861 and 1905, and rose further thereafter. Redemption payments increased the existing tax burden on the peasants: the poll tax was replaced by indirect taxes only in the 1880s, and although some arrears were written off at the same time, redemption dues were finally abolished only in 1905. Huge and accelerating population growth put increasing pressure on resources and on the size of individual peasant holdings.‡ And labour migration faced peasants with a harsh early-industrial labour market in which their labour did not command a high price.

Nevertheless, in the remaining decades of the century the countryside gradually prospered. With the ending of serfdom, and more active and propitious government policies, in both agriculture and industry the economy developed further on the foundations laid in the previous half-century. The agrarian sector successfully fed the exploding population of the Empire. As in the past, there were periodic crop failures and local famines, the worst in 1890–2, and some regions, notably the centre, fared worse than others; but overall, production kept pace with consumption. Buoyant international as well as national demand also stimulated grain production for much of the period, though international terms of trade turned seriously against Russia in the 1870s and 1880s. Peasants played a leading role in the pre-revolutionary agrarian economy: they became responsible for a growing proportion of agricultural production, increasingly adapted to the market, and over time appear to have acquired more disposable income than prophets of doom predicted. Russian crop yields of the period compare relatively favourably with those elsewhere in Europe. Neither did the repartitional commune as a socio-economic structure shackle flexibility or technical advance in agriculture; a more important hindrance was the unfavourable long-term physical and economic environment in which peasant agriculture had to operate.

This generally positive picture of the economy cannot, however, be matched to social consensus or general peasant contentment. Regional variations were considerable. Particularly in the central agricultural provinces, south and south-east of Moscow, many peasant households struggled to make a living. As time went on, peasants' tax

---

‡ The Russian population of European Russia increased from c.17 million in 1762 to 27 m. in 1815, 36.5 m. in 1850, 60 m. in 1897 and 106.5 m. at the time of the revolution. For the Empire as a whole the figures are: 1861 – 73 m.; 1897 – 125 m.; 1917 – 170 m. Growth appears to have been due essentially to natural increase, from both high fertility rates and an unusual tendency towards universal marriage.

and redemption arrears reached huge proportions; it remains unclear how far this reflected refusal, rather than inability, to pay what was due, but either implies peasant dissatisfaction. Across the country peasants remained resentful that they had lost, and landlords held, land which could have been distributed among the growing peasant population. In the 1890s, the authorities finally created an official voluntary resettlement system, offering generous land allocations in Siberia, but resettled peasants were a small fraction of the population increase, and many failed to adapt and returned home. Official enquiries into reasons for peasant dissatisfaction at the end of the century found land shortage at the head of the list; 'black repartition', the complete redistribution of all land, became a central peasant demand in the revolutionary period.

In the post-emancipation decades, the countryside underwent increasing change. While the emancipation regulations had tried to ensure stability and order, the reforms changed the context of peasant life. Growing markets, population pressure on land, and communal interest in maximising income encouraged peasants to seek work away from the village: they were welcomed by the new railway construction companies, the larger commercial farms in the south, the managers of the new factories, the gang-masters and labour-brokers of busy towns. After the Crimean War the government had allocated substantial funds to promote railway construction, and a first phase of growth took place in the late 1860s, another in the 1890s (though without properly addressing the strategic failures laid bare in the war). Now both goods and peasants could travel farther and faster. Towards the end of the century increasing numbers of women also found their way to the towns and factories: light-industrial employers welcomed them – they could be paid less than men, and were less trouble to manage. Peasants consequently gained, and brought home with them to the village, experience of other milieux and other societies – the new conscript army, from which soldiers returned after a few years instead of disappearing for ever; the life of the mushrooming towns, with its new acquaintances, newspapers, and prostitution, alcohol, gambling, crime, disease, to which peasants were exposed in the absence of family and the routines of village life; the trading networks of the great rivers; the dirty, dangerous, crowded factories and their worker barracks. Peasants acquired unprecedented access to education – the new army taught literacy, and the new zemstvo committees set up very successful rural schools. The last pre-revolutionary decades were the time 'when Russia learned to read', especially younger, mobile people, even if illiteracy still remained widespread until the 1930s. As a result of these trends, traditional village values and the habit of unquestioning obedience gradually became eroded. The large extended families favoured by the old estate managements began to break up: sons broke away to form smaller (weaker, and more numerous) independent nuclear units. These younger heads of household, who had a right to their own land allocation, spoke up in competition with the old guard at communal meetings, as did returning factory workers, soldiers and migrants. Over the years peasants were gradually able to lease and buy more land, either communally, or individually outside the commune's holdings – by 1914 peasants held vastly more land than they received as allotments after 1861. Differences of wealth likewise became greater, and more obvious: while some rich peasants, the so-called kulaks or 'fists' (the term *kulak* basically refers to peasant usury), exploited and sought to dominate their fellow villagers, others prospered through enterprise and acumen, laying the foundations of a productive yeoman stratum.

These processes were gradual. In 1900 the great majority of peasants, it seems, still adhered to traditional values. For most peasants, life was still focused on the village, and access to land remained the great issue. But they were much more aware than before of life outside the village. Loyalty to the 'holy tsar', 'little father', was still the norm, but contested by new experiences and ideas increasingly widely spread. In all this the communal organisation of the peasantry remained intact and important. The government continued to regard the commune as a bulwark of stability: during the 1890s 'counter-reforms' its powers were strengthened. The peasants themselves relied on the commune as before for self-government, on the basis of their own customary law, for land management and redistribution, and for mutual support: the *artel* (labour cooperative) and *zemliach-estvo* (association of working people from the same locality) projected communal support structures into the wider world. As before, too, the commune remained the foundation for peasant resistance and solidarity in the face of outside threat or when collective action was undertaken: the communal solidarity of the 1861–2 disturbances reappeared in the 1905–6 revolution.

The impact of 1861 was as great on the land-owning class as it was on the peasantry. Landowners now lost their free labour force, as well as significant, if varying, amounts of land. The government deducted any outstanding debts from the compensation payments; the redemption bonds could not be immediately encashed, and soon declined in market value. The old way of life became increasingly impossible, and by 1905 nobles owned 40 per cent less land than they had in 1861. Nevertheless, this period witnessed not so much the 'decline of the gentry', much trumpeted at the time and later, but rather a redisposition of noble activity. Some estate-owners succeeded in adapting to the new economic situation on the land, either by taking advantage of persisting peasant dependence, or with new farming methods and a reduced lifestyle, or both. As the market in land developed, nobles were buyers as well as sellers; modern methods using hired hands, multiple crop-rotation and machinery coexisted with traditional strip-farming, labour-rent and share-cropping. Many owners retreated from active involvement in agriculture, selling or renting out their land and using the proceeds to launch into other occupations. Most landlords did not favour the development of an independent peasantry, which contradicted their social values and threatened them still further economically. After 1905 the nobility revived as a political force: the newly founded right-wing United Nobility provided strong organised support for the monarchy.

REVOLUTION FROM BELOW: 1905–17

Dress Rehearsal for Revolution: 1905

Faced with mounting social unrest and revolutionary and public opposition in the years before 1905, the government tried to combine concession, diversion and repression. The police swiftly countered overt protest, and had considerable success, too, in infiltrating revolutionary groupings. Serious government commissions on the needs of the countryside recommended change, resulting in 1904 in a decision in principle to relax the hold of the commune; corporal punishment of peasants was abolished in 1902. In 1901 the head of the Moscow okhrana, Sergei Zubatov, was given authority to divert worker discontent into innocuous channels by creating police-controlled trades unions, to articulate purely economic grievances. Initially he had some success, but he could not control the membership, and in 1903 his union was closed down. As tensions rose, the government likewise expected that 'a successful little war' with the

Japanese would defuse public hostility. Instead, military disaster fanned the flames at home.

On Sunday, 9 January 1905, revolutionary events began in St Petersburg. A huge procession-demonstration of workers, organised by a priest, Father Georgii Gapon, ironically a successor to Zubatov, came to the Winter Palace to present a petition to the Tsar. Many of them ex-peasants, the workers carried icons and religious banners, seeking redress in the traditional manner. Nicholas was absent and the police, nervous, fired on the crowd – several hundred were killed or injured: the 'little father' gave his children bullets instead of bread. Public indignation at 'Bloody Sunday' was immense, and the Tsar's personally unapologetic and condescending response ('the demonstrators were misguided') compounded the outrage: the myth of the 'little father' tsar, and the loyalty of the workers, never recovered.

The rest of the year represented a trial of strength between Crown and people, of all social groups: social support for the government withered, except in a small right wing. Strikes and demonstrations spread across the Empire. In the countryside, the peasantry went on the rampage. On the peripheries the national minorities joined violently in the protests flaring at the centre. Mutinies in the army and navy were contained, but the Black Sea battleship *Potëmkin* sailed successfully away to Varna. New organisations emerged to articulate opinion, sectional interests and discontent. At the same time 'soviets' (councils) of workers' deputies appeared, which functioned very much like the peasant commune writ large, with directly elected and recallable deputies. These emerged first in the Urals and the textile town of Ivanovo as strike committees, and spread; later, as state organs faltered under pressure, they expanded their grasp to fill the vacuum of power and administration.

The rising tide of opposition culminated in October in a huge and remarkably solid general strike. St Petersburg workers organised a soviet to help direct it, and the brilliant and talented Leon Trotskii (real name Lev Davidovich Bronstein) soon became Chairman. Government attempts to buy off their opponents with counter-force, appeals for support and weak concessions failed. Finally Sergei Witte, by now Prime Minister, presented the Tsar with an inescapable choice: military dictatorship – with an unreliable army – or concession. Nicholas gave in: his 'October Manifesto', elaborated by Witte, promised an elected national assembly or Duma with legislative powers, and a wide range of civil liberties – a constitution. The

October Manifesto satisfied more moderate public opinion, and split the opposition. After October the government regained the initiative. The Peace of Portsmouth (USA) which had ended the Russo–Japanese War in August also enabled Witte to raise a large international loan, underpinning parlous finances. In December the St Petersburg soviet was arrested: attempts by Moscow workers to stage a rising in its defence were put down bloodily by military force – the army largely did remain loyal.

In the ensuing months a new Prime Minister, Pëtr Stolypin, pursued a dual policy of pacification and reform. Pacification was quite successful. Peasant and worker insurgents were pursued mercilessly – in the countryside 'Stolypin neckties' (the noose) killed hundreds in summary judicial executions. Revolutionary terrorism caused over 4000 deaths in 1906–7; Stolypin's own residence was blown up, though he escaped injury. It was met with severe repression: special regulations were imposed across the Empire, and police information-gathering and recruitment of informers stepped up. Dozens of newspapers were suspended and their editors prosecuted. The promises of the October Manifesto were given practical expression in Fundamental Laws published in May 1906. At the same time peasant redemption payments had been cancelled. Stolypin launched a major agrarian reform (1906, discussed below), and sought the cooperation of the new Duma; however, very much on his own terms. His strategy combined limited reform and strengthening of public institutions, to conciliate main-stream public opinion, with efforts to consolidate the monarchy, including a revival of Russification. As well as peasant land reform, he wanted to make the zemstvo more representative by strengthening it at volost level, to give peasants a real voice in local affairs, and also to introduce it as a Russifying measure into the western provinces. Both of these policies excited widespread upper-class opposition – the zemstvos had become class-consciously conservative since 1905. However, Stolypin failed to persuade any of the four Dumas which functioned between 1906 and 1914 fully to support his proposals, and in the balancing process increasingly lost the confidence of the Tsar. His assassination in 1911 probably forestalled his dismissal. Subsequent prime ministers were less talented and more subservient to Nicholas.

Russian society remained quiescent in the first years after 1905. Industry had not yet recovered from recession and revolution, and production only picked up, and with it the labour movement, in the years before the World War. A police massacre of protesting workers in the Lena goldfields in 1912 gave new impetus to worker unrest. Nearly three-quarters of a million workers struck in 1912, more than a million and a quarter in the first half of 1914. By this time the revolutionary parties, who had played a minor part in 1905, were well established among the industrial workforce, and in particular the Bolsheviks (the left wing of the revolutionary Social Democrats) benefited from worker militancy; but they were less important in the rising opposition than local conditions and workers' growing consciousness, which was reflected in increasing calls for political as well as economic change. In summer 1914 large-scale worker demonstrations in St Petersburg demanded a democratic republic, an eight-hour industrial working day, and expropriation of gentry land.

The Stolypin Land Reform

In 1905, as the country burst into uproar, the peasantry initially hung back: but then a vast peasant movement erupted, both in the centre and on the non-Russian peripheries, communally organised, with collective responsibility – everybody must take part – and directed against landowners' estates, property and sometimes lives. Contemporaries remembered the sky red with the flames of burning manor houses. The celebrated claim that '1861 caused 1905' has been generally discounted as excessively simplistic; but the festering discontent about land and justice found violent expression. As we have seen, this was countered, once the revolutionary wave had broken, by an equally violent government response. However, it was now clear that, far from being a bulwark of stability, the commune was in fact a weapon of revolution.

The major land reform initiated by Stolypin in 1906 was designed to address these problems – to relieve land shortage, to break down the commune, and free enterprising peasants from communal constraint. His 'wager on the strong' offered extra land and private ownership of individual communal shares. He hoped to create an economically strong and politically conservative class of yeoman farmers, farming their own consolidated individual plots and with a new voice in the zemstvos, who would pull the countryside up by its bootstraps while supporting the autocratic regime. Stolypin and his officials brought to the consideration of the peasantry their own vision and their own agenda: the perpetual problem of power in the 'peasant state'. However, local officials were encouraged to be flexible, to seek the cooperation of the peasantry, and to focus on workable rather than doctrinaire solutions. They laboured in the countryside, surveying, rationalising, consolidating. But the immense task needed many years of calm for successful conclusion, and it provoked hostility from many commune-minded peasants, and from landowners. In the short term, the proposed changes answered the needs and hopes only of a minority, principally more prosperous peasants and the unsuccessful who could now sell up and leave the land. The greatest number of consolidations took place in the fertile south-west, where individual tenure was also more familiar. In central Russia, even for consolidators, the commune still had major attractions. Some peasants therefore consolidated their land-holding without leaving the village. And some communes themselves adopted new methods – some movement towards better crop rotations and cooperative farming, which the land-surveyors eagerly encouraged, can be observed at this time. The achievement of Stolypin's reform can be measured in different ways; but it can scarcely be regarded as an outstanding success, and especially not in political terms. By 1916, when it was suspended, the majority of households still had communal tenure. In the revolution of 1917–18, when all external constraints collapsed, the peasantry in most places imposed its longed-for 'black repartition', forcing consolidators back into the commune, taking over local lords' estates, and equalising holdings.

World War I

The coming of the first World War completely changed the domestic political situation. In the first decade of the twentieth century Russia's international position had not strengthened: in particular it had been humiliated by Austria and Germany over Bosnia and Herzegovina in 1908 (a 'diplomatic Tsushima', according to the hostile press), and failed to protect Slav interests in the Balkan Wars of 1912–13. The risky decision to mobilise in July 1914 was prompted by the need to demonstrate great-power strength and credible support for allies, as well as to satisfy domestic opinion. Subsequent diplomatic negotiations with its French and British allies over war aims also assigned Russia a gratifyingly predominant position at Constantinople and the Straits in the event of victory. As with other belligerents, the outbreak of hostilities prompted a great outburst of patriotism, among the public and in the Duma, which defused opposition across the country. Only a fringe of extreme socialist 'Zimmerwaldists', including V. I. Ulianov (better known as Vladimir Ilich Lenin), denounced the war as imperialist and wished for Russia's defeat. The expectation, in Russia as among other belligerents, was of a short war.

However, events proved otherwise. The initial Russian advance into East Prussia was stopped by German forces in the disastrous defeat at Tannenberg. In 1915 failures of long-term planning produced desperate munitions and equipment shortages; these were remedied in 1916, but supply remained a problem, and a source of political friction in the rear, throughout the war. Russian Poland was lost to the advancing Germans, the battle with the Austrians for Galicia swung to and fro. Altogether, despite mistakes, the Russian army fought heroically, taking huge casualties, cut off from allied support by German and Turkish control of the relevant sea-ways, gaining successes against the Turks in the Caucasus and equalling the Austrians, but never able to match German power. Recent accounts of the war emphasise the high quality overall of the Russian military performance: none of the belligerents was exempt from errors and set-backs. And Russia did maintain the Eastern Front, forcing Germany to fight a double-fronted war. The costs, however, were colossal. World War I is often overshadowed by the Civil War which followed it: its multiple impacts deserve re-evaluation. Manpower requirements alone mobilised 14,648,000 men during the conflict. The huge losses incurred wiped out most of the well-trained officers and other ranks, and progressively decimated reservists. Noble officer casualties were increasingly replaced by non-nobles with less attachment to tsars and landowners. By 1916, conscription produced three million men of poor quality, low morale and increasingly questionable loyalty; and an attempt at large-scale mobilisation in Central Asia sparked a major rebellion.

In the rear, problems of defeat, war organisation and supply rapidly dispersed the initial patriotic euphoria. Over the course of the war the Russian economy expanded extremely rapidly, with annual growth rates over 110 per cent. But the problems of managing and directing it proved almost insuperable. Worker wage increases did not keep pace with price rises, and there was insufficient food to buy. Rationing was introduced in 1916. In the face of government bungling, public organisations came together to try to coordinate the war effort. The Red Cross mustered wide support. Zemstvo and urban councils created the *Zemgor* commission, to facilitate military supply and labour recruitment, which made a huge contribution, despite ministerial blocking and official interference. Industrialists set up a War Industries Committee to convert industrial production to the needs of the war. These bodies included representatives of all the interests involved, including workers. All the centre parties in the Duma and a majority of the State Council formed a 'Progressive Bloc', led by Pavel Miliukov, which demanded a government of public confidence and further civic reforms to integrate workers and peasants fully into the social and political nation. In August 1915 the incompetent War Minister, General V. Sukhomlinov, resigned.

The End of the Dynasty: February 1917

However, the Tsar was opposed to public participation in what he saw as the exclusive realm of the emperor and his ministers, especially in political matters. Instead he fell back on his narrowly personal and patriarchal view of the ruler's role. He prorogued the Duma, dismissed ministers who had supported the Progressive Bloc, and at the same time – despite the protests of his government – assumed personal command of the army. This step had some logic: coordination between front and rear had been a chronic weakness and Nicholas hoped to bridge the two, and to inspire his troops with his autocratic presence. Politically it was a disastrous miscalculation. Nicholas thereby made himself personally responsible for all Russian military failures. Leaving the capital for army headquarters near Mogilëv in White Russia, he removed himself from central control of the war and of life at the rear; and political power in the capital was left in the hands of his wife, German-born Empress Alexandra, a woman of reactionary views, poor judgment, and unsavoury associates. The government fell into incapacity and disrepute, as incompetent ministers followed each other in quick succession, and its critics and opponents mounted an increasingly hostile campaign. Supplies of food and other essentials broke down in the rear; peasants hoarded grain for which there was no profitable market because of military distortions of the commercial economy; Russia's railways failed under the strain as military freight destined for the Front blocked shipments from the centre of the country to the civilian peripheries and the capital. In 1916 workers began striking again against worsening conditions: 1400 strikes were registered that year. In the capital production started falling, food and fuel were in short supply, inflation outpaced wage rises. Rumours circulated about 'that German woman' – just as the British royal family changed their family name Saxe-Coburg-Gotha at this time to Windsor, so Alexandra's German origins suddenly became a public issue. In general, as tensions grew, German citizens and nationals came under increasing persecution; St Petersburg had already been renamed Petrograd in 1914. Things went from bad to worse. In November 1916, Miliukov spoke in the Duma (in session once more) to accuse the government of incompetence, treason, or both.

The end came suddenly. 1917 opened with a 50,000-strong strike to commemorate Bloody Sunday. In response, to maintain order, the government created a special Petrograd Military District. Industrial turbulence continued, with a lock-out at the huge Putilov metallurgical plant on 22 February. The next day was marked by demonstrations for international Women's Day, and against food shortages; in the days following, protests mounted, as did clashes with police and increasingly vacillating troops, whom Nicholas had ordered to restore calm. Despite appeals from the President of the Duma to the Tsar for a ministry of public confidence, he declared the Duma dissolved. On 27 February troops fraternised with the rioters, who seized the Arsenal and the Winter Palace. The Duma now created an interim government, which reflected the make-up of the abortive Progressive Bloc. At the same time the Soviet of Workers' Deputies re-emerged and was soon joined by soldiers as well. Its famous 'Order no.1' called on all soldiers to take charge of their units through elected committees and to send representatives to the Soviet: the Soviet thus effectively took control over military forces in Petrograd. At the same time it declared its conditional support for the provisional government: 'dual power', of the workers and the political classes, was established. The Petrograd Soviet was spontaneously duplicated across the country, as soviets sprang up in towns throughout the Empire. The Tsar set out from headquarters towards the capital, but his train had to be re-routed to Pskov. On 2 March, the day that the Duma announced its new administration, the Tsar in his railway carriage bowed to the *fait accompli* and abdicated, for himself and his ailing son, in hopes of saving the monarchy under a more acceptable ruler. He proposed as successor his brother, Grand

Duke Mikhail; but the army command would not guarantee Mikhail's safety, and he declined the offer. The Romanov dynasty ceased to rule.[§]

The immediate critical factor for the Tsar's survival, in 1917 as in 1905, was the response of the armed forces. Now both the Petrograd garrison and the army at the Front proved unwilling to obey their officers in propping up the autocratic regime. The Tsar's political incompetence had discredited the system; and Nicholas II's ideological position and his inability to grasp political realities had made the autocracy and its mechanisms increasingly an irrelevance and a hindrance in national life. His political outlook, moulded in his youth by Pobedonostsev, emphasised autocratic divine right and the direct patriarchal relationship between ruler and *narod* which he believed to have existed in 'Holy Russia' before Peter I. His son was named after Tsar Aleksei Mikhailovich, and Court events used seventeenth-century dress and symbolism. Refusing to reform the Church as an institution, he sought true sanctity among its simple representatives in the dubious but charismatic person of the Siberian peasant *starets* Grigorii Rasputin. The latter had made a disciple of the mystically inclined Tsarina in 1905 by stopping the haemophiliac bleeding of Tsarevich Aleksei, and became her and the Tsar's personal and political confidant. He had a disreputable lifestyle, and his influence became an increasing scandal, until he was assassinated by desperate courtiers in 1916. After 1905 Nicholas's conduct in the new political and social situation perpetuated the exclusion and alienation of most of society from the political process, and neglected the chance to broaden the base of government support. Fundamentally, the February revolution reflected the pressures of war and social conditions acting upon long-term factors and grievances. Whether political concessions by Alexander II and Alexander III, or whole-hearted acceptance by Nicholas of his constitutional role after 1905, could have saved the regime and allowed Russia to evolve peacefully into some form of democracy has been passionately debated. Such evolution was not impossible, although whoever had guided Russia's government at this juncture, fundamental structural problems of

---

[§] The Tsar and his family were taken into custody; in July 1918, during the Civil War, when White monarchist forces advanced on Yekaterinburg/Sverdlovsk in the Urals where Nicholas was being held, the local Bolshevik authorities, possibly on orders from Moscow, executed the entire Imperial family.

society and the economy would have made themselves felt in the wartime crisis. But the intransigent autocracy had become incapable of managing the increasingly complex society which had emerged after 1861.

THE FLOWERING OF CIVIL AND URBAN SOCIETY: 1861–1917

Education and the Press

The 'great reforms' of the 1860s impacted sharply on the life of educated and urban society. Over the following decades the independent 'public sphere' and public opinion, of which first signs could be found under Catherine II, now emerged mature, despite official constraints. The newly reorganised universities, run by their faculty with greater autonomy and expanded student numbers, still only served a tiny proportion of the population; but they became a ladder of education, social awareness and intellectual change. In the last four decades of the century student numbers increased roughly fourfold, to some 16,000, and their social origins became more diverse. Many students hoped that education, and above all, the sciences, would give them meaningful answers to life's questions which traditional Church teaching increasingly failed to provide. The scientific discoveries of the time were eagerly followed. As early as 1862 Turgenev's controversial masterpiece *Fathers and Children* highlighted a generational shift of attitudes and popularised the term 'nihilist' for his hero, the medical student and 'new man' Bazarov, who would accept no values or mores that he had not proved for himself. In the novel, Bazarov ended in confusion and death. Chernyshevskii responded with *What Is To Be Done?* (1864), another 'tale of new people', a badly written novel of revolutionary utilitarianism and women's liberation. It was the first of a number of third-rate but influential radical novels, and distinguished by its accent on the 'woman question', a major strand of public debate in the period after the 'great reforms'. In the 1870s, radical students discovered the peasants' cause: as we shall see below, thousands of young idealists went off to the countryside in the summers of 1872–4 to salve their consciences by befriending, helping and educating the peasantry. Less radical students also found their lives changed by the university experience, both in what they studied and in what they discovered for themselves: many were poor or under-prepared, and the student body created its own discussion and study circles, mutual aid funds, book pools, often in response to poor facilities and teaching. Demands for improved conditions in the universities, both material and political, led to student clashes with authority in the years 1899–1905. At the same time, the new autonomy in the universities encouraged research and scholarship. Modern historiography, for instance, came of age with the work of Sergei Solovëv, founder of the 'state' school of Russian historians, and his pupil Vasilii Kliuchevskii, both professors of St Petersburg University. Solovëv's son Vladimir became an influential idealist-religious philosopher, also teaching at St Petersburg, until suspended in 1881 after appealing for clemency for the assassins of Alexander II. In the natural sciences universities replaced the Academy of Sciences as research leaders. By the end of the century Russia's scientific community was producing world-class research, though the national infrastructure was still inadequate for a great power, and Russia remained technologically dependent on Germany. World-class figures included Ivan Pavlov (of dog fame), Russia's first Nobel laureate in 1904, and Dmitrii Mendeleev, discoverer of the periodic table, who held the St Petersburg Chair of Chemistry 1865–90.

The more flexible censorship law of 1865, and widening readership, facilitated the further expansion of the print media. The public impact of journalism increased, the press covering the whole political spectrum. In 1900 Russian-language newspapers and periodicals numbered over 600. Excessively independent publications still ran into trouble with the censors; but skilful editors could survive. *The Contemporary* was closed down in 1866; its contributors went to a new journal, *Notes of the Fatherland*, which successfully continued the radical tradition, until it too fell victim to harsher conditions in 1884. Other new newspapers, articulating right-wing or nationalist viewpoints supportive of the regime, were also disciplined, but were very successful, above all the *Moscow Gazette* edited by the conservative Mikhail Katkov, which acquired serious influence in government circles. Katkov was an enthusiastic supporter of the Russification policies practised particularly under the last two tsars. An alternative or complementary ideology was Pan-Slavism, a different nationalist approach which sought the liberation and unity of all Slav nations under Russian leadership. First emerging in the 1830s, Pan-Slavism became an important ideological current in the second half of the century and up to the revolution, particularly popular in some Court and army circles, but also supported by such as Dostoevskii. Russian Pan-Slavs envisaged the Slavs as the new force in Europe, and also preached the eastern civilising mission of the tsars' Slav empire. But like Katkov's Russian nationalism, Pan-Slavism had little to say to non-Slavs or non-Russians within the Empire, or even to other Slavs wary of Russian dominance. Neither doctrine could be an effective force for cohesion in the multi-ethnic Empire, nor successfully underpin great-power status abroad.

New Professional and Social Organisations

Besides the press, the new institutions of local government – municipal councils and zemstvos – also provided forums in which educated people could talk together, and develop a sense of civic purpose. Zemstvo committees, noble-dominated, rapidly established themselves in the majority of Great Russian provinces, and employed growing networks of professionals (teachers, doctors, nurses, foresters, agronomists, statisticians), known as the 'third element'. Their unspectacular work of administration and development brought huge changes over time to the areas where they operated, even though the government hamstrung them in the 'counter-reforms' of the 1890s. Their urban counterparts, the new municipal councils, presided over a tremendous boom in urban growth in the decades before World War I as industrialisation took hold, markets expanded, and the growing rural population, increasingly free to move, came to the towns in search of work. The mushrooming cities of the late nineteenth and early twentieth centuries eluded central government attempts to control town planning and expansion, with their constant population movement, unofficial settlement and building, and chaotic economic activity.

Another result of the 'great reforms' of the 1860s was the emergence of autonomous professions and professional organisations. Teachers proliferated in the new schools. The judicial reform created an independent bar for the first time, which aimed to set new standards of legality and due process. Like lawyers, most doctors had hitherto been government employees or individual practitioners, but now they acquired their own corporate organisation. The surgeon Nikolai Pirogov presided over the foundation of a systematic public health organisation and a new independent medical profession. The post-war urge to autonomous civic activity expressed itself likewise in a rapid increase in voluntary organisations. Over 750 private charities were founded between 1856 and 1880.

These changing frameworks of public life and new areas of civic activity tended, however, to conflict with autocratic traditions of social control which were increasingly reasserted after the early, liberal reform years. The medical profession found its attempts to improve public hygiene blocked by local governors, and its wish to discuss medical issues in national congresses regarded with political suspicion by government. Judges were irremovable, but those who showed excessive independence could find themselves assigned to unattractive backwaters, or their pension rights under review. The zemstvo claimed autonomy in raising and spending local taxes, wished like the doctors and lawyers to discuss its professional concerns in national conventions, and also became a channel for liberal constitutional hopes; but the government, determined to retain control of all affairs at national level, responded with bans on national gatherings, restrictions on zemstvo taxation rights, and – except under pressure – curt rejection of constitutional ideas. Such clashes with entrenched political authority pushed even political moderates to the conclusion that professional rigour and social improvement could not be separated from political change. The government persisted with increasingly severe restrictions on public activity, and with Russification measures in the increasingly restive borderlands. After 1881 Alexander III reasserted autocratic authority and the new police clamped down on expressions of dissent – a time, consequently, of 'small deeds' for moderates and liberals. The mood began to change in the following decade. During the famine and cholera epidemic on the Volga in 1891–2, professionals and volunteers worked hard, and with success, to alleviate popular suffering. Their labours relied considerably on local official help, but their achievement gave a sense of having supplied an official failing. In the wake of the 1890s 'counter-reforms' this gave new impetus to social activity, and new confidence to those wishing to make a difference in public life.

At the same time, the mass of the population were developing new entities of their own. The continuing separation between social classes was a fault-line in Russian society which opened into a chasm in the revolutionary years. Both rural and urban workers continued to regard the educated parts of society as alien and suspect, an attitude justified by government failure to give due weight to worker and peasant interests. In the towns this was most obvious in the weakness of labour regulation. Large-scale industrial development in the second half of the century was accompanied by the common evils of early industrial society and uncontrolled urbanisation. Although industrial workers were very few in comparison with the peasantry until after the revolution, the workforce grew rapidly in absolute numbers. But the rising generation of factory-owners had the ear of government. Factory inspection and labour legislation came little and late, in the 1880s, with some further regulation in the following decade; conflicts between managements and workforces increased. The first serious industrial strikes in Russia took place in the late 1870s, and from then onwards strike action was a permanent part of the industrial scene. Exploitation was rife, wages and living standards low, labour organisations illegal. Industrial troubles reached a new pitch with the slump of 1900–3. Working men found their own centres of sociability. They gathered in taverns (where their discussions were monitored by police agents). A more sober milieu was the Sunday school, which had appeared in the mid-century: people of all ages sought education there, and radicals were happy to volunteer as teachers. *Zemliachestva* were used for social as well as labouring purposes, and cooperatives played a similar role in town and country. After 1905, when freedom of association was guaranteed, trades unions mushroomed, and although many were shut down again in the years that followed, others survived, becoming a permanent part of working life. All these were working-class bodies with which members of the middle classes had little connection.

The Tsar's authority, still strong among the lower classes and in the countryside before 1905, increasingly lost its power in educated and urban circles. Nor was the troubled Orthodox Church in a position to promote acceptance of tsarist infallibility, although Orthodoxy still remained the base-line of most Russians' world-view. While St Petersburg parish priests (for instance) were active and successful, the institution itself at this time offered no leadership. Moves by some of the liberal intelligentsia to find a common language with the Church foundered on ecclesiastical inflexibility. Under the pressures of 1905 the long-serving Over-Procurator of the Synod, Pobedonostsev, the embodiment of reaction, was dismissed; but the Tsar then aborted well-founded proposals for Church renewal, depriving the institution once more of the opportunity to play an effective public role. Only after the February revolution, freed from the dead hand of tsarist control, did the Church take effective charge of its own affairs. In August 1917 a Church council finally met, in the Kremlin, and decided on the restoration of the Patriarchate; on 5 November 1917 Metropolitan Tikhon was elected Patriarch of Moscow.

While political associations were still illegal in the years before 1905, professional and academic associations became increasingly politicised; student disturbances were common. The radicals were organising into revolutionary parties. The Bund, an underground Marxist Jewish workers' organisation, appeared in Vilna in 1897. The foundation of the Marxist 'Russian Social-Democratic Labour Party' (*RSDRP*, 'SDs') in 1898 was aborted by arrests, and it had to be refounded in London in 1903. The neo-Populist 'Russian Party of Socialist Revolutionaries' (*RPSR*, 'SRs') emerged from prolonged negotiations, mainly in Berlin, in 1901–2. In 1903 the former Marxist Pëtr Struve created a liberal Union of Liberation, an umbrella organisation for zemstvo and professional activity. It too held its constituent meeting abroad, in Switzerland, but soon became active at home, organising constitutional 'banquet campaigns' and leaflets. During the revolutionary year 1905 itself, numerous new forms and examples of social organisation emerged. Liberals and professionals, railway workers and book-keepers, women and Jews organised themselves into campaigning unions; the professional associations came together in May in a Union of Unions. An All-Russian Islamic Union appeared in Nizhnii Novgorod in August. The Constitutional Democratic Party (*KDP*, 'KaDets'), a new liberal organisation led by Pavel Miliukov, emerged in October, just preceding the foundation of the extreme-right Union of the Russian People. The first general working-class organisations also took shape. Besides the St Petersburg Soviet of Workers' Deputies, and the railway workers, book-keepers and waiters, peasants created a short-lived All-Russian Peasants' Union, with SR support, in 1905. The civil liberties granted that year supported the further growth of public organisations and activity in the following years, despite the post-revolutionary police clamp-down.

The Arts and Literature

The arts and literature of the post-emancipation decades likewise showed a growing public awareness. Initially in the post-emancipation period they stood under the sign of critical realism, but the influence of the growing Russian national and nationalist mood soon made itself felt. This was also the time of the mature writings of Turgenev, Tolstoi and Dostoevskii. The last quarter-century of Imperial Russia became the 'Silver Age', a period of remarkable cultural revolution in all fields, marked by a decisive rejection of the previously dominant realist code in favour of free individualism, aestheticism, *fin-de-siècle* experimentation and mystical imagination.

In the 1860s, however, the new realist 'Itinerant' school of artists (*Peredvizhniki*, alternatively 'Wanderers' – so named for their travelling exhibitions) felt called to depict the Russian land and people as they were in daily life. Besides the moving pictures of common people given prominence by Soviet art criticism, they produced landscapes and portraits. Their art constituted the mainstream of painting in Russia from the 1860s to the 1890s. It was championed by the influential critic Vladimir Stasov and they gained the patronage of the merchant magnate Pavel Tretiakov, who bought their works for his private collection, later given to the nation as the great Tretiakov Gallery (Moscow).

In music the developments of the previous decades were consolidated with new institutions. The Russian Musical Society was founded in 1859, and rapidly established branches across the country. The brothers Anton and Nikolai Rubinshtein founded the St Petersburg and Moscow Conservatoires, respectively, in 1862 and 1866, both of which became centres of training and musical excellence: a native musical profession was now possible. Anton was a musical Westerniser, unlike most of his Russian contemporaries. Milyi Balakirev, already mentioned, was the centre of a St Petersburg circle uniting the so-called 'Mighty Handful', the composers Aleksandr Borodin, César Cui, Modest Musorgskii, and Nikolai Rimskii-Korsakov. All still amateurs, they were united in their dedication to Russian and folk sources, which were represented in both their musical compositions and their choice of libretti. Pëtr Chaikovskii (Tchaikovsky), an early graduate of the St Petersburg Conservatoire, was appointed to the new Moscow Conservatoire in 1866 as professor of harmony, but soon gave up teaching for composition alone. His works, as popular in Russia as abroad, integrated Russian with European forms, and although he wrote successfully on

Russian themes, he never fully identified with the nationalist trend. The last outstanding practitioner of traditional styles was Sergei Rachmaninov, a brilliant pianist and prolific composer, who spent the second half of his life, after 1917, outside Russia. At the turn of the century, younger composers joined in the search for new forms of expression: Aleksandr Skriabin explored Symbolist mysticism, Sergei Prokofiev avant-garde dissonance. Igor Stravinskii's music looked to Russian popular sources, but reworked them into almost unrecognisable forms. His ballet suites *The Firebird* (1910), *Petrushka* (1913) and *The Rite of Spring* (1913), commissioned for Sergei Diaghilev's Ballets Russes in Paris (1909–29), established him as leader of the musical avant-garde.

Diaghilev's balletic triumphs in France rested on his artistic innovation, skills as impresario, and on the strong traditions built up by the Imperial ballet in Russia. Earlier, Diaghilev had been instrumental in the establishment of the 'World of Art' group of artists, formed in Russia in 1898 in a reaction against the Itinerants' critical realism. This group, including Alexandre Benois, Konstantin Somov and Leon Bakst, explored the elegant noble past of St Petersburg and Western aesthetic traditions, using innovative colour and design. World of Art and its journal of the same name likewise benefited from the patronage of Savva Mamontov, an enlightened and artistic railway tycoon. As with Tretiakov, economic and social change was now reflected in industrialists' sponsorship of art. Mamontov was devoted to opera, establishing the first private Russian opera company in 1885. In 1870 he purchased the estate of Abramtsevo, near Moscow, and turned it into a centre for the preservation and teaching of traditional arts and crafts: the thinking recalls William Morris in Britain. Abramtsevo's new impulses in applied arts – furniture, textiles, implements – fed into the designs and stage-settings of World of Art and the Ballets Russes.The aestheticism of the World of Art looked forward to Modernism, the Symbolist painters gathered around the journal *Golden Fleece* (1906–10), as well as the less easily categorised work of Mikhail Vrubel. The upheavals of the revolutionary years were also mirrored in the rapidly changing experiments and artistic theories of avant-garde abstract artists, notably Mikhail Larionov, Natalia Goncharova, Vladimir Tatlin and Kazimir Malevich (Figure 12), who became a significant part of the European modernist scene.

Figure 12 Kazimir Malevich, 'Suprematism' (1920–7)
The Stedelijk Museum, Amsterdam.

In literature, the post-emancipation decades were the heyday of the Russian novel. Dostoevskii re-established himself after his return from exile in 1860, notably with *Memoirs from Underground* (1864), *The Gambler* and *Crime and Punishment* (1866), *The Idiot* (1868), *The Possessed* (1872). He struggled constantly against misfortune – bankruptcy, the deaths of people near to him, epilepsy, compulsive gambling – and much work was written under pressure of time and need of money. In his later years, supported by his devoted second wife, he became a respected journal editor, and in the year before his death gained a rapturous reception with his last great novel, *The*

Brothers Karamazov (1880). Tolstoi's most famous work, *War and Peace*, was completed in 1869; *Anna Karenina* followed in 1877. In the 1870s Tolstoi underwent a crisis and conversion experience: the need to justify his life in the face of the overwhelming reality of death drove him first to the Orthodox Church, then beyond to a rationalistic Christianity which found salvation essentially in good works and moral living, and above all in non-resistance to evil. He sought to live the simple life of the peasantry, who knew (he thought) the answer to death; he dressed in peasant garb and walked behind the plough on his estate, and wise peasants feature frequently in his writings. His new beliefs estranged him from state and Church – eventually he was excommunicated – and from his wife. His later multifarious writings were all informed by his moral and religious concerns. His last full-length novel, *Resurrection* (1899), a much lesser literary achievement than much that had gone before, was written to fund the emigration to Canada of the Dukhobor sect, whose refusal of military service had led to government persecution. Tolstoi's long life ended at a wayside railway halt in 1910, after he had attempted to flee from his wife and home in final search of spiritual fulfilment.

By the time of Tolstoi's death, his religious preoccupations were shared by wider circles of the cultural elite. This was particularly true of the extraordinarily powerful literature of the Silver Age, which produced some of Russia's finest writers. Drawing inspiration from the religious revival of the turn of the century, represented in the religious-philosophical works of Vladimir Solovëv, Nikolai Berdiaev and Vasilii Rozanov, Symbolist writers and their contemporaries – almost all from the cultured, intellectual strata of society – mixed formal experimentation with mystical or self-absorbed individualism and imagined townscapes, especially that of the capital. Andrei Belyi's *Petersburg* (1910–16) weaves St Petersburg into a dark mythic vision of Russian identity in a changing world. The intensely personal love lyrics of the young 'Acmeist' Anna Akhmatova (real name Gorenko) are set in the intimate surroundings of Tsarskoe Selo and domestic Petersburg, where she and her fellow poets frequented the 'Stray Dog' cabaret off Nevskii Prospekt. All this was much separate from the harsh realities of the lower classes: later (in emigration) Berdiaev wrote: 'I cannot help realising now that we were living in an ivory tower where mystical discourse was pursued, while below the tragic destiny of Russia took its course.' The clearest political expression of this ideological turn away from the radical intelligentsia position came in 1909, with the explosive publication of *Landmarks*, a collection of 'revisionist' essays in which repentant radicals such as Berdiaev and Pëtr Struve took part. *Landmarks* excoriated the intelligentsia for deifying the *narod*, the masses, whom in fact (the authors said) it did not understand, to the neglect of fundamental values of truth and law and of properly constituted statehood. They called upon the intelligentsia humbly to perfect itself before trying to perfect society. Aleksandr Blok, the outstanding poet among the Symbolists, represented a different vision. Drawn to the Symbolists' mystical realm, he nevertheless sympathised deeply with the coming revolution as he conceived it: *The Twelve* (1918), for example, glimpses a new revolutionary Russia, mystically hallowed by the return of Christ.

At the same time a different, more urban strand in Russian imaginative writing was developing, exemplified in the stories, novels and plays of the medical doctor Anton Chekhov and the Nizhnii Novgorod carpenter's son Maksim Gorkii ('Bitter', real name Peshkov). Gorkii combined romanticism with bitter experience of brutal and poverty-stricken reality at the bottom of the urban heap, as in *The Lower Depths* (1902). At the turn of the century Tolstoi and Gorkii were arguably the best-known writers in Russia: the landowning would-be-peasant aristocrat and the urban intellectual proletarian, each equally at odds with the tsarist establishment.

The Duma and the Government

The upshot of the 1905 troubles, after the government had regained control, was the 'constitutional experiment' of the State Duma. Reluctantly conceded by Nicholas II, it operated in four sequences between 1906 and 1917. The wide-ranging and unprecedented political rights promised by the October Manifesto proved somewhat less generous than expected in their concrete embodiment in the Fundamental Laws of 1906. The Duma could propose and veto legislation, but executive power remained with a government answerable to the Tsar, and the assembly, elected indirectly, could be dismissed at the Tsar's pleasure. The Tsar had significant influence over the composition of the conservative appointed upper chamber, the State Council. And the emergency legislation of 1881 remained in force, giving the state continuing police and administrative control over public activity. Once order was restored, Nicholas wished to limit the Duma's functions to a minimum. As an exercise in the articulation of public opinion, the first Duma (1906) represented 'an extension of revolution in parliamentary form': it showed how far society stood to the left of the Tsar and his coterie. Elected by weighted indirect male suffrage, the first two Dumas confronted the government in adversarial fashion until Stolypin, backed by the Tsar, illegally altered the franchise in July 1907. The resulting Third and Fourth Dumas were sufficiently conservative for the government to be able to work with them, but had their own agenda, so that Stolypin still had to use emergency procedures to promulgate his desired legislation. And in no sense did they represent the country as a whole. The Duma period demonstrated the renewed political dominance of the government and its supporters, but also the fragmentation and increasing polarisation of political views within the public. The Duma itself became increasingly divorced from the principal social dynamics of Russian society as tensions built again towards 1914. Yet when the autocracy collapsed in 1917, it remained as the sole legitimate political authority in the Empire.

THE DEVELOPMENT OF A REVOLUTIONARY MOVEMENT: 1861–1917

Populism

The 1861 emancipation fulfilled the worst expectations of the radical left. It was rapidly followed by suspicious fires in St Petersburg, and anonymous revolutionary proclamations declaring solidarity with the dispossessed peasants. In 1863 a small number of activists joined together in a clandestine grouping which they called *Zemlia i volia*, 'Land and Freedom' – what the peasants should have received. This was the first specifically revolutionary organisation since the Decembrists; its aim was to pursue the cause of revolutionary socialism, to agitate among the peasantry and to link up with radical *émigrés* abroad. The group did not last long: it was broken up by the police and its members, who included Chernyshevskii, were arrested. Other small circles remained, however, especially in the university milieu, and it was to one of these that the failed assassin of 1866, Karakozov, belonged. His attempt, undertaken against the wishes of his fellow conspirators, provoked a severe government reaction; and like the extraordinary case of Sergei Nechaev, a charismatic revolutionary psychopath who used murder to serve his cause, it brought direct action into disrepute.The next years were essentially peaceful: radicals were concerned to prepare themselves for future revolutionary action, and to make contact with and energise the masses, the narod – initally urban workers, and when that gave promising results, peasants too. In this they were inspired by the hugely influential *Historical Letters* (1869) of Pëtr Lavrov, who declared that intellectuals owed a debt to the narod whose labour supported them, and therefore must help them transform their lives: revolution must be the work of the people themselves. In 1872–73, and especially in 1874, thousands of students, called *narodniki* or Populists, fired with enthusiasm and dedication, 'went to the people' in the countryside. But persuading – even communicating with – peasants in the villages proved difficult: there was culture shock on both sides. When the students found a practically useful role that fitted with peasant preconceptions of how such outsiders (schoolteacher, medical worker) should behave, meaningful contact was possible; however, preaching atheistic socialism to peasants who still revered God and the Tsar was a heart-breaking task. And while peasants rarely turned in the strange newcomers, local power-holders (landowners, priests, policemen) were suspicious of them and many were soon detained. In 1877–8 the authorities held two large-scale public trials, of 93 and 177 defendants. Of the latter, 90 were acquitted, and only 28 sentenced to penal servitude; but it was scarcely a revolutionary triumph.

The failure of the 'going to the people' forced the radicals to conclude that revolutionary work must be more controlled and focused: in 1876 a second 'Land and Freedom' was set up, a strictly clandestine and centralised body which sought to build a support network in the provinces. However, the question of how to achieve revolution brought deep differences to the surface, which came to a head in 1879. The 'propagandists' continued to hold that the people must make their own revolution: the role of revolutionaries was to educate and empower them to do so – a long task. The 'terrorists', now convinced that peasant revolution was not a practical prospect, returned to the perspective of Nechaev, the theories of Pëtr Tkachëv and the inflammatory arguments of Mikhail Bakunin, to use terror for revenge, or to strike down the pillars of the state – historically a common delusion among extreme radicals: terror acts do not trigger mass uprisings. They arrogated to themselves the right to act in the people's name. Land and Freedom split in two. 'Black Repartition', representing the propagandists, was led by Georgii Plekhanov. When Plekhanov emigrated in 1880, and devoted himself to Marxism, the field was left to the terrorists of *Narodnaia volia*, 'The People's Will'.

The People's Will worked single-mindedly to kill the Tsar; their goal was to overturn the state. In 1881 they finally succeeded in assassinating Alexander II. But their triumph immediately proved to be failure: its political consequences were the reverse of their intentions. Not only did the state not collapse: the assassination aborted the impending constitution and swung the government to the right. Their leaders were quickly rounded up, and followers hunted down, by the effective new Police Department, the *Okhrana*, established in 1880 to deal with the threat they posed. Five leaders were hanged; People's Will collapsed. Nevertheless, underground Populist circles persisted into the 1890s. To one of these belonged Aleksandr Ulianov, the elder brother of Vladimir Ulianov (Lenin); Aleksandr plotted unsuccessfully in 1887 to assassinate Alexander III, and was executed.

'Controversy over Capitalism' and Debate on Revolution

Meanwhile a different form of European socialism, Marxism, began to make its mark in radical circles. In 1883, in Geneva, Plekhanov and his associates founded the Marxist 'Group for the Emancipation of Labour', and some ephemeral Marxist groupings coalesced inside Russia. Initially the differences between Populist and Marxist thought were blurred. The Populists had always been interested in industrial workers as well as peasants, and were open to Marx's ideas. Besides the clandestine revolutionaries, Populism also produced intellectuals who (like Marx in London) operated within the law. A 'Legal Populist', Nikolai Danielson, published the first translation of *Das Kapital* (vol. 1) into a foreign language, Russian, in 1872 (the thick, difficult book was passed by the censor), and he and others corresponded with Marx about the Russian situation. The Legal Populists argued that revolution based on the existing proto-socialism of Russia's peasant majority would enable the country to avoid the capitalism of the Western industrialising economies. (It was not industry itself, but capitalist exploitation, which was undesirable.) Marx was intrigued and thought their arguments plausible, but urged them to act quickly before capitalism became irreversibly established. After Marx's death, in the 1890s, Engels decided that it was indeed too late: Russia was (he said) already firmly on the road to capitalism. This view coincided with that of the new Marxist Social Democrats who had appeared in Russia in the 1880s, and were interested primarily in the embryonic industrial working class. They sought to demonstrate that Russia's economic development was following the European capitalist pattern. There began a learned 'controversy over capitalism'; argument turned on the absence (Populists) or presence (SDs) of markets in Russia for capitalist production, and especially on the extent to which capitalist relations had already penetrated the countryside. While the Populists saw the peasants united around the socialistic commune, the Marxists argued that differentiation among the peasantry was already far advanced, with an emerging exploiter class and an impoverished or landless rural proletariat. The best-known work in this vein was Lenin's overstated *Development of Capitalism in Russia* (1899). Many of the first Russian Marxists had been Populists or associated with Populist groups: not just Plekhanov and his colleagues, but also Vladimir Ulianov too. The son of an ennobled school inspector, and of ethnically mixed parentage, Ulianov went to study law at Kazan University and, fired by his brother's example, at once became involved in student activism. The evolution of Ulianov's ideas, and the extent of his debt to Populism and terrorism, have long been debated: evident early sympathies with Populism were veiled by the later polemical need to draw a clear line between himself and Populist opponents, as well as to refute charges of Populism levelled by SD rivals. In the 1880s and 1890s the now older Legal Populist generation in Russia became increasingly reformist. The younger neo-narodnik generation was increasingly interested in revolutionary Marxism, for instance A. Skliarenko, whose group Ulianov joined in Samara, on the Volga, after expulsion from Kazan in 1888. It was in Samara that Ulianov read Marx, and became a devoted disciple.

As social and economic discontent became more and more manifest in the Empire during the 1890s, revolutionaries and radicals of all stripes sought ways forward. Expectation of imminent social upheaval fuelled attempts to make contact with the masses, and debates about organisation and strategy. Were the peasants or the workers, or both, the bearers of revolution? Did terror have any place in revolutionary strategies? What type of organisation was needed? Within all tendencies there were exiles and undergrounders, hardliners and revisionists: radical proponents of conspiracy and terror versus reformists, old *narodovoltsy* versus Legal Populists, thoroughgoing revolutionists like Ulianov-Lenin as well as Legal Marxists and 'Economists'. The Russian underground and *émigrés* became notorious among their fellow European radicals for their disputatiousness. Newspapers mushroomed, underground and in exile, with titles such as *Workers' Thought, Russian Worker, Revolutionary Russia*; the most important Social Democrat organ, *Iskra* (*The Spark*, a reference back to the first 'revolutionary spark' struck by the Decembrists), was founded by Plekhanov, Pavel Akselrod and Lenin in Munich in 1900.

Socialist Revolutionaries and Social Democrats, 1900–17

In 1896 the veterans of the 1878 trials finished their sentences and returned from Siberia, giving new impetus to the neo-narodnik tendency at home. This was embodied in the Socialist Revolutionary Party. The SRs looked primarily to the peasant majority, but were always urban-based, did not reject Marxian analysis, and unlike the SDs did not distinguish between different elements of the 'toiling people'. They combined mass organisation and agitation with the use of violence and terror, as a tool of intimidation, revenge and fundraising (banks were a favourite target – some SDs used the same tactic): their 'Battle Organisation' was led by Grigorii Gershuni and the extraordinary double-agent Evno Azev. The talented Gershuni, described as the SRs' Lenin, died from tuberculosis in 1908. The main theoretician of the SRs, and their principal leader, was Viktor Chernov, a powerful thinker but poor organiser; their other outstanding personality was the brilliant agitator Yekaterina Breshko-Breshkovskaia, 'grandmother of the revolution'.

The Social Democrats came together in 1903, first in Brussels and then in London, to relaunch their party. The programme had been drafted by the Iskra group, which envisaged a period of bourgeois government before a dictatorship of the proletariat paved the way to socialism. Wide workers' rights were demanded, while peasants were offered freedom from the commune, and the restoration of 'cut-offs', land lost at emancipation – a minimalist programme reflecting the party's low expectations of peasant revolutionism. The right of the proletarian government to use necessary force was proclaimed: a gesture towards the terrorist tradition. The most contentious point in the programme was the question of party organisation. In his pamphlet *What is to be Done?* (1902) Lenin had declared that while the working class would lead the revolution, it could only do this successfully under the direction of the revolutionary social-democratic party, with its 'scientific' Marxist knowledge and 'correct' theory: by themselves, workers could not develop suitable consciousness and skills. The Iskra draft of party membership criteria reflected this stance: Lenin required 'personal participation' in party organisations. His opponent Yulii Martov on the other hand suggested 'regular personal assistance under the direction of one of the party's organisations', a much looser definition. Lenin lost this vote; but his supporters won on the composition of the party's Central Committee. Lenin accordingly (and tendentiously) claimed the name 'Bolshevik' (Majoritarian) for his faction, while Martov and his sympathisers accepted the name 'Menshevik' (Minoritarian). The difference in wording on party membership seemed slight, but the difference between the two visions was crucial and reflective of broader attitudes, which crystallised after 1905 and led to a formal split in 1912. Mensheviks thought less in terms of tight party discipline than of a broad movement, were more ready to collaborate with other radicals, and to allow history to take its Marxian course. Lenin wanted a disciplined party of full-time professional revolutionaries who would intervene to hasten the historical process; his vision was centralising, voluntarist and authoritarian, in terms both of party control over its members, and of revolutionary control over society. It was intolerant of rivals, and gave no thought to checks on the party leadership. Ultimately this approach ran the risk of despotism, of a dictatorship not *of* but *over* the proletariat: as Trotskii later remarked, without control mechanisms 'The party organisation takes the place of the party itself; the Central Committee takes the place of the party organisation; and finally "the dictator" takes the place of the Central Committee.'

After the 1903 SD Congress, the squabbling and in-fighting continued. As tension built in the country, argument raged on matters of organisation and tactics. Despite their optimism about the revolutionary potential of the masses, all the revolutionaries were taken by surprise by the events of 1905. They took advantage of the developing situation as best they could. The SRs helped coordinate peasant actions in some parts of the countryside and supported the creation of the Peasant Union. Both SRs and Mensheviks – who with their broader base did initially better than the Bolsheviks – had a voice in the St Petersburg Soviet. Lenin, watching from abroad until he felt it safe to return home after the October Manifesto, advocated immediate worker seizure of power. The events of 1905 fundamentally changed his perception of both the peasants and the national minorities, and convinced him of the weakness of the bourgeoisie. But in the aftermath of the revolution, all revolutionary parties suffered heavily, and were decimated by arrests and members' disillusionment. Many of the revolutionary leaders and intelligentsia went or stayed abroad for years, quarrelling and jockeying to enforce their particular line. In Russia the collapse of worker resistance was parallelled by a decline of revolutionary activity in the years 1907–11. As *Landmarks* appeared, in 1909, the SRs were rocked to their foundations by revelations about the long-standing treachery of their star terrorist Azef. The SDs suffered similar betrayals, as the police became more skilled at turning revolutionaries, though these proved less traumatic than the Azev affair: in the most notable SD case, Lenin stubbornly refused to believe the mounting evidence. Many Mensheviks turned to legal activities. Between 1906 and 1910 the number of affiliated SD members fell from 150,000 to 10,000, of whom fewer than 10 per cent were Bolshevik; and in 1910 there were no underground newspapers at all left in production. In 1912 Lenin told an audience in Switzerland that there would be no revolution in his lifetime.

However, after 1910 the economy and the strike movement, and with them revolutionary activity and peasant discontent, revived. By mid-1914 there was a widespread sense of crisis, both political and social, in the country, and a rising tide of opposition to the authorities. There has been much debate as to whether the World War actually halted a slide towards revolution, or in the end was its precipitating cause. In Russia in 1914, as in other belligerent countries, many revolutionaries were affected by the national enthusiasm. Between 1914 and 1917 revolutionaries worked to expand membership and influence, with some success, but such efforts were undermined too by police intervention, the drafting and relocation of activists, and the masses' distrust of intellectuals and preoccupation with daily survival. The February Revolution, like 1905, took them by surprise. The initial strikes by women textile workers went against local revolutionary advice. The upheaval was not the result of revolutionary leadership or plot (although the revolutionaries joined in at once when it began, and the rapid creation of the Soviet came from Menshevik and SR prompting). But it opened unprecedented perspectives. In February 1917 most revolutionary leaders were abroad – Lenin and his colleagues in Switzerland, and Trotskii in New York, began urgent efforts to get back to Russia. On the spot in Petrograd even those leading Bolsheviks present – the first, returning from internal exile, were Iosif Stalin ('Man of Steel', pseudonym of Iosif Vissarionovich Dzhugashvili) and Lev Kamenev ('Stone', real name Rosenfeld) – initially supported the Soviet's stance of conditional cooperation with the new government. Lenin, however, had already been formulating more radical ideas. On his return he presented his 'April Theses', demanding immediate creation of a Soviet government. They have been compared in importance to Martin Luther's Wittenberg theses of 1517. Calling for immediate Soviet seizure of power, they unleashed furious argument among Bolshevik colleagues. But they resonated with ideas already stirring in Petrograd, and were very shortly accepted as Party policy.

6

1917–1953
Russian Empire and Soviet Union: From Pariah to Superpower

The Duma-based Provisional Government which inherited power in the February Revolution failed to satisfy mass aspirations, and progressively lost popular support to the resurgent Bolsheviks, who in October overthrew it in a Petrograd coup. The Bolsheviks under Lenin survived the ensuing bitter civil war, and consolidated a new authoritarian and violent Communist order. By the end of the 1920s Stalin had gained control of Party and government, and the 'Stalin Revolution' inaugurated mass collectivisation, rapid industrialisation and cultural change, presiding also over huge social mobility and mass terror. The Soviet Union triumphed in World War II and the terrible 'Great Fatherland War' on the Eastern Front, establishing its control over much of Eastern Europe. Stalin reasserted tight domestic control and international confrontation after 1945; he died in 1953.

'BUILDING SOCIALISM'

The October Revolution

The new Provisional Government which took office in Petrograd in February 1917 included representatives of most political complexions, except the extremes. It started with general if qualified support, but bore huge expectations. It also faced huge tasks: the war, food supply, land for the peasants, the aspirations of the workers and the nationalities – and above all the organisation of an elected Constituent Assembly, to which, as a *Provisional* Government, it correctly assigned constitutional and other fundamental questions. Its administrative grasp was also uncertain. One of its first moves had been to disband all coercive tsarist institutions, notably police organisations; in the localities the authority of existing administrative bodies was increasingly fragile, and the army was less and less reliable. The Provisional Government's policy of continuing the war, to keep faith with its allies and in hopes of fruits of victory, was not popular, and also meant that urgent social and economic questions had to be subordinated as before to war needs. While the Provisional Government recognised the right of Poland to independence, it did not favour that of Finland and Ukraine, negotiating a compromise in July with the new nationalist Rada (Council) in Kiev but ordering the Finnish Diet dissolved when it proclaimed its autonomy.

Initially, the Soviet acknowledged the Provisional Government and accepted its policies within limits. The Soviet leadership was dominated by the popular Mensheviks and SRs. Both rapidly gained members after February: by the autumn Menshevik membership had grown from a few thousand to 200,000, while the SRs, who claimed a million members in town and country, were by far the largest political party – Bolshevik support was initially much smaller. Neither party wanted the poisoned chalice of political office. Yet as the Provisional Government's difficulties mounted, it sought increasingly direct support from the other side of the 'dual power', and in successive reshuffles Menshevik and SR Soviet representatives were drawn into membership of the cabinet. Consequently the moderate revolutionary parties found themselves propping up the 'bourgeois order'; they became associated with government policies, and government's failure to satisfy pressing popular aspirations. A new June offensive ordered against the Austrians turned into a costly retreat, which sparked growing desertions and mass demands for a purely defensive war or none at all. In August the Germans broke through Russian defences on the Baltic and took Riga. The only large party standing outside the government's problems were the Bolsheviks. They argued that the establishment of 'Soviet power' in Russia would trigger international revolution and end the war. The Bolsheviks actively sought the collapse of existing structures in order to create a world socialist society on the ruins of capitalism: they welcomed the prospect of civil war, and encouraged local activism to break down the existing order.

Mass disillusionment with the government and its left-wing supporters swelled. Peasants began to take land matters into their own hands: a few cases of seizure of gentry land were reported already in March 1917, and they became increasingly numerous and violent, especially after the harvest. 'Workers' control' was enforced in increasing numbers of factories: 378 enterprises in July, 573 in October. Bolshevik support mushroomed – membership approached 300,000 by 1918. The economy was collapsing, with growing inflation, falling food supplies, business failures and unemployment. The June defeat prompted mass demonstrations in Petrograd in favour of immediate 'Soviet power', with some Bolshevik support. The government, now headed by the SR Aleksandr Kerenskii, still had enough authority and military strength to suppress this 'July days' opposition by force, and arrested leading Bolsheviks: Lenin was accused of being a German spy (Bolsheviks did receive German money), and fled into hiding in Finland. In late August Kerenskii, worried about government lack of muscle, ordered his new Commander-in-Chief, the disciplinarian right-wing General Lavr Kornilov, to bring troops to Petrograd; but then he recognised the possibility of a military take-over and countermanded the order. Kornilov pressed on nevertheless, and Kerenskii had to call upon the Soviet itself and Bolshevik agitators to stop his troops: the general was arrested (but later released). The episode alienated mass opinion still further. In September the Bolsheviks finally gained a majority in the Petrograd Soviet; most urban soviets across Russia soon followed suit. Kerenskii attempted to rally moderate opinion in a national assembly known as the 'Pre-Parliament', in anticipation of the Constituent Assembly, but this talking-shop only made matters worse.

Lenin, still in hiding, campaigned furiously among his still reluctant Bolshevik colleagues for an immediate take-over in the name of the country-wide structure of soviets which the party now largely dominated. The Bolshevik Central Committee eventually agreed, but tied insurrection to the second All-Russian Congress of Soviets, set to meet on 25 October (Old Style): the Bolshevik *coup d'état* could thus be legitimated by Soviet authority. A perfect vehicle became available when the Petrograd Soviet, concerned at a possible German or right-wing army attack on the capital, created a 'Military-Revolutionary Committee' capable of directing military operations. On the night of 24/25 October, the MRC under Trotskii's control coordinated the armed take-over of key points in the city by Bolshevik forces. There was no great commotion: on 25 October Petrograd went about its normal business. Government ministers blockaded themselves in the Winter Palace, which was stormed and the ministers arrested. The insurgents met no effective opposition – a vacuum of power. One SR memoirist commented that 500 good troops could have swept the Bolsheviks from the streets of Petrograd. Kerenskii escaped to seek such military aid, but his subsequent attempt to mount a counter-attack with loyal army forces was foiled. The army was disintegrating.

The Congress of Soviets duly ratified the transfer of power declared to it by the Bolsheviks. But uproar followed when it became clear that Lenin rejected the common left-wing conception of a broad-based socialist administration, and was bent on an exclusive Bolshevik government. The Mensheviks and many SRs denounced the Bolshevik take-over as a crime, but then foolishly and fatally played into Lenin's hands by walking out, thus leaving the Bolsheviks to arrange things as they pleased. In a famous vitriolic phrase, Trotskii consigned his opponents to the rubbish heap of history. The Bolsheviks established an exclusive 'Council of People's Commissars' (*Sovnarkom* – acronyms became a typical feature of Soviet administration) to run the country, with Lenin as Chairman and Trotskii as Commissar for Foreign Affairs. Commissar for Nationalities' Affairs was Stalin, whom Lenin had once called his 'wonderful Georgian'. Stalin brought to the post his own non-Russian experiences of an impoverished and violent Georgian childhood as the son of a drunken cobbler, uncompleted education in an Orthodox seminary, successful clandestine organisational work among the workers of Baku, and Siberian exile. Sovnarkom was joined in December by the Left SRs, the radical wing of the SRs which had constituted itself into a separate party.

The Bolshevik Revolution was an epoch-making event. It inaugurated an unprecedented attempt at authoritarian social engineering in the largest country on the planet, a doctrinaire challenge to the whole existing capitalist order which had world-wide ramifications and shaped the agenda of world politics for most of the next century. The new government moved quickly to set out its broad programme. A

Decree on Peace appealed to the world for a 'just, democratic peace' to end 'the greatest crime against humanity', the World War. Trotskii, like Lenin, thought that socialist revolution in Russia and the publication of its secret treaties with other 'imperialist' powers would provoke international revolution. The Decree on Land was stolen wholesale from the popular land programme drawn up after February by the SRs on the basis of peasant mandates – for once this reflected genuine peasant aspirations. It declared that all land should belong to the people, and encouraged the seizure of non-peasant land; however, the exact nature of future land ownership was left deliberately and misleadingly vague. This in reality gave the peasants the free hand they wanted – the government was in no position to do anything else. Regulations were promulgated for worker control in industry (which meant supervision rather than direct management), together with confirmation of the eight-hour day. A cascade of further decrees followed, aiming to change radically the face of social life, and in December came creation of the 'Supreme Council of the National Economy' (*VSNKh*), attached to Sovnarkom, with coercive powers to direct the economy. All banks, state and private, were amalgamated into one nationalised People's Bank, presaging the repudiation of shareholders' rights and foreign debts in February 1918. On 2 November a Declaration of the Rights of the Peoples of Russia, drafted by Lenin and Stalin, abolished all distinctions based on nationality and religion, called for the creation of a voluntary union of nations, and acknowledged minorities' rights of secession; Poland's independence had already been confirmed. Bolsheviks had no intention of allowing the former Empire to disintegrate, but expected the national minorities to join in the coming socialist revolution, which should render national distinctions and boundaries obsolete. A Bolshevik-dominated Congress of Ukrainian Soviets declared a Soviet Republic of Ukraine on 11 December and shortly ousted the Rada; a week later Sovnarkom arranged Finnish independence.

On the news from Petrograd, 'soviet power' began to assert itself elsewhere in the country. A Bolshevik rising in Moscow finally secured the Kremlin on 3 November. By 1 November soviets had taken control, generally more peacefully, in several Volga cities and in Tver, Riazan and Rostov-on-Don; Ufa in Bashkiria, Baku, centre of the Caspian oil industry, and Tashkent in Central Asia were also in soviet hands. In the winter of 1917–18 rural soviets sprang up across the country at township (volost) level. At the same time opposition began to gather. The few feeble anti-Bolshevik actions in Petrograd were fruitless, but in November an anti-Bolshevik 'Transcaucasian Commissariat' emerged in Tiflis (Tbilisi) in Georgia, including Mensheviks, and in Novocherkassk (Cossack country) Generals Kornilov and Alekseev began organising a 'volunteer army'. Simultaneously, Sovnarkom was taking steps to consolidate its monopoly of power. Already on 28 October a decree had banned 'counter-revolutionary' newspapers; fierce censorship was introduced. As the 'volunteers' gathered, a warrant was issued for the arrest of KaDet leaders on grounds of fomenting civil war. On 7 December Sovnarkom created the 'All-Russian Extraordinary Commission for Struggle Against Sabotage and Counter-Revolution' (*CheKa*), a new secret-police organisation headed by the Polish ex-nobleman Felix Dzierzynski. It had very wide and ill-defined powers, and became the foundation of Soviet political control in Russia. It was formally renamed GPU (State Political Directorate) in 1922, and later went through further nominal and institutional metamorphoses – OGPU, NKVD, NKGB (People's Commissariat of Internal Affairs/State Security), MGB, KGB (Ministry/Committee of State Security), and after 1991 FSB (Federal Security Service).

Meanwhile, the long-delayed elections to the Constituent Assembly had been taking place: the Bolsheviks thought it unwise simply to cancel this long-promised 'bourgeois' assembly, and expected in any case to achieve a majority. It soon became clear, however, that they were decisively outvoted by the SRs' rural constituency: the SRs gained 58 per cent of the vote. Lenin published 'Theses on the Constituent Assembly' in December, demanding that it fully accept Soviet (Bolshevik) power. When it met in January 1918 and failed to do so, it was declared dissolved and the left-wing guards providing 'security' closed it down. A week later the third All-Russian Congress of Soviets, Bolshevik-dominated, met in Petrograd, adopted a 'Declaration of the Rights of the Labouring and Exploited Peoples', and proclaimed the Russian Soviet Federative Socialist Republic (RSFSR): the first Soviet constitution was approved in July 1918.

At the same time, negotiations had begun with the Central Powers to end Russia's part in the Great War. The Bolshevik/Soviet takeover in Russia had so far failed to unleash the promised European revolution; after the events of 1917 the Russian ex-Imperial army was in a state of collapse, and Sovnarkom had authorised demobilisation. The Soviet side nevertheless demanded a 'just peace' without annexations or reparations, and with rights of national self-determination. Not surprisingly, this did not please the adversary. Sovnarkom moved the capital to the relatively greater safety of Moscow, and began building a new workers' and peasants' Red Army under Trotskii as People's Commissar for Military Affairs. Trotskii sought meanwhile to stall diplomatic negotiations – 'neither peace nor war' – and to appeal to the world proletariat over the heads of the capitalist warmongers: this bemused the diplomats, but produced little proletarian response. Finally the Central Powers lost patience, made exorbitant demands and resumed their advance, which Sovnarkom was in no position to resist. Lenin's realism prevailed over advocates of continued 'revolutionary struggle': the Left SRs left the government in disgust, and the Treaty of Brest-Litovsk which ended Russia's war in March 1918 deprived Sovnarkom of all the Empire's western territories, one-quarter of its population and cultivated land, and three-quarters of its coal and metals. German occupation of Kiev restored the nationalist Ukrainian Rada. These colossal losses were a tremendous blow to Sovnarkom's prestige as well as its strength; and Russian withdrawal from the war prompted intervention by the Western Allies who saw their second front and stocks of military aid disappearing. Very fortunately for Lenin, Allied operations were restricted to the peripheries, action by their war-weary troops was minor, and overall the intervention proved ineffectual. Equally fortunately, in November 1918 the final defeat of the Central Powers allowed the Bolsheviks to denounce Brest-Litovsk; and the Allied interventionists, while imposing huge reparations on the defeated Germans at Versailles, pulled their troops out of Russia without seeking to extract anything further from its government.

The new regime had seized power in the expectation of mass national support and international revolution. Its specific policies were fluid. Lenin's utopian 1917 pamphlet *State and Revolution* had proposed that once a revolutionary socialist order was consolidated, the technical sophistication of modern capitalism would make daily tasks of government simple enough to be carried out by 'any literate person': 'under the leadership of the armed proletariat' and with 'worker control' it would be possible to 'organise the whole economy on the lines of the postal service'. Other writings emphasised contingency: the prime task was to establish socialist, proletarian power, the rest would follow.

October 1917 manifested two revolutions. A Bolshevik *coup d'état* at the centre overturned the existing government and inaugurated a new political order. But Lenin and his colleagues were able to carry out and consolidate their take-over only because far more fundamental changes taking place within grassroots society had emasculated existing structures of state power and authority. Moreover, the changes taking place were acted out differently in towns, in the countryside, and in the borderlands of the national minorities. The Bolsheviks did not create, but approvingly followed and encouraged the local activism of peasants, workers, soldiers and others who in the melt-down of 1917–18 rejected all unacceptable external authority and formed their own institutions to pursue immediate interests and desires. Peasant and worker horizons were largely local; their concerns did not focus on national issues, and so conflicted with policies which sought to balance interests nationwide and in international terms. In the absence of the Bolshevik take-over, the summer of 1917 might well have ended in some other radical upheaval. One of the striking features of the revolutionary years was the growing expression of popular anti-intellectualism, and animosity against all *burzhui* ('bourgeois bastards'): people with education or money, wearers of spectacles, non-labouring 'white-hands', even prosperous peasants. The soviets which emerged in both towns and countryside were genuine conduits of local mass feeling and opinion. The Bolshevik slogan 'All Power to the Soviets', which appeared to embody and legitimate this grass-roots activity, represented all things to all people and rallied mass support behind maximalist programmes until the implications of Bolshevik rule became apparent during the Civil War.

Civil War

Brest-Litovsk freed Sovnarkom to concentrate on domestic resistance, which was crystallising after the Constituent Assembly fiasco. The Civil War – or wars – of 1918–21 were fought in Russia between three broad groups, the Bolshevik Reds (who renamed themselves 'All-Russian Communist Party [Bolsheviks]' in March 1918), the anti-Bolshevik Whites, and the so-called Greens, who represented local, peasant interests. The moderate revolutionary parties, SRs and

Mensheviks, fell between the Red and White stools, unwilling to join the reactionary Whites, alienated from the Reds, and unable to turn their continuing widespread support into any other effective form of power. Practical opposition to the Bolshevik take-over was a mixed bag, starting with an SR-led 'Committee for the Defence of the Constituent Assembly' (*KomUch*), established in Samara after January 1918. But principal leadership against the Bolshevik centre came from senior tsarist military officers, who recruited properly-constituted 'White' armies on the peripheries of the Empire. Elsewhere – in Central Asia, the southern Caucasus, Bessarabia, Finland, the Baltic provinces – Whites, nationalists, socialists and others fought with Reds for local control. Admiral Aleksandr Kolchak established a White government in Siberia from which to attack westwards. The Volunteer Army, now under General Anton Denikin, moved into Ukraine and advanced north towards Moscow; from Estonia General Nikolai Yudenich's White forces marched on Petrograd. The potentially deadly White challenge was fought over two years, with fluctuating success. But the new Red Army finally defeated and executed Kolchak; it threw Denikin and his successor Wrangel back into the Crimea and retook Ukraine; and it drove Yudenich back in disarray into Estonia. While the White generals were able to call upon the personnel and skills of the former tsarist army, and some aid from the Allied intervention, their campaign had critical weaknesses. Career military men, they neither understood nor respected politics, and failed to conciliate and rally mass support. Their policies amounted to restoration of an indivisible monarchical state and of landowners' property: a stance which alienated the national minorities among whom they were based and the peasantry on whom they relied for food and recruits. Numbers of committed White supporters were small in comparison with the Reds. Supply problems were intractable, and Allied help marginal; compulsory requisitioning of foodstuffs, brutal terror against suspected Reds and opponents, further alienated even potentially sympathetic local populations. Based far apart around the periphery of the Empire, they had to operate over vast distances, and had difficulty coordinating their actions against the centre.

The Reds' great achievement was to construct an army capable of matching the Whites, and to support it on campaign. To do this they had to reverse their previous practice of undermining state structures and encouraging grass-roots autonomy and localism, opportunistic policies which had won them their greatest popularity. Centralisation and compulsion were in any case inherent in Bolshevik ideology and long-term strategy, as well as Lenin's tactics once in control. Discipline became the order of the day, both at the centre and in Red-controlled territory. Military hierarchy, conscription and the death penalty were restored in Trotskii's new Red Army; to the rage of revolutionary purists, Trotskii also inducted ex-Tsarist officers – some 30,000, checked by political commissars, the first of many 'bourgeois specialists' used by the Bolsheviks, and who made a critical contribution to success. Munitions workers were placed under the same military discipline. Peasants had to provide recruits, and a new ruthless requisitioning system demanded foodstuffs, as well as other military essentials. The Reds owed their survival to a number of factors. They appealed adeptly, through highly effective propaganda, to the defence of grass-roots revolutionary gains which the Whites clearly threatened. Positioned in the European centre of the Empire, they controlled most remaining industry, and defended a compact territory which also provided a sound base for offensive operations. Trotskii, ranging the country in his armoured train, proved a brilliant if brutally ruthless military organiser and leader. The Reds were also murderously merciless in combatting internal resistance: the CheKa killed at will. But above all, the Reds beat the Whites because most of the population regarded them as the lesser evil. Only when the White danger had clearly been broken did popular grievance boil to the surface, and the peasant Green threat and worker opposition become of major concern.

While the Red Russian centre warded off German and White invasion, the Finns fought a civil war of their own. Although the Marxist Reds were much the largest political party in Finland, the Whites were popular, and had superior military skills and leadership, especially in the figure of the tsarist General C. Mannerheim. They received German help, while intervention from beleaguered Moscow was not forthcoming. The Red Finns lost; in October 1920 a peace treaty finally confirmed White Finnish independence. A similar picture emerged in the Baltic provinces. Baltic Bolsheviks – especially the Latvian Rifle Brigade – played a significant part in Russian events; at home they were less successful. As the defeated Germans withdrew in late 1918, Red regimes were established in Latvia, Estonia and Lithuania, but failed to maintain themselves: the RSFSR signed treaties of peace with all three newly independent 'bourgeois' states during 1920. The Romanian population of Bessarabia merged with neighbouring Romania. Besides the Ukrainians, some other national minorities succeeded in asserting temporary self-determination. The southern Caucasus was cut off from the Soviet centre by the Whites, and had strong anti-Bolshevik parties of its own; separate regimes appeared in Georgia, Armenia and Azerbaijan (the Soviet Baku 'commune' was overthrown). But the successful Red advance against the southern Whites was continued into the Caucasus, reincorporating the three states into Russia in 1921. The 'railway campaigns' over vast and empty Central Asia followed a comparable pattern. Tashkent became the centre of a Soviet Republic, which survived until Kolchak's defeat in Siberia opened the way to Red victory over local anti-Bolshevik forces, pro-Bolshevik revolt in Khiva and Bukhara, and Red consolidation across the region. A very important factor in Red success in the borderlands was the support of Russian workers and Russified natives in the principal towns.

Poland was a special case. Both the Provisional and Soviet governments recognised its right to independence. After the defeat of the Central Powers, Poland reconstituted itself, with its capital in Warsaw. Its new nationalist leadership under Jozef Piłsudski also asserted claims to the ethnically non-Polish (Lithuanian, Ukrainian and Belorussian) eastern borderlands, former Polish territory, still under Russian control. The Poles launched a major invasion in April 1920, but were pushed back to the Vistula by the Red Army. Lenin wished to use the defeat of 'White' Poland as a stepping-stone to 'revolutionary' Germany: a Red Army advance into the heart of Europe should fire European revolution. He had expected Polish proletarians to welcome brotherly revolutionary liberation. The Poles saw instead a new imperialist Russian oppressor, and Piłsudski's very competent army turned the tables on the now over-extended Reds, driving them back in their turn to Minsk. An October armistice was confirmed by the Peace of Riga in 1921.

The failure in Poland was a severe check to Bolshevik expansionist and revolutionary hopes. In March 1919, freed from the threat of the Central Powers and the World War, Lenin had inaugurated *Comintern*, the third socialist and first Communist International, at a Moscow congress attended by small numbers of international delegates and safely under Bolshevik control. He closed the proceedings with the ringing assertion that 'The victory of the proletarian revolution around the entire world is guaranteed. At hand is the foundation of an international Soviet republic.' But the revolutionary attempts and social unrest in Europe which raised Bolshevik millenarian hopes proved abortive; now the Polish fiasco showed the limits of the appeal of Russian proletarian internationalism. European revolution remained stubbornly absent. The Reds' success in consolidating their hold within most of the former Russian Empire led to the formation of a new Russian (*rossiiskii*) Soviet state, isolated (despite much sympathy among labouring folk in other countries) in a hostile or indifferent world: in December 1922 a First All-Union Congress of Soviets met to ratify the formation of the federal Union of Soviet Socialist Republics.

Internal Consolidation and War Communism

As civil war developed in 1918, the Bolsheviks took steps to secure their internal position. The 1918 RSFSR constitution confirmed the Executive Committee (*VTsIK*) of the All-Russian Congress of Soviets as the supreme organ of state power, with its President, at this point Lenin's close ally Yakov Sverdlov, as Head of State; VTsIK appointed Sovnarkom. But in practice power rested with the Bolshevik/Communist Party Central Committee. As the latter's responsibilities grew, the need became apparent for greater administrative capacity and specialisation. In 1919 the Eighth Party Congress adopted a new Party programme and new structures: a special Central Committee Secretariat; a Political Bureau (*Politburo*) as a 'cabinet' for practical government matters, and an Organisational Bureau to oversee Party organisation and membership. Stalin was given charge of the *Orgburo*.

The Party also moved against political opposition. After the suppression of the Constituent Assembly, rival parties' newspapers and presses were closed, and soviet elections which failed to produce Bolshevik majorities overridden. The Left SRs had become bitter opponents of the Bolsheviks after Brest-Litovsk. During the Fifth Congress of Soviets in Moscow in July 1918, they attempted an uprising; the situation had to be saved by Lenin's loyal Latvian Rifle Brigade. When an assassination attempt was made on Lenin in August 1918, a Left SR was held responsible, and Sovnarkom responded with a wide-ranging 'Red Terror'. The CheKa was given free rein. Executions became widespread. Terror was extended to potential as well as real opponents, and used simply for intimidation:

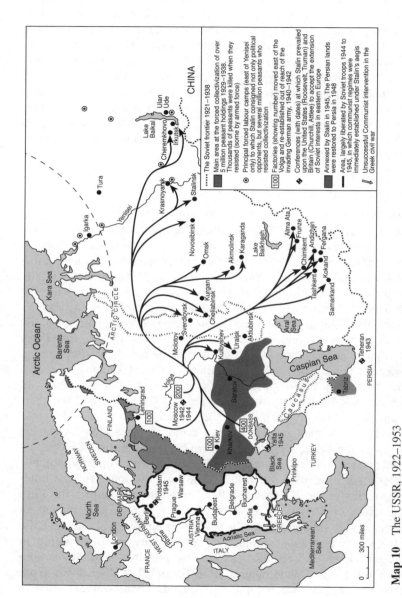

Map 10 The USSR, 1922–1953

© Sir Martin Gilbert, *The Routledge Atlas of Russian History* (London and New York, 2002), no. 113.

Dzierzynski's Latvian CheKa deputy M. Latsis declared that the only question to ask about an accused person was 'what class does he belong to?', while Lenin cabled to one local Bolshevik centre: 'Hang no fewer than a hundred well-known kulaks, rich-bags and bloodsuckers (and make sure the hangings take place in full view of the people).' Concentration camps (a British invention) were established, with forced labour. Show trials were organised against SR leaders. The numbers killed by the CheKa ran into tens of thousands, possibly more. Such massacres were largely uncontentious among the Party leadership.

A major potential threat to Communist hegemony lay in the newly revitalised Orthodox Church. Atheistic, millenarian, anticlerical Bolshevism could not tolerate a popular rival ideology, especially one deeply rooted and well-organised at grass-roots level, and associated in socialist minds with tsarist authority and capitalist exploitation. The Church reciprocated the hostility. In January 1918 the new Patriarch Tikhon was provoked to pronounce anathema on atheists who abused power – a transparent reference to Sovnarkom – and called his priests to passive resistance: street demonstrations followed. Four days later Sovnarkom issued its long-meditated decree 'On the Separation of Church from State and School from Church'. At this difficult time, Lenin wished to be avoid alienating the masses by attacking religious 'prejudices', and therefore refrained from direct action against believers, nor did he touch Tikhon, despite extreme-left pressure. But such measures as the opening of saints' tombs, to debunk holy cults, were pursued. And he had no compunction regarding incidental terror: according to Church figures, 28 bishops, thousands of clergy, and some 12,000 ordinary believers were killed between 1918 and 1920. Attitudes to non-Orthodox confessions and faiths were less stringent, since many had previously suffered persecution or disadvantage – Nationalities Commissar Stalin wrote a special appeal to 'the Muslim workers of Russia and the East'; but the separation decree applied to them too. In 1920 however new anti-religious structures were organised, notably the Party's Agitation and Propaganda Department. In 1922, the authorities fuelled a violent anti-religious campaign. Tikhon was arrested and, with government encouragement, more radical clergy set up a pro-Communist movement within the Church, the 'Living Church' (a.k.a. 'Renovationists'), which persisted until the 1940s. Tikhon was released in 1923 only after self-criticism and expressions of loyalty. In 1925 a League of Godless (later Militant Godless) was created to conduct atheist propaganda. On Tikhon's death the same year, the government prevented his replacement; in 1927 Metropolitan Sergii, having declared loyalty to the regime, was recognised as *locum tenens*, a position he held until raised to the Patriarchate by a wartime Church Council in 1943.

Violence and terror were also inflicted on the peasantry, both as a matter of ideology and in hopes of improving food supplies. Already in February 1918 Lenin was speaking of 'ruthless war against the kulaks', and although he sought to protect 'middle peasants', definitions of who these groups were, or what constituted grain 'surpluses', were fluid. A Food Dictatorship was established and *prodrazvërstka* imposed, a system of confiscating alleged surplus grain according to regional quotas, with worker and CheKa units descending on villages and violently seizing peasant grain at derisory prices; 'committees of the village poor' (*kombedy*) were set up, to inform on fellow villagers and identify grain holdings – a rural dictatorship of the proletarian peasantry. With their help the requisitioning system was very successful – deliveries quadrupled during 1917–19 – but its basis was largely guesswork, completely inequitable and extortionate, leaving many peasants with no reserves and nothing to eat. The huge 1921–2 famine in the Volga region and the south-east killed some five million, prompting international relief efforts. Nor were requisitioned stocks remotely enough, even so, to feed the towns, half of whose supply came from the illegal 'bagmen', black-marketeers who traded sacks of urban goods for peasant grain, despite CheKa countermeasures. And the kombedy proved so corrupt and divisive that they were disbanded within the year.

Economic chaos grew. As the civil war disrupted production and transport, and cut central Russia off from traditional sources of supply, large-scale factory production tailed off, and inflation made money worthless. There were some, so-called Left Communists such as Nikolai Bukharin, who welcomed the collapse of free-market exchange as part of a move to true socialism, when all resources would be allocated by state action in a moneyless economy. The exigencies of war reinforced this tendency, necessitating increasingly direct state control. Under the emerging order, later known as 'war communism', private trade ('capitalist speculation') was outlawed. VSNKh presided over centralisation and nationalisation in industry, and the subordination of worker power to managerial authority and strict discipline. The worthless money was phased out – everything should be done by book-keeping transactions and in kind between producers' and consumers' communes. Even tiny workshops, and windmills, were taken into state ownership, although such things – like the economy as a whole – could not possibly be adequately run by the new officialdom of leather-jacketed commissars. The logical last step was the militarisation of labour: as Red victory neared in 1920, Trotskii proposed the formation of 'labour armies' of demobilised conscripts.

Civil war, Bolshevik terror and economic collapse destroyed the last vestiges of social cohesion and the old order. Survival became the primary task. Towns emptied, as people fled to the villages where there might be food. Townspeople were joined in the countryside by deserters and demobbed soldiers. In Petrograd all wooden buildings had been pulled down, and the wooden pavements torn up, for fuel. In 1919 official industrial value was 66 per cent less than in 1918. By 1921 international trade had collapsed, gross industrial output stood at one-third of 1913 levels, coal production at even less.

Civil War between Reds and Greens: The Peasant Revolt

Peasant reactions to the new situation were initially cautious; they sharpened as the White threat ebbed. An adverse swing in urban–rural terms of trade had compounded the unbearable tax and requisition burdens; the growing political centralisation had destroyed the power of both opposition parties and peasants in the soviets, and enabled intolerable local dictatorship by Bolshevik cadres. In 1919–21 Sovnarkom was confronted across the countryside with spreading outbreaks of armed resistance. Peasant action ranged from village riots through banditry to full-scale sophisticated military operations helped by army deserters and ex-soldiers; pro-peasant mutinies also occurred among Red Army units, and Green commanders operated extensive guerrilla campaigns. Insurgent villagers would throw out local officials, create their own soviet and militia, and spread revolt to neighbouring villages. The 'caftan war' of March–April 1919, one of several major risings on the Volga, raised a skilfully organised but poorly equipped army of 20,000 conscripts, and involved altogether some 150,000 people. Its aim was soviets without Communists, a return to the first period of soviet power when the peasants had been left to themselves; the insurgents routed initial Red forces sent against them, and were crushed only by major local Bolshevik mobilisation. Some of the most successful peasant commanders were former Soviet officials or ex-Red Army officers. Nestor Makhno, the fabled Green Anarchist and Ukrainian guerrilla leader, had commanded a Red division against the Whites in 1919. The SR Aleksandr Antonov, leader of the major Tambov insurgency, the *Antonovshchina*, had been a Soviet police chief in 1917–18. A. Sapozhkov, a Red commander with a distinguished record, including the suppression of 'kulak uprisings', became a supporter of Volga peasant resistance to requisitioning and led a whole army division into anti-Communist mutiny, which took two months to suppress. These peasant-based movements stood in the tradition of Razin and Pugachëv, local risings based in vast steppe areas, reflecting peasant values and mentalities, and lacking the resources, if not the skills, to withstand state counter-force in the long run. Their causes lay in the Bolsheviks' terroristic assault on the fundamental relations of Russian society, in the basic contradictions between the new rulers and the ruled in the 'peasant state'; and they posed a potent threat to the new regime which Lenin recognised as 'far more dangerous than all the Denikins, Yudeniches and Kolchaks put together, since we are dealing with a country where the proletariat represents a minority'. In March 1921, as Orlando Figes put it, 'the Bolshevik government surrendered before its own peasantry' – at least in economic terms: while deploying superior armed force against peasant resistance, Lenin pushed through the New Economic Policy.

The NEP

First Bolshevik doubts about prodrazvërstka were voiced in 1920, but broad Party opinion, including Lenin, remained hostile to change. Only gradually did the extent of peasant resistance persuade Lenin otherwise, leading finally to a proposal for *prodnalog*, a grain tax set at lower levels than the prodrazvërstka quotas, and beyond which peasants should have the right to trade their grain. But peasant resistance was by now symptomatic of wider popular opposition: mass disillusionment and grievance was coming to the boil. Most serious was the action of the 14,000 sailors and workers at the Kronshtat island naval base outside Petrograd, in 1917 a bastion of Bolshevism. On 28 February 1921 the base erupted in an anti-

Communist mutiny – a 'bolt of lightning' for the government, illu-
minating inescapably the true state of affairs. Trotskii ordered a
concerted military response; loyal government forces attacked across
the ice on 7 March. The day after the attack began, the Tenth Party
Congress opened in Moscow. Lenin threw his authority behind not
just prodnalog, but a whole new course in economic policy: the
Congress reluctantly recognised that forms of hated 'capitalist'
economic activity were the only means to defuse the situation while
the country recovered from years of war – a temporary though open-
ended retreat. The New Economic Policy (*NEP*) was to be based on
an 'alliance' between workers and the 'toiling' (non-kulak) peasantry. It was combined with harsh measures to restore order in the
provinces, and strict political control: other political parties were
finally banned – trials of SR leaders were held soon after – and rigorous inner-Party discipline was demanded, with the proscription of
'factions' of all kinds.

NEP marked a sharp change. The decision to allow peasant trade
in food products led ineluctably to broad private trade between town
and countryside – peasants could not run large-scale commercial
operations by themselves; in 1924 the prodnalog was commuted to
monetary payment. The same logic was applied to other sectors,
where the state retained direct control only of the 'commanding
heights of the economy' – banks, large-scale industry, foreign trade
– and allowed private enterprise at lower levels. Soon the nationalisation of small-scale industry was formally revoked, and freedom
decreed to set up handicrafts and small enterprises of fewer than 20
workers. In 1922 an RSFSR Land Code came into force, shortly
followed in other republics, declaring all land state property, forbidding trade in land – although this was widely evaded – and allowing
peasants to choose their manner of cultivation. The new economic
framework, together with the cessation of military activity, produced
gradual recovery. Rationing was abolished in November 1921.
Initially the sudden re-introduction of commercial relations caused
chaos and wild inflation, but from 1923 the economy slowly
improved; the currency was stabilised, and a balanced national
budget achieved, from 1924. The social disruption of revolution and
civil war was compounded by wide-spread unemployment.
Agriculture recovered faster than industry, which caused considerable problems in internal trade. But by the mid-1920s output and
industrial wage levels were around those of 1913; by 1928 the land

area under cultivation was slightly greater. However, the new situation confronted the Bolshevik leadership with fundamental questions
of principle: decisions on social and economic development, on
political and social control, relations with the outside world and
between the constituent domestic parts of the Soviet polity, the
nature of the new Party and Soviet government themselves. Lenin in
his final days suggested that the NEP might last 'for generations',
though his recorded statements are not unambiguous. The underlying
problem was how to construct the new socialist state.

The Death and Afterlife of Lenin

The resolution of these issues was complicated by Lenin's incapacity and death. In March 1923 he was finally crippled by the last of
three strokes; he died on 21st January 1924, at the age of 53.

Lenin after death at once became the object of a veneration which
turned into a cult (adulation to which in his lifetime he had always
objected). His body was embalmed and enshrined in the now famous
mausoleum constructed for him on Red Square in Moscow. The
Party wished to capitalise on his undoubted charisma among large
parts of the populace – he had regularly received petitioners in the
Kremlin; even malcontents saw him as a 'good tsar' surrounded by
evil ministers, and for xenophobic Russian anti-Semitism he was a
Russian among Jewish Commissars. He became the presiding genius
of the Soviet Union, his writings the source of the doctrine of
Marxism-Leninism which replaced Orthodoxy as the official Soviet
belief-system. Marxism-Leninism and the Lenin cult performed the
social, political and psychological functions of a religion, especially
as the 1920s gave way to Stalinism. Petrograd was renamed
Leningrad. Statues of Lenin were erected throughout the country.
The mausoleum and Leninskie Gorki, where Lenin spent his last
days, became shrines. Reference to Leninist holy writ soon became
obligatory in all spheres of public activity, and the official image of
Lenin himself evolved a saintly personal aspect which imitated Jesus
Christ: infallibility, understanding, gentleness, frugal simplicity, love
of children. 'Lenin,' Soviet citizens were told, 'is always with us.'
Anything that could sully the icon – Lenin's casual murderousness
and disregard for human life in political matters, his extra-marital
involvements, partial Jewish ancestry – was unmentionable. His
historical contribution remains highly contentious. As principal

founder of the Soviet Union he was one of the remarkable figures of
his age. His selfless – obsessive – dedication to his cause, great intelligence and extraordinary ability to grasp the complex dynamic of
unfolding events made him an outstanding leader, and he demonstrated brilliant political and administrative skills. He possessed
energy, endurance, rhetorical power and personal charm. He was
however a utopian bookman, whose universe was construed essentially in terms of theory, however skilfully and realistically flexible
he may have been in practical matters; a sectarian, whose fanatically
unshakeable belief in his own rightness and righteousness led him to
construct his own narrow and vicious morality, provoke schism with
all opponents, and disregard the humanity of others and the multi-
fariousness of social phenomena. His approach to politics, and to
violence and terror, was conditioned by his early environment and
the commitment of his brother and, if extreme, was nothing very
unusual for the time; nor were its long-term outcomes then immediately obvious. But he presided over the creation of political structures and a political culture which made possible the future
development and ultimate failure of the USSR.

Political Problems of the 1920s

Lenin's decline heightened a power struggle among the Communist
leadership which would continue through the 1920s, principally in
terms of personal alliances around policy choices. During the Civil
War Stalin had been in charge of the Southern Front at Tsaritsyn
(later Stalingrad, now Volgograd), where he had thrown his weight
about and used terror methods with some effectiveness, but had
clashed with Trotskii's overall direction of operations. The rivalry,
personal and political, between Trotskii and Stalin became fundamental in the following years. Stalin's position as head of the
Orgburo, a low-profile administrative post which he ran very effectively, enabled him to control appointments and build a personal
constituency among Party and Soviet members which gave him
increasing power. The Communist Party emerged from the Civil War
very different from the mass movement it had been in 1917: battle-
hardened, but with a newly recruited membership devoted to revolutionary change and accustomed to obey the leadership. The 1921 ban
on 'factions', such as the Democratic Centralists who sought to
combine centralised rigour with greater inner-Party democracy, and

the Workers' Opposition which called for greater worker involvement in Party activity, played into Stalin's hands. In April 1922 the Central Committee elected him General Secretary, heading the Secretariat. Only very late – too late – did Lenin focus on the growing bureaucratisation of Party life, on Stalin's 'crudeness' and rough treatment of those in his way (including Lenin's wife, Nadezhda Krupskaia), and on the growing extent of Stalin's power. On his sickbed he drew up a 'Testament', warning about the state of the Party and recommending Stalin's removal as General Secretary. At the Politburo meeting to consider this document, Stalin acknowledged errors. Trotskii, aware that he was seen as the most likely Bonaparte among the leadership – Russian parallels with the French Revolution were a constant Bolshevik preoccupation – did not press the matter. Unity was maintained; the Testament was suppressed and Stalin remained General Secretary. Lenin was initially succeeded by a *troika* of Stalin, and Lev Kamenev and Grigorii Zinoviev (real name Radomyslskii), whose power bases lay in the Leningrad and Moscow Party organisations respectively.

During the following five years the issues of policy, and of the leadership succession, were fought out. Socialist revolution had taken place in the most peasant and least developed of the capitalist powers, and world revolution had not followed. What to do? There ensued a great debate, both among technical experts who produced pioneering theory – the Soviet experiment was, after all, unique – and among the politicians. All Soviet leaders wished, of course, to build socialism. Trotskii, on the 'Left', maintained that since world revolution was essential, all efforts should be directed to achieving it, by radical policies at home and abroad. This position was broadly shared by Zinoviev and Kamenev. The 'Right', best represented by the former Left Communist Bukharin, editor of the Party newspaper *Pravda*, held that in the absence of world revolution, socialism should be built up gradually by domestic consolidation: wishing to extend the NEP and conciliate the peasantry, he was derided by critics for wishing to 'ride into socialism on a peasant nag'. A middle position, which came to be identified with Stalin, was that of 'Socialism in One Country': given the hostile international environment, radical policies should be used to build Soviet strength rapidly at home. In the manoeuvrings of those years, Stalin allied himself first with one grouping, then with another, while keeping a relatively low public profile and consolidating his control of the Party membership. He presented himself as keeper of Lenin's heritage and of Party regulations. By 1927 he had established his dominance. Trotskii and his followers, and several other leaders, were expelled from the Party; in December the Fifteenth Party Congress condemned all 'deviations from the general Party line' as interpreted by Stalin and approved a policy of heavy industrial development – the outline of the coming Five-Year Plans. Bukharin and his allies Aleksei Rykov and Mikhail Tomskii continued to argue in favour of the NEP, but by November 1929 had lost their Party positions and made a public recantation. Stalin's birthday on 21st December 1929 brought press adulation which marked the beginning of his 'cult of personality', although he was still by no means omnipotent. Trotskii was expelled from the Soviet Union and ended in Mexico, where in 1940 a Stalinist agent murdered him with an ice-pick.

Collectivisation

Stalin's growing political dominance paralleled developments in the economic sphere. Specialists in the Commissariat of Finance (*Narkomfin*) and State Planning Committee (*Gosplan*) gradually accumulated enough expertise and statistical information to draft a long-term state economic plan. The Right–Left political argument over NEP was mirrored in planning debates – slow balanced advance versus 'teleological' rush towards prioritised goals. Many Party members had only very reluctantly tolerated the 'bourgeois' success of 'NEP-men' and prosperous peasants. By 1926 the reconstruction of old industry was largely complete and growth slowed, sharpening the question of capital investment for new. Government price controls persistently distorted the free market, and in 1927 caused a food-supply crisis: peasants responded to price cuts by withholding grain from sale. Stalin also used the international situation – a spy scare and breach with Britain in 1927 – to justify forced-rate economic advance in terms of capitalist encirclement. As he would argue in a famous speech in 1931, 'We are fifty or a hundred years behind the advanced countries. We must make good this distance in ten years. Either we do so, or we shall go under.'** To highlight the

---

** War came exactly ten years later. The imminent threat has been used to justify the 'Stalin Revolution': without rapid and ruthless industrialisation, in this view, Soviet victory over the Nazis would have been impossible. Contrary calculations have suggested that a steady development of NEP, without the wild disruptions of collectivisation and the

danger, in 1928 the first demonstrative move was made against alleged internal enemies. The 'Shakhty' show trial arraigned 53 innocent engineers, 'bourgeois specialists', as 'wreckers', capitalist saboteurs: five were shot. In the following two years alleged nationalists and potential separatists were attacked, with show trials against a mythical 'Union for the Liberation of Ukraine' and an imaginary 'All-People's Union of Struggle for Russian Regeneration'.

The Party's solution to the long-term problems posed by the grain crisis was now immediate mass collectivisation. Cooperative and collective forms of agriculture to be introduced by gradual, voluntary means had long figured in policy debates, but the Party now returned to its violent class-based Civil-War strategy of 'struggle against kulaks', to stamp its authority on the whole complicated problem of the peasantry. Under the NEP, as Bolsheviks saw it, petty-bourgeois peasants held the towns to ransom. Collectivisation would finally bring necessary state control over the countryside, and modernise and increase agricultural output; it also aimed at 'eradication of kulaks as a class'. An All-Union Collective-Farm Centre and All-Union Land Commissariat were established to oversee the process, which began in late 1929. In November the government recruited 25,000 volunteers, urban workers and militants to go and win the new civil war for grain and socialism. The campaign was masterminded under instructions from the centre by local Party committees and their Secretaries, who also mobilised poor peasants and members of the Komsomol youth movement. They called communal meetings and pressured peasants to sign resolutions calling for collectivisation. 'Kulaks' were excluded and their property confiscated. Divided into three categories of harmfulness, they were given other poor land outside the collective farm, or were deported – crammed into cattle trucks, shipped in their hundreds of thousands by the GPU to Kazakhstan, the Far North or Siberia, for settlement or forced labour. The GULag labour-camp system in its developed form dated from 1929. 'Kulak' identity was fluid. Together with other 'exploiters', kulaks had been identified, listed and disenfran-

---

waste, inefficiency and often shoddy products of the Five-Year Plans, without the Terror's wholesale murder of peasant producers, competent specialists and skilled officers, and the suppression of initiative and common sense, without the despotic misjudgments which left the USSR undefended in June 1941 and presented western territories to the Nazis on a plate – that such a development might have achieved equal results. These are speculations.

chised under the 1918 constitution; now 'kulak' was as much a political as an economic category – attitudes to collectivisation were all-important. The catch-all term *podkulachnik* (sub-kulak, pro-kulak peasant) was introduced to hound lesser uncooperative peasants. Peasants tried to pre-empt disaster by selling off property, killing and eating livestock, fleeing for shelter to the towns. Some enthusiastic collectivisers enforced pooling even of clothing and furniture. In many places atheist activists took over and desecrated churches and arrested the priest: church bells were carried off for industrial scrap. In June 1930 all village communes were dissolved, their functions transferred to soviets and the collective farms. Rumours circulated among the peasants that women were to be held as common property, or that the inevitable coming famine presaged the Last Days. Often villagers resisted, and collectivisers were murdered; full-scale revolts occurred, many of them led by women.

The collectivisation process nevertheless continued, with some fluctuations, and minor incentives as well as naked coercion, until by the mid-1930s the vast majority of all peasants was collectivised. How *kolkhozy* (collective farms) should be organised and function was worked out as things went along; after a first attempt in 1930, a model kolkhoz charter was finally adopted in 1935. Initially the government's assault resulted in an absolute shortfall of grain to feed the country. During collectivisation rural millions died – in the new chaotic collectives themselves, during deportation or in labour camps, or in the famines that struck borderlands where collectivisation was particularly unsuitable, strongly resisted, or implemented with totally excessive quotas. In nomadic Kazakhstan the population declined by 20 per cent between 1926 and 1939, cattle were decimated and the sheep population almost wiped out. In fertile but recalcitrant Ukraine in 1932–3 the authorities deliberately connived at a secret famine by exporting or withholding food and preventing starving peasants from leaving, while all news outlets were blocked. Cannibalism occurred. Estimates of total famine deaths range from 4 to 6.5 million.

Collectivisation shattered the old peasant way of life and successfully subordinated countryside to town and government. The new agricultural sector was completed by state-run 'Machine Tractor Stations', which leased out (and therefore controlled access to) big farm machines, and by larger state farms (*sovkhozy*), run on industrial lines. But collectivisation bound the peasantry to a 'new serfdom';

and until the 1970s collective-farm peasants were denied the internal state passports, reintroduced in 1932, without which Soviet citizens had difficulty moving about. (The tsarist passport system had been abolished in 1917.) Collectivisation thus consolidated the Soviet 'peasant state' and the gulf between town and countryside. Moreover, its economic purposes were only partly achieved. Quite apart from the famines, in some respects it was disastrous. Peasants slaughtered livestock, or it died from neglect in the new farms. Union-wide, 70.5 million head of cattle in 1929 shrank to 49.3 million in 1935 and dairy and livestock production did not recover for decades. Animal draught power was similarly affected, while there were few tractors yet to replace it. Collective farm productivity was low, and farmers' 'private plots' (legal family allotments or smallholdings averaging 0.3 hectares, a peasant form of production) became the principal means of survival for their owners, as well as a significant national source of fruit and vegetables, not otherwise adequately provided by state producers. However, collectivisation did solve the state's grain-supply problem in the medium term: in the later 1930s harvests recovered and increased somewhat, enabling the growing urban population to be fed. Food rationing, introduced in 1928–9, was abolished in 1935. And while the extent of cross-investment between agriculture and industry remains controversial, low procurement prices, which constituted a tax on the peasantry, made a contribution to industrial growth.

The Five-Year Plans

The First Five-Year Plan (*piatiletka*) ran from October 1928, although only officially confirmed in 1929. Very optimistic production targets were proposed, and the decision was taken to complete it in four years. Reasoned doubts and objections were swept aside in favour of revolutionary enthusiasm: 'there are no fortresses Bolsheviks cannot storm'. This was the spirit of Aleksei Stakhanov, the Donbass ex-peasant miner, whose exploit in hewing 102 tons of coal in one extended shift in 1935 created the figure of the 'Stakhanovite' superman 'shockworker'. Huge investment was undertaken, funded by massive foreign and domestic loans and increased taxation. Necessary imports were paid for by exporting grain, while peasants starved. Vast industrial projects arose, which sucked in not only the NEP unemployed, but huge numbers of migrant peasant workers, who toiled under savage new labour discipline. Equally vast urban housing programmes were envisaged, to accommodate them. Metallurgical plants were developed, the impressive Moscow metro constructed, hydroelectric dams, tractor production to underpin collectivised agriculture. New territories were opened up for exploitation. The Volga-White Sea canal (*Belomorkanal*), praised by Soviet propagandists as a product of heroic Soviet creativity and redemptive labour, was in fact the work of unredeemed prison gangs, and too shallow to be very useful; however, the new Urals city of Magnitogorsk, constructed in the wilderness around a 'magnetic mountain' of exceptional ore deposits, was the work of idealistic technicians, *Komsomoltsy* and young socialists labouring in the most primitive conditions – though here too GULag workforces were used. In general, conditions for workers were dismal. But all this was to be set against the capitalist Depression and the hungry 1930s in the West (the Soviet government and Comintern tried to support foreign labour movements, of which capitalist governments were very fearful). There was waste, hardship, inefficiency and growth imbalance; production and quality standards were low, with everthing geared to fulfilment of the norm. But despite the confusion and ludicrous hyper-optimism, the first piatiletka achieved impressive results. Thus actual coal production in 1927–8 was 35.4 million tons. The second, so-called 'optimal' version of the Plan envisaged 75.0 million for 1932–3, and this figure was further 'amended' and inflated to 95–105. The actual 1932 figure achieved was 64.3 million, an increase in production of 82 per cent in four years; all branches of heavy industry increased by similar amounts or more, consumer goods less spectacularly. The problems thrown up by this frenetic industrial surge forced more realistic adjustment of targets in the Second Five-Year Plan (1933–7), but it and the Third Plan (1937–41) continued the élan, building on knowledge and experience acquired, until interrupted by the war. At the same time military requirements became increasingly prominent. Concurrent military development was, however, gravely compromised by the social and economic upheaval, and by the primacy of political over military factors.

Events during the years of collectivisation and the Five-Year Plans amounted to a renewal of revolution in Russia, often called the 'Stalin' or 'Cultural Revolution' – in Soviet terminology the 'Great Breakthrough'. Changes in economy and society went much deeper than in 1917–21, laying the ground-plan for the mature Soviet society that would exist, of course with further development, until 1991. An integral part of the Stalin Revolution was a demand for ideological loyalty and reversion to overt terror.

The Great Terror

The mass terror of the collectivisation campaign and the search for 'wreckers' on the eve of the Five-Year Plans presaged an internal orgy of cruel and bloody repression throughout the Soviet Union in the 1930s – arrests, murders, torture, forced confessions, show trials, executions, deportation, long prison and camp sentences in inhuman conditions. The Soviet elites were decimated, and millions of ordinary citizens engulfed. The apogee has come to be called the 'Great Terror' (some historians prefer the less emotive term 'purges'). Gathering momentum from 1932, the Terror really took wing in 1934 after the assassination of Sergei Kirov, Leningrad Party Secretary and potential rival for Stalin's post of General Secretary. Stalin may possibly have engineered the murder; he moved instantly to use it as pretext for widespread purges. Over the next five years the secret police struck at all groups of the elite, at their families and associates: industrial managers, cultural figures, national minority cadres, senior army ranks, diplomats, Old Bolsheviks, ordinary members of the Party and its hierarchy. Stalin's close colleagues, members of the Central Committee and Politburo, were subjected successively to humiliating show trials where they publicly confessed to absurd charges before being shot. The wife of the Soviet head of state, Mikhail Kalinin, was dispatched to the GULag; Viacheslav Molotov (Skriabin)'s wife would follow in 1949, while both men stayed in Stalin's entourage. Other Kremlin wives were executed. Even members of Stalin's own family circle died. Repeated weeding of the Party membership left thousands of ex-members fatally vulnerable to charges of wrecking and espionage. Terror reached its height in 1937–8; in the midst of it Lavrentii Beria, a Georgian, one of the NKVD's darkest angels, was appointed First Deputy Commissar. In 1937 torture, already widespread, was formally sanctioned; and a Party resolution on 'Anti-Soviet Elements' assigned regional arrest quotas to the NKVD, with 28 per cent to be shot. The camp regime also became temporarily far more deadly – usually, unlike German camps, the GULag was not specifically designed for extermination.

Official figures show 681,692 people executed in those two years alone; total excess deaths from all causes may have been 1.5 million. They included much of the officer corps of the Red Army. Finally in 1939 Stalin called a pause: Nikolai Yezhov, head of the NKVD, who himself had liquidated his predecessor, Genrikh Yagoda, was shot and replaced by Beria, and the repressions slowed. At this time numbers in the prison and penal system as a whole approached 3 million; and while the statistics remain controversial, recent estimates suggest total excess deaths in the 1930s, from all causes, of 10–11 millions. Stalin had not given up terror – he used it until the end of his life. But the Great Terror was extreme.

Like collectivisation and the coming war with Germany, the Terror was a human and social catastrophe. The hellish, enclosed, twilight world of the Stalinist repressions and the Dantesque universe of the GULag have been captured in classic memoirs, works of literary fiction, and cinema. As a phenomenon the Terror was as outlandish, demonically and inventively cruel and unpredictable, and as destructive, as the oprichnina of Ivan IV, a Tsar whom Stalin, much interested in Russia's past, greatly admired and adopted as model. Its causes and rationale have been strenuously debated, as has the extent of Stalin's personal role. He was intimately involved and personally responsible – he orchestrated events, and signed many death lists himself. Terror continued until he died, and was quickly wound down thereafter. Those who emphasise his personal directing role point out that he used terror to reassert Party pre-eminence over the People's Commissariats running the Five-Year Plans, and over other major power bases in the state, the NKVD and the armed forces, and to terrify ordinary people out of any thought of resistance. The purges also allowed Stalin finally to consolidate his personal political position, still not fully secure in the early 1930s despite his triumph in the leadership succession struggles. From 1939 onwards, however, he was and remained the undisputed master of Party and country: significantly the Party Congress, supposed to meet every three years, did not convene between 1939 and 1952. Terror enabled Stalin to dispose of senior Party members who knew things about him and his record from his early days. It allowed him to attack (though never to eliminate) the elusive support and patronage networks common in Soviet institutions, which fostered loyalties to other people. And it reflected important dimensions of Stalin's personal character – he was vain, vengeful, deeply suspicious, paranoid; comfortable with conflict, brutality and indiscriminate killing; and he savoured the humiliation of rivals.

But Stalin was not alone in running the Terror. All the leadership, including those purged, assented to and were complicit in it. The OGPU/NKVD became an autonomous institution with a large staff, a career structure, and its own momentum. Its successive directors had their own agendas, and its GULag empire, using slave labour, was a significant part of the developing Soviet economy; in the latter, terror also provided a motor to replace market-driven incentives. Terror had been part of Communist practice since 1917 and before, and had important social underpinnings. Even under NEP, in the less fraught years 1921–8, some 450,000 people were arrested on suspicion of 'counter-revolutionary activity'. Marxism-Leninism, with its claim to a uniquely correct 'scientific world-view', divided the world into progressive and reactionary elements set against one another in Manichean class struggle. Bolsheviks were thus always under threat – a siege mentality was never far beneath the surface. They were also called to render total devotion to their cause and to the Party which led it. In 1929 the leadership added to the religious certainty of the scientific world-view the fervour of a crusade or jihad, to fortify the Russian holy places of world socialism against the capitalist Moloch. So the '25,000-ers' went forth to confront the kulak infidel, while the workers of Magnitogorsk pitched their tents in the wilderness to build a new Jerusalem. The same was true in other fields where a resurgence of radical idealism reacted against the multiple retreats of the NEP years. These young enthusiasts, Stalin loyalists, followed the Stalinist version of the revolution. Moreover, many made their careers by stepping into the shoes of those purged, forming a new generation of leaders who believed in and profited from the system. These 'yuppie' vydvizhentsy ('people moving out [of their former sphere]') have been described as a 'new class'; they provided the rulers of Russia through to the 1980s. Some 'revisionist' historiography has sought explanations of the purges less in the actions of Stalin and the leadership, more in the latter's response to grass-roots social phenomena, and has emphasised popular support for, and engagement with, the line formulated at the centre.

In 1936 Stalin claimed that socialism had been built in its fundamentals, and the Stalin Constitution of that year underpinned the new social formation. Yet as socialism was consolidated, Stalin warned, class struggle would intensify – 'the more success we have, the more embittered will the remnants of the destroyed exploiter classes become, the sooner they will resort to extreme forms of struggle'. Martin Luther had said the same about the Devil's response to the triumph of the Reformation; and the Devil worms his way in everywhere – as Stalin knew from his youthful studies as an Orthodox seminarian. The Terror looked increasingly like the witch-crazes of early-modern Europe. Hostile elements with extraordinary powers to harm – 'Enemies of the People' – lurked in every shadow. Denunciations became a feature of Soviet daily life: the dark side of the traditional Russian petition culture. A constant concern of the Party leadership, as Party membership ballooned after 1921, and again 1928–33, was to ensure that those enrolled were true believers and loyalists: the Party itself might be riddled with careerists and subversives, hence the repeated membership purges. But by 1929, as Stalin's birthday tributes in *Pravda* imply, in Stalin's own mind and that of many Soviet citizens Stalin had become the embodiment and guardian of Party truth. The 'cult of personality' was the positive pole of social mobilisation, terror the negative. As Beria put it, 'an Enemy of the People is not only one who commits sabotage, but anyone who doubts the rightness of the Party line': such doubts were a betrayal of the Leader himself and his wisdom, a capital crime. Families and friends were drawn by association into the guilt of those accused. The latter also included foreign Communists who had sought refuge in Moscow, and their kin; and terror was extended abroad, to White *émigrés* in Paris, to anti-Fascist Spain, where the NKVD repressed non-Communist Republican fighters, and in 1940 to find Trotskii in Mexico – his kin, too, was exterminated. Terror was also applied to the populations of territories annexed on the eve of the Great Fatherland War, and then again to the Soviet population itself in the desperate drive to defeat the German invader after 1941.

PARTY, SOCIETY, AND IDEOLOGY, 1921–41

Party and Nomenklatura

The political structure over which Stalin presided, set out in the federal 1924 Union constitution, and elaborated in the Stalin Constitution of 1936, was predicated upon the political grip of the Party (from 1925 the 'Communist Party of the Soviet Union'). The basic administrative structure remained the pyramid of elective soviets culminating in the

All-Union Congress of Soviets, and two national Soviets, of the Union and of Nationalities, which were the nearest equivalent to a parliament. As before, the Congress of Soviets elected its permanent Central Executive Committee (VTsIK), which now had a Praesidium or inner cabinet and formally appointed Sovnarkom. Suffrage was universal, but weighted, and until 1936 excluded members of 'non-toiling' classes. Actual power lay, however, with the Communist Party. The Party structure rested upon 'primary organisations' ('cells') located in all basic units of economic, military or administrative activity. It mirrored the soviet structure in electing deputies upwards through district, provincial, regional, republican levels to the All-Union Party Congress; but 'democratic centralism' bound members to accept decisions of higher Party bodies. Each Party level had its own executive Committee with an executive Secretary: the highest instance was the Central Committee elected by the Congress, which in turn elected the Politburo (replaced under Stalin by a larger Praesidium). At each level the Party Secretary was the most powerful person in his bailiwick. Party committees at all levels had the power of nomination (strictly, 'recommendation', since posts were notionally elective) to principal posts in both Soviet and Party organisations below them, formalised in 1923 under the name of *nomenklatura,* and they held lists of these posts and of suitable nominees. This gave them total control over the work of both Soviet and Party organisations at lower levels, and over the membership as a whole. The highest body directly charged with appointment matters was the Orgburo, on which Stalin based his rise to power. Party members were obliged to fulfil Party directives, in return for which they could expect advancement and advantages. Members of the nomenklatura shared in the Party's power and had access, increasingly, to exclusive material privileges. Like the Imperial Table of Ranks, the nomenklatura appointment network was an enduring part of the system.

In its ideological stance, structure and articulation of political power, the Soviet Party regime has been compared to the Imperial autocracy. There was continuity in their common claim to divine right, omnicompetence, powers of social mobilisation, and containment of dissent. Stalin liked to compare himself privately to Ivan IV and Peter I; his reign also had features in common with that of Nicholas I. The nomenklatura in this comparison equates with the pre-revolutionary Imperial nobility, the dvorianstvo. They were both privileged elites whose rationale was service, ostensibly to the state or the Party, in practice to the leader or leadership group, who at once dominated and tyrannised over them, and depended upon them. Their administrative roles and relations with the mass population were very similar. The Communist solution to controlling and administering the country was thus not as different as appears from what had gone before. In both systems, moreover, persons were more important than institutions – law and legality were ostensible and superficial, and what counted were connections, client and patronage networks (even if due process and institutional effectiveness had been growing in the pre-revolutionary decades). As in the Empire, so in the Union, the centre had difficulty in enforcing its will upon the provinces and peripheries, where local power-holders and their networks pursued their own agendas; one purpose of Stalin's terror was to compel compliance.

Another, related analytical approach, used by both Western Weberian and Soviet Marxist historians, has called both the dvorianstvo and the nomenklatura as a whole a ruling class, a self-perpetuating elite which dominated society in its own interests. A subset of this analysis has focused on the revolutionary intelligentsia as an exploitative class: an idea that has a long history, and several different versions. In Lenin's own time the relationship of the intel-ligentsia to the German working-class movement concerned Karl Kautsky, and the Russian revolutionaries were denounced in these terms by the Polish radical Jan Machajski, whose book *The Intellectual Worker* (1904–5) found echoes in Milovan Djilas's *The New Class* (1957), and Mikhail Voslenskii's *Nomenklatura* (1980), an insider account of the Russian *apparat*.

Integrating the Nationalities: 'Indigenisation' and its Problems

Soviet control of national minorities also posed problems. In 1917 non-Russians composed about half of the Empire's population (56 per cent in 1897, 47 per cent in 1927). The Bolsheviks had denounced the Russian Empire as a 'prison-house of the peoples', and were aware of the dangers of 'Great Russian chauvinism' in their own relations with minorities; but they expected that socialist revo-lution and industrialisation would progressively erase separate national consciousness and ethnic differences. Meanwhile the Communist solution to the organisation of a multinational state, announced in 1923, was tripartite. First, the 'national-territorial' principle declared each nationality separate but equal, on its own territory; the federal Soviet Union would consist of nationally based constituent republics and regions. Nationality was one identifier registered in the new internal passports issued from 1932. National groups of any size who lacked a recognised territory of their own were in principle to receive one, and many such territories were created. The compact Volga-German settlements, for instance, were organised into the 'Autonomous Soviet Socialist Republic of the Volga Germans' (1924–41) within the RSFSR. Attention was also paid to minorities scattered among other nationalities: thus the far-flung Ukrainian diaspora acquired Ukrainian soviets and schools across the RSFSR, besides its own homeland in the Ukrainian SSR. Moscow hoped that a liberal territorial-based policy might also attract minority conationals in neighbouring countries, for instance Ukrainians in Poland. There were of course problems. The identity of the approximately two million Soviet Jews, for instance, was bound up with religion and potentially with Zionism, and the deep-rooted tradition of Russian anti-Semitism reappeared in Soviet forms, especially in 1948–53. A Soviet Jewish 'homeland', the Jewish Autonomous Region of Birobidzhan, was established in 1934 in the Far East, on the unquiet Chinese border. This was tantamount to banishing Jews to an alien, inhospitable and undeveloped region, and accordingly never aroused Jewish enthusiasm: in 1979 only 5.4 per cent of its quarter-million population were Jews. The Party's policy of enshrining national difference as an organising principle in order to defuse national tensions in fact perpetuated potential divisions and rivalries which would ultimately become fatal to the Union in the 1980s. According to the 1924 constitution, nationalities had the right of secession from the Soviet Union; but Moscow ensured that this was not exercised.

To confirm national-territorial political autonomy, the second plank of policy gave each full republic of the federal USSR its own Communist Party. Central political control was assured, however, by the subordination of republican Parties to the Communist Party of the Soviet Union based in Moscow: the Russians (who controlled the Union-wide CPSU) were the only territorial nationality without a Party of their own.

Third, national independence and equality were to be strengthened by *korenizatsiia*, 'indigenisation'. National languages and cultures were to be encouraged, and ethnic-minority cadres trained and promoted to leading positions in the Party, trades unions and government, where as good Party members they would support Moscow's policies in the localities. Indigenisation was a response to the underdevelopment and hostility of non-Russian peoples, and tensions between Russified towns and non-Russian countryside. In deliberate contradistinction to Tsarist 'Russification' policies, national cultural and linguistic as well as territorial autonomy was to legitimate 'soviet power' and reconcile the nationalities – especially their peasantries – to the new state: development was to be 'national in form, socialist in content'. During the NEP this policy was especially conciliatory in Muslim areas. In the First Five-Year Plan massive investment in the republics (higher than in the centre) was very successful in building industry and drawing in large numbers of ethnic-minority workers, so that the industrial labour force became predominantly local, rather than Russian as before. The Soviet authorities also encouraged education in the local vernacular, undertook sweeping literacy campaigns, and systematised and modernised indigenous languages: a huge effort with far-reaching social effects. The numbers of ethnic-minority cadres in Party positions increased. However, these measures had unforeseen results. Especially in the less developed eastern regions, the new emphasis on local languages split local cultural consumers from their Russian-speaking Russian neighbours, and led them to expect development in terms of their indigenous culture and values. Non-Russian identities were strengthened, and national differences politicised – thus Ukraine developed a clear national identity and national elite for the first time in the 1920s (even though in Ukraine and Belorussia the Russian language remained strong). Moreover, under pressure new ethnic-minority Party cadres tended to espouse local interests: their focus became less the international proletariat as defined by Moscow than their own national community, while local Russians began to complain of forced de-Russification. These tensions first came to the fore after 1929, when collectivisation required the assertion of central state authority and also placed huge pressures on minority regions – resistance was greatest among non-Russians. While still affirming the principle of indigenisation, Moscow now attacked 'local chauvinism' and 'nationalism' and placed new emphasis on the liberating as opposed to oppressive significance of things Russian: in the socialist context, after the abolition of Imperial oppression, these now supposedly opened the way to higher cultural levels. In 1932 a terror campaign targeted 'national communist' cadres who tried to defend their peasantries against excessive grain requisitioning (most notably the Skrypnyk case in Ukraine): many were executed. Korenizatsiia, still advocated in principle, was thus severely limited in practice, and repression presaged far-reaching changes of direction in the ensuing pre-war decade, with ethnic cleansing of border areas and administrative Russification of the RSFSR. In the peak terror years of 1937–8 some 20 per cent of all arrests and over 30 per cent of all executions derived from ethnic-minority issues.

Other Social Transformations

From the outset the Bolsheviks wished to transform the social life and culture, as well as the economic life, of the proletariat: to dismantle what they saw as the oppressive social institutions and attitudes of bourgeois society – Church, family, marriage, illiteracy and ignorance, ill health, women's subordination. A socialist society moving towards a 'machine utopia' needed optimal material conditions and a new mass consciousness, conducive to culture, discipline, and awareness of the common good. In this the regime and its supporters were moving to some extent with the grain of wartime and revolutionary changes, and much was attempted in the 1920s, though results were patchy. The scientific future was heralded by the 1920 *GOELRO* plan for electricity generation: Lenin declared that 'electrification plus Soviet power equals Communism'. Labour legislation of 1922 confirmed the eight-hour working day and decreed paid holidays, sick and unemployment pay, medical provision, collective wage bargaining and dispute arbitration – a welfare state well ahead of its time in Europe. The 'Women's Section' of the Party headed by Lenin's close friend Inessa Armand sought to transform women's lot. New codes on marriage and the family (1918, 1926) made divorce and abortion available on demand. Women were encouraged to demand respect from their husbands, while workplace refectories and crèches would reduce housebound chores, foster the collective spirit, and allow women to take jobs and participate in public life. Collectivism took other shapes – social automotion came to the Soviet Union in the form of trams and buses rather than private cars; the housing shortage was addressed by grouping new flats 'communally' around a shared kitchen (also convenient for information-gathering informers).

Education and literacy, for both sexes, were a major preoccupation and one of the greatest areas of Soviet success – though it transpired that they did not necessarily equate to enhanced political consciousness. Literacy campaigns were mounted in town and country, with impressive effect. In 1897 40 per cent of males aged 9–49 were literate. Soviet censuses showed 70 per cent in 1926, 94 per cent by 1939. Women, and the nationalities, followed after. The coming of Soviet education and women's liberation to Kirgizia is heroically depicted in Chingis Aitmatov's story, filmed in 1965, *The First Teacher*. The People's Commissariat for Enlightenment (*Narkompros*) under Anatolii Lunacharskii opened education to all, though with class restrictions, and created programmes to improve worker qualifications; the school curriculum of the 1920s included strong practical and vocational elements. The early *Proletkult* movement sought to create a new, original, proletarian culture, but this did not find official favour; instead, conventional high culture, cast in appropriately Communist discourse, became universally accessible through vast production of cheap newspapers and books, and the development of theatre and the new radio and cinema. Approved (but *only* approved) social organisations were encouraged and mushroomed – both grass-roots activities like theatricals and sports clubs, and national organisations like the Komsomol youth movement and League of Militant Godless. From the late 1920s a new Central Standing Commission on Religious Questions (1929–38) oversaw, and tried to control, a much harsher anti-religious policy. Official trades unions were fostered, but became in the Soviet system state-controlled channels of industrial discipline rather than independent safeguards of worker well-being. The focus of urban social organisation increasingly became the enterprise or work-place, which controlled access to material benefits such as housing, child-care, holidays and rest-homes, and in which managers and workers had a common interest in stability and security of employment.

These social transformations, real and potential, were impressive, inspiring and far-reaching. As with all social change, practice did not always match vision; but change was demonstrably possible. At the same time the aftermath of the Civil War made life very hard. Under NEP urban unemployment was rife; wages were low, urban housing poor; crowds of orphaned street-kids roamed the cities, defying attempts to place them in under-equipped orphanages. Strikes were discouraged as damaging to production, not only by employers but by trades unions too; collective wage bargaining gave way in practice to local deals.

The countryside under NEP also felt some of these changes, but to a lesser extent. The Soviet population still remained overwhelmingly rural: 82 per cent of the 147 millions recorded by the 1926 census. In the revolution the peasantry had resolved the land problem according to their own values, dividing land among those who worked it. Even many former landlords had been allowed to stay on, provided they were prepared to farm for themselves, effectively to become peasants. As late as 1927, 10,756 such ex-landowners were registered in the RSFSR alone. The village communal gathering, while formally regulated by the Land Code and now more inclusive than in tsarist times, ran its affairs in its traditional way, and in practice was largely its own master in the localities, more so than at any other time in its history: government intervention was weak and rural soviets underfunded. Nevertheless, the revolution had brought new movement to the countryside. Officials of the People's Commissariat for Land (*Narkomzem*) continued the work begun by Stolypin's officials in encouraging land rationalisation and more advanced agronomy, and now was added propaganda for collective methods – cooperatives, communes and collective farms – though this had made relatively little headway before mass collectivisation. New experiences brought other changes. In the Tambov village of Viriatino near the mines of the Donbass, if we may believe an approved and positivist Soviet account:

During the NEP years steel began to be used as a roofing material. . . . A considerable improvement in [house] furnishings began in the [later] 1920s. More emphasis was placed on cleanliness; the walls and floors of the wooden dwellings were washed more frequently and the walls of the brick cottages were whitewashed two or three times a year. Tables were always covered with tablecloths; oilcloth became very popular. It became a widespread practice to hang curtains at windows [and . . .] in front of . . . the stove. . . . Walls were papered, or decorated with posters and pictures depicting the civil war. Photographs were starting to become popular as wall decorations. The influence of the urban bourgeoisie . . . turned out, however, to be one of the most tenacious survivals of capitalism, and the living room was usually coarsely or tastelessly decorated.

This may be compared with the sketch of rural Volga conditions written by an English famine-relief worker a few years before (Samara, 1924):

> Actual living conditions are almost indescribably miserable, and even those of the richer peasants would be utterly condemned in any part of England. . . . The best houses have some appearance of solidity and comfort, being built of trimmed logs, well jointed, with a short iron roof, inner walls lined with matchboarding, and floorboards well raised from the ground. The average log hut has a thatched roof, unlined walls, and floorboards often laid onto the earth. Meanest and most wretched of all is the mud hut, with walls that crack in summer and are washed away in the spring floods, and a floor of beaten clay or earth. . . . A brick house . . . is rarely seen. The lack of a convenient water supply makes cleanliness difficult even in summer, and in winter water is avoided as much as possible. Winter indeed throws into relief the miserable conditions . . . . The husbandman sits discussing . . . with neighbours, all smoking vile-smelling home-cured tobacco screwed up in newspaper. The housewife is busy spinning flax or hemp . . . and children sit dumbly around the wall. Doors are kept vigorously closed, windows are hermetically sealed, and the atmosphere cannot be described, its poisonous quality can only be realised by experience. The only [evening] light . . . comes from a paraffin lamp, often home made. . . . The universal habit of chewing sunflower seeds and spitting the husks onto the floor adds to the untidiness and filth of the hut.

The mobilisation of 1929–32 produced vast social mobility, the relocation of millions and rapid urbanisation; social turnover was further facilitated by famine and purges. These developments were accompanied by far-reaching changes in education. From 1930 primary education was made obligatory, and curriculum and teaching methods became more traditional – school uniforms were restored in 1937. Pupil numbers in general schools rose from 11.6 million in 1927 to 21.4 million in 1933. Higher education was also affected. From the late 1920s wide-ranging efforts were made to train up a new generation of 'Red specialists', to eradicate the regime's long-standing reliance on 'bourgeois specialists'. Promising young workers nominated by official bodies (Komsomol,

Party or trades union) were sent to technical higher-education institutes where they could both receive education and training, and be prepared for administrative responsibility. These 'yuppies', already mentioned, some 150,000 people, made up one-third of all higher-education students in 1929–32; on graduation they quickly found posts in all areas of public life, many of them in the nomenklatura, and their support of the system which so markedly advanced their social status was a significant factor in the developments of the Stalin years.

The biggest social movement was from the countryside into the towns. Twelve million peasants made this transition. Viriatino peasants who had worked seasonally in the Donbass mines now settled there permanently. The mass influx of peasants produced a notable 'ruralisation' of urban centres, and sometimes friction with established workers who monopolised the best jobs. However, peasant town culture evolved under the impact of urban experiences, becoming an amalgam of both; this was noticeably reflected in dress, and in liking for the urban kitsch complained of at Viriatino. It also tended to accelerate generational conflict, as urbanised children diverged from the village mores of their families. Nevertheless, the peasant world-view persisted in the towns as well as the countryside – urban peasants consorted with their own countrymen, friends and relatives, and the radical state-led vision underlying the 'cultural revolution' took less hold here than anywhere else.

Thus while Stalinist believers worked to further the socialist millennium, the popular masses were more resistant to Party discourse and its attendant thought-patterns. Moreover, the new social values proclaimed in the 1920s had unforeseen consequences. Family cohesion was undermined by harsh domestic conditions and labour migration, and divorce rates rose rapidly, while women reacted to the double burdens of work and household by limiting their families – abortions rocketed and the birth-rate shrank. The Second Plan gave slightly more attention to consumer needs. In the mid-1930s official rhetoric began to move back to more traditional values, a 'retreat' from previous revolutionary radicalism. Schooling became more academic. The family was exalted, as a model for good order both social and political, divorce and abortion were made more difficult, and women were now called to be model housewives as well as workers. The Party's Women's Sections were closed on the grounds that the 'women's question' was solved. Materialism was approved – as Stalin put it: 'Life has become better! Life has become more joyous!' This was particularly true for the nomenklatura, who in the times of shortage now increasingly acquired privileged access through special outlets to *defitsitnye* goods and food: a re-establishment of hierarchy paralleled by the reintroduction of wage differentials in industry. The need to enforce central control after 1929 and the increasingly threatening international situation after 1933 contributed further to a new emphasis on the Russian centre and Party mythology. Immediate defence concerns required a focus on the Soviet motherland, national unity under Russian leadership, and military preparedness. Military training and physical fitness programmes were increased. Mass culture was also harnessed to the new Russian nationalist mood – a folk-song olympiad was held in Moscow in 1935. The Russian past, decried in the revolutionary tradition, now became a source of patriotic unity and common endeavour: history teaching in schools emphasised the heroic rather than the exploitative, while the cinema moved away from collective heroes and began to glorify individual Russian national leaders, from *Peter I* (1937) to *Ivan IV* (1941–6).

The Arts

The immediate post-revolutionary years were a time of ferment and great productivity in the arts. The new state immediately nationalised all artistic institutions, and viewed cultural activity as an important tool in its relationship with the population. In the 1920s the Party took a pluralist line, allowing expression within reason of individual or group ideas, while blocking factional attempts to establish theoretical or political dominance, since this would not be under Party control. This applied to all art forms – literature, music, ballet, film, painting – and they followed a common pattern of evolution in the first half of the century. In literature, several groups continued the radicalism of the pre-revolutionary avant-garde and campaigned for new revolutionary forms. The earliest was the leftist Proletkult, which evolved into the quarrelsome *RAPP* (Russian Association of Proletarian Writers); this persuasion included Mikhail Sholokhov, noted for his Cossack epic *And Quiet Flows The Don*. Others were the Futurists, led by the ebullient literary revolutionary Vladimir Maiakovskii, which evolved into *LEF* (Left Front of Art), and the Imaginists around the 'peasant poet' Sergei Yesenin. Radicalism of another sort inspired the Formalist critics grouped in *Opoyaz* (Society for the Study of Poetic Language), who approached literature as a stylistic exercise; the brilliant theorist and critic Mikhail Bakhtin was associated with them. Besides these groupings, a range of variously talented authors more or less in sympathy with the regime produced impressive works of drama, prose and poetry in the 1920s, mostly on revolutionary and civil-war themes. They included Mikhail Bulgakov, whose later masterpiece *The Master and Margaret* (1930–40) could not, however, be published until 1966; the humourist Mikhail Zoshchenko; the novelists Aleksandr Fadeev, Konstantin Fedin, Leonid Leonov and Boris Pilniak; the satirist Yevgenii Zamiatin, in trouble for his Orwellian dystopia *We* (1927), published abroad, until he could emigrate in 1931; and Andrei Platonov, probably the most significant prosaist of this period. Maksim Gorkii, who had a chequered relationship with the Bolsheviks, lived abroad from 1922 until 1928; he then became a sort of literary icon until his (suspicious) death in 1936. The Jewish community of Odessa produced a number of outstanding artistic talents: Isaak Babel's moving and technically brilliant short stories centred on his experiences in the Civil War (*Red Cavalry*, 1926) and Jewish life in Odessa (*Odessa Tales*, 1931), while the pseudonymous Ilf and Petrov wrote hilarious and best-selling novels satirising the NEP, *The Twelve Chairs* (1928) and *The Golden Calf* (1929–33). In poetry, the older tradition was best represented by four established poets of outstanding talent: Boris Pasternak, who made his name with *My Sister Life* (1917); the former Acmeists Osip Mandelshtam and Anna Akhmatova; and Marina Tsvetaeva, who lived abroad from 1922. None of them fitted easily into the Soviet mould. Akhmatova could no longer publish in the 1920s; in the 1930s, when her son was involved in the purges, she found a new voice to articulate popular suffering in her powerful *Requiem* (1935–40/61, not immediately published). During the 1930s Pasternak devoted himself to translations; Tsvetaeva, who returned inopportunely in 1939, committed suicide in 1941.

The relatively liberal 1920s ended with 1928 and the First Five-Year Plan. RAPP briefly gained political command of literature, but in 1932 a decree 'On the Reconstruction of Literary and Artistic Organisations' suppressed autonomous groups in favour of Party-controlled Unions for each branch of culture. The Writers' Union was created the same year; at its first Congress in 1934 it adopted the doctrine of 'Socialist Realism'. This rather vague concept required writers to write realistically but positively about the challenges and triumphs of revolutionary socialist construction; literature – and all art – must be inspiring, optimistic, reflecting the heroic potentialities of Soviet society, 'party-spirited' in following the Party line, and critical only of individual, not systemic, shortcomings. Socialist Realism remained the compulsory format of Soviet art until the 1980s, exerting a powerfully deleterious effect on quality. In private, some writers and artists went on producing 'for the desk drawer'. Socialist Realism was also designed to inculcate Soviet patriotism and during the 1930s it fully accommodated the turn to nationalism.

Many writers were caught up in the purges. Mandelshtam died in a camp in 1938; Babel was shot in 1940. During the war, however, pressures eased, and members of the Writers' Union joined the war effort as journalists, publicists and propagandists. Akhmatova was able to publish again. Widely popular war novels and poetry appeared, notably Aleksandr Tvardovskii's long poem *Vasilii Tërkin* (1941–5). In 1946, however, a vitriolic attack by Zhdanov upon Zoshchenko and Akhmatova (in fact a symptom of political in-fighting) signalled a return to an extreme form of socialist-realist control, and the last Stalin years are reminiscent in their dogmatic sterility of the last period of Nicholas I.

The course of Soviet music, opera and ballet followed that of literature closely, with an Association of Proletarian Musicians (*APM*) confronting the Association for Contemporary Music (*ASM*), and the creation of a Union of Soviet Composers in 1932. Prokofiev left Russia in 1918, returning in 1932. During the NEP diversity reigned; traditional compositions contrasted with the modernising scores of Dmitrii Shostakovich, the outstanding Soviet composer, who made his debut in 1925 with his First Symphony – the first Soviet work to be noticed abroad. Soviet opera and ballet took off at the same time. Western influences remained strong throughout the 1920s. Shostakovich worked with both contemporary and 'proletarian' trends, and after 1932 had considerable difficulties: his Fifth Symphony (1938) was sub-titled 'A Soviet Artist's Creative Reply to Just Criticism'. Much composition revolved around revolutionary and Bolshevik themes, and historical patriotism appeared in 1930s music too. A significant talent emerged at this time in Aram Khachaturian, outstanding among several noteworthy Soviet Armenian composers. Jewish Odessa also contributed significantly to Soviet music, with the composer Glier, the violinists David and

Igor Oistrakh, and the pianist Emil Gilels. During the war both Shostakovich and Prokofiev composed prolifically: Shostakovich's hugely popular Seventh Symphony (1942), dedicated to his besieged Leningrad and widely performed abroad, expressed in David Oistrakh's words 'the prophetic affirmation . . . of our faith in the eventual triumph of humanity and light'. The post-war clamp-down struck music too. Tchaikovsky and nineteenth-century Russian music became the declared models; Prokofiev and Shostakovich were denounced for 'formalism'; the latter's Eighth Symphony (1943) was suppressed for nearly ten years.

The budding cinema was extremely popular in pre-revolutionary Russia; Bolsheviks regarded it as the ideal art form for their purposes of mass propaganda and education. Russian cinemas were nationalised a year after theatres, in 1919, and the world's first state film school established, followed in 1922 by a state production body, *Goskino* (from 1924 *Sovkino*). It presided over the 'golden age' of Soviet silent cinema and the work of Sergei Eizenshtein, Vsevolod Pudovkin and others. The famous *Battleship Potëmkin* was made in 1926, but was more popular with foreign audiences than with either the Soviet authorities or Soviet masses: during the 1920s easily accessible American and German films were most popular. As in other spheres, close control was introduced in 1928, and Socialist Realism followed soon after, coinciding with the coming of cinematic sound. As war approached, a series of heroic military historical films focused (as already noted) on individual heroes: after *Peter I* came *Alexander Nevskii* (1938), *Suvorov* (1941), *Bogdan Khmelnitskii* (1941) and *Kutuzov* (1944), as well as *Ivan the Terrible*. In the post-war clamp-down the film industry suffered in the same way as other fields: the second part of Eizenshtein's *Ivan the Terrible* was one casualty. Jewish producers were forced out of the industry.

In the visual arts, the revolution attracted enthusiastic support from many of the avant-garde, and new associations proliferated. The Visual Arts department (*IZO*, 1918) of Narkompros patronised this trend, employing avant-garde artists and constructors in the new experimental Institute of Artistic Culture and as teachers in the Higher State Art-Technical Studios (*VKhuTeMas*,1920). Initial modernist projects stayed mostly on paper – Vladimir Tatlin's famous 1919 design for a huge monument to the Third International, commissioned by Sovnarkom, proclaimed the new industrial pretensions of Constructivism (Figure 13). But the reconstruction of the

Figure 13   Vladimir Tatlin, 'Monument to the Third International' (1919)
From the personal collection of Professor Lindsey Hughes.

NEP years opened wide opportunities and allowed private architectural practice; impressive new buildings were erected by such architects as Konstantin Melnikov, Panteleimon and Ilia Golosov, and the Constructivist Vesnin brothers. Poster art, which had played an important propaganda role in the Civil War, was developed further through the 1920s. As in other artistic fields, politically committed painters (the Association of Artists of Revolutionary Russia, *AKhRR*, 1922) promoted a left agenda, but without preventing artistic diversity: the Society of Easel Artists (*OST*) painted scenes from contemporary Soviet life for the emerging NEP art market. The coming of Socialist Realism affected art and architecture equally. A new All-Russian Academy of Arts was set up under Isaak Brodskii, leader of AKhRR, which promoted increasingly severe representational painting. The Itinerants were back in fashion, and what was left of the avant-garde tradition survived only unofficially in private circles. Brodskii and his successor Aleksandr Gerasimov specialised in portraits of the Soviet leadership. Architecture in the 1930s came under the same close state control. The vast urban construction programmes of the First Five-Year Plan produced vigorous debates on both architectural needs and town planning; the latter failed to meet the intense pressures on accommodation created by industrialisation, despite such urban solutions as the pioneering and fully-integrated Moscow City Plan of 1935. The characteristic official style of the Stalin period became 'Stalin neo-Baroque', a proliferation of decorative Soviet and neo-Russian motifs on grandiose neo-Classical structures, culminating in the 'wedding-cake' sky-scrapers constructed in principal Russian cities (and Warsaw), such as the new 1953 Moscow State University complex (Figure 14). Typical of the period's sculpture is Vera Mukhina's famous *Worker and Female Collective-Farm Worker*, designed for an international exhibition in 1937 (Figure 15).

The Natural Sciences

The new Soviet regime was deeply committed to the development of science, and immediately extended the existing research establishment and the Russian Academy of Sciences – from 1925 the Academy of Sciences of the USSR: Union republics also each had their own Academy. Relatively large numbers of scientific workers were women. The First Five-Year Plan included further rapid expansion of

Figure 14   Moscow State University, new building (1953)
Source: From the personal collection of the author.

research and development, both to service the new industry being created and to achieve Soviet technical self-sufficiency. The Soviet scientific establishment became huge, but under Stalin it had to work in international isolation and under ideological constraint. The outstanding area of initial success was physics. Nobel prize-winners Pëtr Kapitza, Lev Landau and Nikolai Semënov began their careers in post-revolutionary Petrograd, and later made critical contributions to the successful Soviet atomic-bomb project, insulated from ideological pressures, in the 1940s. The expansion of medical facilities brought an increase in medical research and particular success in epidemiology; in 1944 an Academy of Medical Sciences was created. In the 1920s Nikolai Vavilov (brother of another distinguished physicist) established a network of agricultural research institutions under the All-Union Academy of Agricultural Sciences, building successfully on pre-revolutionary achievements. But the critical importance of agriculture and the crusading fervour of the late 1920s and 1930s opened the way for purveyors of unorthodox quick fixes such as the quack horticulturist Ivan Michurin and the pseudo-geneticist Trofim Lysenko who first came to prominence in

Figure 15   Vera Mukhina, 'Worker and Kolkhoznitsa' (1937)
Source: From the personal collection of Professor Lindsey Hughes.

1927–9. Vavilov died in prison in 1943. Lysenko's 'agrobiology', which claimed that genetic traits could be acquired as well as inherited, was patronised by Stalin and exercised a malign dominance over Soviet genetics, as well as undermining biochemistry, until the 1960s. Botanists realised the dream of P. S. Pallas, setting in train a great 30-volume description of *The Flora of the USSR* (1934–64), but their director Viktor Komarov was a lesser Lysenko who imposed his Stalinist views. Both psychology and psychiatry were subordinated to Party control and used for political and penal purposes (as in the reign of Nicholas I) until the 1980s; Freud's theories were excommunicated already in the 1920s. The Terror of the 1930s seriously affected scientific work. Apart from ideological controls, numerous scientists were repressed – but their services could still be co-opted: much wartime aircraft design, for example, was carried out in special camp or prison facilities.

THE COMING OF THE 'GREAT FATHERLAND WAR'

International Relations, 1917–41

The Bolshevik government began its international activity in 1917 by seeking world revolution and the subversion of the capitalist powers; Comintern was the fullest expression of this strategy. In pursuit of its exclusive, Bolshevik vision of revolution, Comintern required its member Communist Parties to work against, not with, other less radical socialists, thereby splitting European left-wing movements. When world revolution failed to materialise, however, the USSR had to reach a diplomatic accommodation with other states, both to ensure Soviet security and to find essential trading partners. Initially, while some states and individual entrepreneurs were willing to deal commercially with the maverick regime, Moscow did not find ready diplomatic acceptance. In the 1920s Soviet Russia's closest partner was its former adversary Germany, then also an international pariah. The 1922 Rapallo treaty restored normal German–Russian diplomatic and commercial relations and facilitated collaboration, especially in the military field where Germany laboured under restrictions imposed at Versailles. The German army established military bases and training areas on Soviet territory, and German industry constructed advanced plants in Russia for military-related production. Both sides benefited in strengthening their armed forces – the Germans also in gaining knowledge of terrain they would fight over in World War II.

In the following decade the USSR developed diplomatic relations with the other powers. The only serious security threat came from Japanese expansion in the Far East. Tensions generated by the Japanese invasion of Manchuria in 1931 were finally resolved decisively in Moscow's favour by Soviet victory at Khalkin-Gol in August 1939; a non-aggression pact was signed with Japan in 1941. The advent of the Nazis to power in Germany in 1933, materially assisted by the quarrels of the German Communists with the Social Democrats, had transformed the USSR's international position and strategy. In face of the Fascist threat it joined the League of Nations in 1934, and switched Comintern to promoting united left-wing Popular Front alliances, especially in Republican Spain, to which the Soviet Union alone among the powers gave active support against Franco. This did not, however, prevent the NKVD's Spanish repressions already mentioned; and the Terror, especially the 1937 purge of Red Army officers, raised serious questions abroad about Soviet moral standing and military competence. The latter doubts were apparently confirmed by the dismal Red Army showing against Finland in 1940. Meanwhile Franco's success, the passivity of the League of Nations, and especially Hitler's aggressive actions made new security arrangements essential. Maksim Litvinov, pro-Western Commissar for Foreign Affairs, laboured to promote 'collective security'. The Soviet Union, like France, had treaty obligations to Czechoslovakia, and seems to have been prepared to honour them if fighting had started. But it was not invited to the 1938 Munich conference at which Neville Chamberlain cut his deal with Hitler. Soviet offers of a major security treaty in April 1939 received a lukewarm reception from France and Britain, who doubted both the sincerity of any agreement, and its practicality and value. Finally, in August 1939, a low-level, dilatory Franco-British delegation sent to Moscow demonstrated the half-heartedness, and the military unreadiness, of the Western allies. Stalin promptly replaced Litvinov with Molotov and made his peace with Hitler, who had been pressing his diplomats to reach an accommodation with Russia before the planned German invasion of Poland. For the Soviet side this was a 'Brest-Litovsk in reverse', a high-risk short-term strategy to which they could see no viable alternative, whose purpose was to gain time. On 24 August 1939 Molotov and Ribbentrop, the German Foreign

Minister, signed a non-aggression treaty, with a secret protocol dividing Eastern Europe into spheres of influence and giving Stalin freedom of action in the Baltic states, Finland, eastern Poland and Bessarabia.

In September 1939 German, and then Soviet, forces invaded Poland, from opposite sides. To eliminate any possible opposition to Soviet power, thousands of Poles were imprisoned, tortured and shot, including the army officers murdered in the notorious Katyn massacre. Further, by November 1940 Nikita Khrushchëv, in charge of the operation, had deported 1.17 million people to Soviet labour camps. Stalin also forced the three Baltic states of Estonia, Latvia and Lithuania to sign 'mutual assistance' agreements, allowing Soviet troops into their countries. Similar demands on Finland were rejected, unleashing the 'Winter War' (November 1939–March 1940) in which the Finns gave the ill-prepared Red Army a bloody nose. Soviet numbers finally told, but the peace confirmed Finnish independence and Soviet gains were limited. In 1940, as German forces swept triumphantly through Belgium and France to the Channel and drove the British into the sea at Dunkirk, Soviet troops invaded the Baltic states and repeated the Polish scenario. Thousands were murdered outright, many more – some 127,000 – deported to Siberia; puppet Soviet republics were created. Shortly before, as a by-product of the Nazi–Soviet pact, the Baltic-German population of Latvia and Estonia left the lands they had dominated for over 700 years and migrated 'home into the Reich', in fact to German-held Polish territory. Bessarabia (Moldavia) was also annexed to the Soviet Union at this time.

The Great Fatherland War

As soon as he had defeated France, in mid-1940 Hitler began to plan an attack on the USSR. A vast invasion would turn the area up to a line from Astrakhan to Archangel into a colonial German satrapy, with the residual Soviet population pushed eastwards beyond the Urals. Stalin clung obsessively to his belief that the 1939 pact guaranteed him for the moment from German aggression; despite the failure of further negotiations, and accurate and multiplying intelligence warnings, he refused to believe the imminence of danger. When the blitzkrieg invasion struck in a three-pronged attack on 22 June 1941, Soviet forces were accordingly taken wholly by surprise. The

Germans achieved overwhelming air and land superiority, and captured huge numbers of prisoners; inappropriate Russian tactics also caused huge casualties in the field. By September German Army Group North had surrounded Leningrad, which then endured a horrific 900-day siege; by November Army Group South had captured Kiev and occupied Ukraine, and Army Group Centre was 12 miles from Moscow. Lenin's corpse and the government were evacuated eastwards, but Stalin stayed in the capital: a symbolic stand of great importance. Hitler, however, changed his priorities, diverting armour to Leningrad and the southern push towards the Caucasus and the Caspian oil-fields. This, and a savage early winter, saved Moscow. The Soviet side thus kept its main command and communications centre. It also successfully reconstructed its economy after transplanting essential industry and workers wholesale to the distant rear (some 2600 enterprises and 25 million workers and their families – a dazzling feat); in February 1942 the entire Soviet population was placed on a mobilisation footing. In the later stages of the war the USSR out-produced Germany in war machines and *matériel*, and matched it in quality, while British and American lend-lease provided items in short supply: an economic achievement which was key to ultimate Soviet victory. In 1942 Hitler's eastward advance was countered by the encirclement of his huge Sixth Army at Stalingrad: on 31 January 1943, after fighting of unimaginable bitterness and destruction, Field Marshal von Paulus and his remaining 91,000 men surrendered. This was the turning-point of the war, reinforced by the great tank battle of July at Kursk, north of Kharkov, 'the largest set-piece battle in history', when the now highly effective Soviet armour destroyed the German Panzers. The German campaign turned into inexorable retreat: Soviet forces rolled westwards and southwards into Romania and Bulgaria, Hungary, Austria and Czechoslovakia, and reoccupied the Baltic States. In June 1944 the Allied landings in Normandy opened the long-awaited Second Front (thereby also preventing total Soviet domination of post-war Europe); on 25 April 1945 American and Soviet troops made contact in Germany, on the river Elbe. By then, Soviet forces were already fighting their way into Berlin: the Red Flag was raised over the Reichstag on 30 April and Hitler committed suicide. The final surrender ceremony, involving all the principal combatants, took place in Berlin on 9 May. The future shape of Germany and Europe was decided by the 'Big Three', Churchill, Stalin and Truman, at the

Potsdam Conference finally convened on 15 July: the conference demonstrated the new realities of power, the dominance of the USSR and USA. A week after it closed, the Soviet Union declared war on Japan, fighting a short and extremely successful campaign before the final Japanese surrender.

The cost of Soviet victory in the 'Great Fatherland War' was immense, both in lives and material destruction. 34.5 million men and women were mobilised. The number of Soviet deaths (military and civilian) has been much debated: current consensus suggests between 25 and 27 million. The Nazi–Soviet struggle constituted the core of World War II, dwarfing in numbers, deaths and barbarity the Allied experience on other fronts (German wartime deaths are estimated at 5–7 million, British 0.39 million, American 0.3 million). With all credit to British and American achievements, it is clear that Nazism was defeated in the Soviet Union. This war was an armed clash of ideologies without parallel since the Thirty Years' War, which gave it a particular edge of brutality, 'a war to the death between two world systems'. It was the confrontation of two vast terror machines, a majority of whose victims, at least proportionately, were from non-Russian and non-German nationalities. Hitler made a strategic mistake in his mistreatment of the East European populations which came under his control. In some places German troops were welcomed as liberators, and he found many collaborators, out of fear, hatred of Communism, or hopes of national renewal: in all some one million 'Soviet' soldiers fought for the Germans. Partisan activity was sometimes hostile to both sides, and guerrilla resistance to Soviet domination was widespread in Eastern Europe after 1945 (in the reoccupied Baltic States, bands of 'Forest Brothers' fought on in the countryside against the Soviet occupiers until 1956 – the last recorded Estonian guerrilla killed himself on capture in 1978). But in the war's later stages the large-scale anti-German, pro-Soviet partisan movements, driven in part by German brutalities, made a very significant contribution to Soviet operations. The Germans made extensive use of slave labour – seven million people were taken to Germany from occupied territories. Both sides exploited their prisoners of war in similar ways.

Like other invaders before him, Hitler was defeated also by the Soviet Union's climate and its vastness, which stretched his resources and supply lines perilously, whereas the Soviet forces, retreating, came closer to their supply bases. The Soviet command economic system and administrative dictatorship were well-suited to the focused mobilisation of men and materiel, organising the colossal transfer of industry to the rear even as the war began, and the distribution of resources and development of production as it progressed. The Party apparatus undoubtedly played a mobilisational role – for once Party and masses were at one in the war effort. Above all, the Soviet population was fighting a war of survival for its homeland and its people, which most of those involved did with immense courage, sacrifice and endurance. For many the war brought relief from the authorities' terror – despite and because of the dire circumstances, it became possible to talk and act humanly once again. Boris Pasternak wrote that the war 'was a period of vitality and in this sense an untrammelled, joyous restoration of the sense of community with everyone'. In the crisis the government further invoked past Russian heroes of national resistance and the support of the Church, which was now (1943) permitted a Patriarch once more; and previously silenced writers were enlisted for the war effort – Akhmatova's writings and broadcasts elicited a huge response. The army's prestige was raised by the restoration of tsarist ranks and insignia, and downgrading of political commissars. Stalin succeeded in making himself the focus of the national will. For all his absolute authority, and his undoubted qualities which greatly impressed Western observers, he was an amateur military commander, like Hitler, and made serious errors in running his war. But unlike Hitler, Stalin learned from his mistakes and gave latitude to his professional commanders, notably Zhukov; they in turn, as Frederick Kagan puts it, 'continually reinvented' the Red Army, with critical success as the war wore on. (At the peace, Stalin adopted the highest possible title of 'Generalissimus'.)

Besides the 'carrots' of national and religious fervour, the regime applied the stick of well-practised terror methods to the Soviet people, in wartime as in peace. The GULag made a significant contribution to the war effort, through mining, lumbering and construction; prisoners produced 15 per cent of all Soviet ammunition, and uniforms, foodstuffs and other goods. The quarter-million NKVD troops, rarely in action themselves, were ordered to shoot front-line soldiers who retreated or showed 'cowardice', and in 1941 anyone taken by the enemy was declared to be a traitor. As before, the apparatus rooted out domestic sedition wherever it was found; the war effort still did not take precedence over the crushing of thought-crime, real or imaginary. Thus in 1945 artillery Captain Aleksandr Solzhenitsyn's incautious critical letter to a friend had him removed from the Front and into the camps (and on to his Nobel Prize for literature and distinguished oppositional career). Both the Nazi forces and the NKVD practised slaughter in occupied areas; the monstrous German treatment of Soviet civilians was reciprocated by vengeful Soviet troops as they advanced into Germany itself in 1945.

Repression was applied to whole Soviet populations whom Stalin came to regard as Enemies. During hostilities nearly 950,000 Soviet Germans from across the Soviet Union were shipped eastwards to Siberia or Kazakhstan. When Soviet forces recovered the south, Crimean Tatars, Kalmyk and Caucasus mountain peoples – Chechens, Ingush, Karachai, Balkars, Meskhetians – followed the Soviet Germans. Over 1.5 million Chechens were deported, of whom at least a quarter died. The Crimean Tatars, most implicated in collaboration with the enemy, received the harshest treatment; 413 medals were awarded to the NKVD troops involved in the action against the 'traitors'. Further deportations, followed by collectivisation, accompanied the re-establishment of Soviet power in the Baltic States. The hatred sown by these actions and subsequent Soviet settlement policies became a powerful disintegrating factor in the last Soviet years. Brutal treatment was meted out likewise to Soviet soldiers caught in encirclements, and after 1945 to repatriated Soviet prisoners of war. Many POWs and displaced persons were sent back against their will, even when this was not mandated by law. By 1953 nearly 5.5 million had been repatriated; some were shot, many went to camps or forced labour, the rest remained under surveillance. A notorious case was that of 50,000 Cossacks serving on the German side under White *émigré* commanders, who surrendered to the British. Not all were subject to repatriation, and their danger was obvious, but the British authorities tricked them into surrendering their weapons and turned them all over to the NKVD.

RECONSTRUCTION, COLD WAR AND THE DEATH OF STALIN: 1945–53

The Post-War Settlement and Reconstruction

The Great Fatherland War, the victory over all obstacles and the expansion of Soviet armed strength turned the Soviet Union into one of the world's two superpowers. This success justified the Soviet regime in the eyes both of revolutionary idealists, who saw revolution and Soviet power vindicated, and of more sceptical Soviet citizens, who consoled themselves for hardship and terror with the re-establishment of imperial power and world prestige. For many the sense of shared war-time endeavour and joint achievement bound them to the society, country and system which had accomplished this exaltation and triumph. Whatever the motivation, the all-engrossing, desperate, Union-wide war effort and overwhelming military success became the greatest legitimation of the Soviet regime. They validated the potency and permanence of what had been achieved in the first 30 years of Soviet power, and enabled it to survive the fall of Stalinism.

In the post-war international settlement, the USSR absorbed Polish territory, moving its boundary westwards; and Stalin established Communist 'people's democracies' in the countries of Eastern Europe under Soviet control, largely by force. They constituted a buffer zone against the capitalist powers, an extension of Soviet socialism and a further imperial realm. This new Soviet 'outer empire' was directed by *Cominform* (Communist Information Bureau) which replaced Comintern, then by *Comecon* (Council for Mutual Economic Assistance [CMEA] from 1949). Churchill's 'Iron Curtain' speech of 1946 recognised Europe's new divisions, a new confrontation of 'world systems' in which the Soviet Union was joined in 1949 by revolutionary Red China, although the Soviet monopoly of Communist truth was already challenged by the emergence of Tito's ideologically independent Yugoslavia. Soviet armed forces stood as a guarantee of socialist security, and of Soviet order in Eastern Europe. They were also the proof of the Soviet Union's superpower capacity, though its potency in this respect had been seriously undermined by American acquisition of the atomic bomb. That, and the development of long-range delivery systems, made obsolete all previous calculations of territorial gain and loss. A balance was restored with the Soviet acquisition of nuclear capacity in 1949, leading to the Cold War military stalemate in Europe between NATO (North Atlantic Treaty Organisation), established that year, and the Communist forces of the Warsaw Pact (1955).

The weakness of West European economies, and fear of the Soviet expansionism manifested in Stalin's support for Communists in Greece and Iran, prompted the establishment by 1947 of the US

Marshall Plan of economic assistance to Europe, and the Truman Doctrine pledging American support for Western democracies against subversion. Marshall Plan assistance was in principle available to the USSR and its allies too, but such American intrusion into internal affairs was rejected. Instead, the Soviet Union drew maximum advantage and reparations from the areas of Germany it occupied, and started on the restoration of its shattered country from its own resources, with social mobilisation in further Five-Year Plans. Industrial reconstruction progressed rapidly, reaching pre-war levels before the end of the decade; however, the political situation prevented technical modernisation of the sort achieved by post-war Germany or Japan. Essentially industry was recreated with all its 1930s imperfections, especially as the available post-war workforce was underskilled and in short supply. Agriculture in the depressed, underpaid and undermanned collective farms, starved of investment, required much longer to recover; famine recurred in Ukraine and Moldavia in 1946. The colossal urban destruction of the war had compounded 1930s housing shortages, and urban living conditions for the masses remained grim. Cities razed in the fighting were rebuilt quickly, but almost everywhere housing remained of low quality and in acutely short supply, as did foodstuffs and consumer goods: housing and consumer production continued to take second place to heavy industry.

At the same time, ideological limits relaxed during the war were tightened again. The reversion to Russian national values observed in the 1930s, and Stalin's wartime espousal of the heroic Russian past, were now wedded to the role of the Party in the great victory: Russian nationalistic chauvinism, reinforcing the domestic *status quo*, became the official Party line. Stalin renewed the old pressures on intellectuals. As already noted, the Culture Commissar and Leningrad boss Andrei Zhdanov persecuted writers and composers whose work he denounced as 'formalist', decadent and insufficiently Party-minded. While allocating all the resources necessary for urgent nuclear research, Stalin sponsored Lysenko, declared Western cybernetics and the ideas of Einstein to be an 'idealist' delusion, and propounded his own unique theory of linguistics to enhance the international role of the Russian language. Most of the criticised 'cultural workers' were not harmed physically, but lethal terror also reappeared. Senior military commanders were executed on trumped-up charges, although the most distinguished of those attacked, including Zhukov, were only demoted. When Zhdanov died (probably of drink and heart trouble) in 1948, the so-called 'Leningrad affair' directed against his clients by Malenkov brought the execution, among others, of Nikolai Voznesenskii, head of Gosplan and hero of the wartime economic achievement. After the Zionist foundation of Israel in 1948, prominent Jews also found themselves in the firing-line, denounced as 'rootless cosmopolitans' and CIA agents. Solomon Mikhoels, director of the State Jewish (Yiddish) Theatre and chairman of the very successful wartime Jewish Anti-Fascist Committee, was assassinated (then given a state funeral). His theatre and the JA-FC were closed, other Jews were executed for alleged conspiracy. In 1953 a supposed 'doctors' plot' was uncovered: senior Jewish physicians were charged with murdering Zhdanov and planning the deaths of other top politicians. Stalin was apparently meditating further major purges, including among the top leadership; but the rising tide was halted by his sudden death in early March 1953.

Stalinism

From the outset, the Bolsheviks claimed to be building an unprecedented kind of society, and this claim took on new significance with the extraordinary Soviet developments of the 1930s, especially when contrasted with the contemporary capitalist crisis. Moreover from the late 1920s the Soviet regime proclaimed its own version of Soviet reality, assiduously propagated both at home and abroad: an heroic vision which minimised systemic and human weaknesses and described the Soviet present in terms of Marxist-Leninist teleology and crusading popular fervour to build the future: Socialist Realism applied to real life. Like Bolshevik true believers, many outsiders, especially 'fellow-travellers' (sympathisers with Communism), accepted this mythic version of Soviet society: notorious British examples included the distinguished and influential sociologists Beatrice and Sidney Webb, whose two-volume work *Soviet Communism: A New Civilization?*, very favourable to the Soviet Union, appeared in 1935. The concept of the Stalinist USSR as a discrete and superior civilisational form had great attractive power. It was marked after all by its own 1936 'Stalin' constitution and a normative belief system, embodied in the holy writ of the very Stalinist *History of the All-Union Communist Party: A Short Course* (1938); it had its own art, architecture, economic and political organisation. In his striking study of the city of Magnitogorsk, Stephen Kotkin identifies Stalinism (somewhat over-emphatically) as 'a quintessential Enlightenment utopia, an attempt, via the instrumentality of the state, to impose a rational ordering on society' while simultaneously overcoming the class divisions of the nineteenth century. For believers, what Magnitogorsk shared with its American precursor, the steel town of Gary, Indiana (Kotkin argues), 'was a sense that they constituted . . . an entire civilization, *and* that their civilization could rightfully lay claim to being the vanguard of progressive humanity'. But this idea could only prevail at the expense of present reality, through selective Manichaean vision and the class-based moral dehumanisation which it engendered in practice: attitudes whose consequences themselves negated the civilisational and philanthropic impulses also to be found in the Enlightenment.

For the masses of little people, less concerned with Communist belief than the pressures of daily life, 'everyday Stalinism' became, as Sheila Fitzpatrick has demonstrated, a struggle for existence. With collectivisation and the closing down of NEP private enterprise, there began an era of chronic shortages; it became normal to spend hours in queues. Red tape proliferated, incompetent, rude and arbitrary 'yuppie' bureaucrats struggling to master unfamiliar tasks. Repressive mechanisms of state control expanded, more secret police to handle collectivisation and the growing GULag, the renewal of tsarist 'administrative exile', not to mention the Terror. Ubiquitous police informers and lack of privacy in communal flats at home counterpointed the closed frontiers and censorship which isolated ordinary Soviet citizens from the outside world. Personal networks and the *blat* 'economy of favours' (discussed below) became increasingly essential to normal living, and every expedient was explored to mitigate the harshness of the material daily grind and constant pressures from the authorities. In these times, in Fitzpatrick's words: '*Homo sovieticus* was a string-puller, an operator, a time-server, a free-loader, a mouther of slogans, and much more. But above all, he was a survivor.' Indifferent to all this, Stalin consistently pursued a vision of a powerful modern state, and he left the Soviet Union a superpower. It was however a particularly inhumane creation, and one which bore the seeds of its own downfall.

A perennial controversy over the nature of Stalinism has been the question of continuity. Was Stalinism the logical outcome of Lenin's

Bolshevism, or its negation? Lenin himself did not suffer from the personal vanity, vengefulness and paranoia which drove Stalin. Nevertheless, the two shared the same understanding of the nature and necessities of power, and recent archival discoveries have emphasised Lenin's contempt for human life and willingness to use violence to achieve his ends. From this point of view the Stalin Revolution reprised against real or perceived internal obstacles the Civil War and Red Terror waged under Lenin against the Bolsheviks' political enemies; as well as Stalin's personal particularities, it also reflected structural problems in the Soviet system itself. Critics of the continuity thesis have claimed by contrast that Stalinism's defining characteristics were the extremism of Stalin's rupture with the existing order and his emasculation of the Party on which Lenin relied; and that Stalinism was merely one of several possible outcomes after Lenin's death. In fact, here continuity and difference were not mutually exclusive.

In seeking to understand Stalin's Soviet Union, its critics found a usable interpretative model in the concept of totalitarianism. As the 1930s 'Europe of the Dictators' threw up authoritarian regimes from Portugal to Russia, and from Italy to Estonia, ideological differences of Right and Left seemed less significant than some dictators' attempts to control the totality of national life. Like Soviet Communism, the one-party Fascist state imposed exclusive ideological dominance and coercive control of education, media, national borders and international contacts, and attacked persons and institutions which represented alternative values or came between it and its citizens. Its purpose seemed to be to atomise society, penetrate all areas of social activity, and achieve total unmediated mastery of the population. 'Totalitarianism' became the dominant Western explanatory model of the USSR in the early Cold War period. Later scholarship pointed out, however, that such total control was in fact only ever an aspiration: neither Hitler nor Stalin actually achieved their goal. The state's reach and grasp, in the chaotic order created by the state's own actions, were never complete; interest groups and alternative options continued to exist; and despite important successes, the regime failed to eradicate alternative value systems or prevent its own elites and rank-and-file citizens from pursuing private agendas within the parameters of Party policy. Stalin's Terror could not totally destroy the networks on which the Soviet system depended, nor overcome the power of national and religious identity. Moreover, as we have seen, some modern 'revisionist' historiography, focused on the Soviet grass-roots in the Stalin period, has sought to understand the phenomenon in terms of interaction between apex and base, in terms of leadership reactions to social movements: one extreme formulation has even suggested that Stalinism was simply 'the evolution and fruition of a popular consciousness', of a new popular awareness of the social possibilities offered by Communist ideology. Such writing has re-emphasised the extent to which Stalinist policies served the interests of emerging social groups, the new 'yuppie' technical intelligentsia and nomenklatura already discussed, without whose support the system could scarcely have functioned, and who determined the political consensus of the post-Stalin years. Another view has suggested that since (directly or indirectly) these vydvizhentsy were largely of peasant origin, the new political and social culture created by the Stalin Revolution reflected in fact the coarse, conflictual mores of the rural patriarchal household and the peasant village, a peasant colonisation of state power-structures: in Nicholas Vakar's words, 'under Stalin a new revolution was accomplished in the course of the 1930s by which former peasants engrossed political power'. Power now fell to Party members risen from the masses; and peasants who obtained power had no compunction in exploiting other peasants, in village, kolkhoz or Party executive committee. At the apex of power, this was certainly the case of Stalin's principal successor, the former peasant shepherd-lad Nikita Khrushchëv.

7

1953–1991
The Soviet Union as World Power: Retreat from Utopia

The power struggle following Stalin's death was won by Nikita Khrushchëv, undisputed leader from 1957. The dismantling of Stalin's terror system began at once; Khrushchëv initiated public 'de-Stalinisation' in 1956. He fostered international *détente*, presided over Russia's first space and missile triumphs, and supported consumer and agrarian interests. However, his mistakes and unpredictable style of rule alienated his Praesidium colleagues, and he was replaced by Leonid Brezhnev in 1964. The new watchword was stability. Brezhnev and his colleagues grew old together until Brezhnev's death in 1982; finally in 1985 control passed to the younger generation, Mikhail Gorbachëv. Under Brezhnev the Soviet Union came of age as a great power, consolidating its position in Europe and the wider world, and reinforcing order and stability at home, despite the post-terror emergence of dissident voices. However the stagnating economy, growing unrest in the 'outer empire', failure in Afghanistan and the spiralling costs of the Cold War laid bare the fragility of Soviet strength. Gorbachev sought to remedy the situation by reform of sclerotic Party structures; but his relaxing of controls, mobilisation of popular support and renunciation of coercion led to the collapse of the 'outer empire', then of the Union itself.

THE ADVANCE TO 'DEVELOPED SOCIALISM': 1953–85

The New Leadership and De-Stalinisation

Stalin's body was embalmed, and placed with Lenin in the Red Square mausoleum. His death produced mixed emotions; there was widespread fear and uncertainty across the country – what could come next? As in 1924, among the surviving leaders issues of succession and of policy immediately became critical. One of the abiding problems of the Soviet system was the absence of an accepted and effective mechanism of smooth political leadership change and succession. Now the first need of Stalin's heirs – just saved from the imminent threat of further purges – was to ensure their own power position and personal safety, and to prevent any one individual from dominating. The most dangerous potential dictator was the man who controlled the secret police, the clever, sadistic Beria. On 26 June Beria was arrested during a Praesidium meeting, shortly tried (as a 'British spy'!) and shot; senior police officials were also executed. The security police was severely pruned, renamed KGB, and brought more closely under the control of the Central Committee. The leadership's physical safety was assured; and thereafter no disgraced leader was executed.

Besides resolving the issue of terror among the leadership, Stalin's heirs had to resolve it within the Soviet Union as a whole. Stalin had been devoted to the GULag system. In 1952 the Ministry of Internal Affairs which ran it controlled 9 per cent of all capital investment, more than any other single ministry, and the 1951–5 piatiletka proposed to double this. But the camps were increasingly difficult to sustain – a huge, violent and underproductive well of forced labour, which was also growing restive. Camp strikes and uprisings became frequent in the post-war years. In 1952 two million camp workdays were lost in this way; the culmination was the 40-day, highly organised strike at Kengir in Kazakhstan in 1954. Moreover, terror prevented the rational discussion and solution of real problems in society and in the economy at large. The leader most aware of these circumstances, and initially most active in confronting them, was Beria himself, though his purposes remain unclear. Within days of Stalin's death he aborted the most grandiose 'white elephant' camp projects of the piatiletka, amnestied minor prisoners, forbade violence (torture) against persons arrested, and halted investigations of the alleged 'doctors' plot'. After his arrest, many of these policies were continued: 1.2 million prisoners were amnestied in 1953. They included numerous ordinary criminals, whose release unleashed a crime wave (memorably reflected in A. Proshkin's poignant 1987 film *The Cold Summer of '53*). In 1954 the authorities began major changes to the camp system, and started rehabilitation of released detainees, an on-going process which was accelerated by Khrushchëv's denunciation of Stalin in 1956, though the camps were retained in modified form until the end of the Soviet period. Cautious literary signs of liberalisation appeared: Ilia Erenburg's best-selling *The Thaw* (1954) was complemented by Valentin Ovechkin's *Weekdays in the District* (1952–6), detailing the problems, particularly agricultural, of provincial life. Nevertheless, liberalisation was not uncontested, and the process could not go too fast, in case it implicated or destabilised the surviving leadership. 'Socialist legality' was proclaimed, but 'de-Stalinisation' was never a whole-hearted process: those released or rehabilitated had to be satisfied with limited concessions, under fear of further repression.

Initially after 1953 a collective leadership emerged. The power-play between individuals and factions was intertwined with policy issues. The material position in the country was dire. While industry had more or less recovered, agriculture was barely producing enough food for the population – the grain harvest in 1949–53 was below 1913 levels. The war and the terror had skewed the Union's demographic and gender balance. The normal amenities of urban (let alone rural) life were under-resourced or absent; lack of basic consumer goods and services, and the need to queue for hours to acquire even subsistence items, distorted labour productivity.

The policies for overcoming these problems now became part of the battle for power. Initially Malenkov, an advocate of greater emphasis on consumer needs whose base became the Council of Ministers, was in the ascendant; but he and his allies were increasingly overshadowed by Khrushchëv, First Secretary of the Party Central Committee from September 1953. Khrushchëv looked after the interests of the military and heavy industry, and cultivated his base in the Party. All the leadership was agreed on the need to raise agriculture: farm procurement prices almost tripled 1952–8, and farmers' incomes rose faster than those of workers. Khrushchëv was particularly associated with the 'Virgin Lands campaign', agricultural expansion in the vast steppe-lands of Kazakhstan; thousands of volunteers were recruited to farm them – a last mobilisation to parallel Magnitogorsk. The scheme initially was a great success; soon, however, much unprotected ploughed steppe turned into dust-bowls.

Khrushchëv sought to use the issue of Stalin's legacy to outmanoeuvre his rivals. By 1955 the enormities of events under Stalin had been formally documented in detail and he took the risk, against Praesidium opposition, of speaking out about them at the Twentieth Party Congress in February 1956. But revelation was to be strictly controlled. Khrushchëv's 'secret speech' denouncing the cult of personality and Stalin's crimes was delivered at a special closed session of the Congress and only selectively publicised at home and abroad. Moreover, it concentrated primarily on attacks and crimes against the nomenklatura elite, from 1934 onwards, and exculpated current Praesidium members: collectivisation and the Five-Year Plans were thereby endorsed, the wider terror passed over, and the question of other leaders' personal complicity avoided (Khrushchëv himself had butchered Ukraine, as well as Poland). With Stalin dethroned, Lenin was exalted as the beacon of Soviet inspiration: a Communist true believer, Khrushchëv intended the Soviet one-party state to be preserved, in more humane and legal form. The 'secret speech' rapidly became known, and caused sensation. Abroad it sparked major unrest which threatened the Soviet 'outer empire'; at home it promised welcome relief from further terror, but its threat to many established interests also provoked growing opposition. Khrushchëv gained in stature, but was left exposed by the reformist implications of his position, and in 1957 his rivals in the Praesidium sought to sack him. However, outvoted, he turned the tables on them by appealing to the Central Committee, packed with his supporters. They reversed the Praesidium's decision, and it was Khrushchëv's rivals, now dubbed 'the anti-Party group', who were expelled. Humiliation replaced the Stalinist bullet: Molotov became Ambassador to Mongolia, Malenkov manager of a Kazakh power-station. From 1957 until 1964 Khrushchëv was firmly in charge. Initially he was partnered by Marshal Nikolai Bulganin as Chairman of the Council of Ministers, but in 1958 the latter resigned. Collective leadership lapsed: Khrushchëv assumed Bulganin's post as well, engrossing the same positions as the later Stalin. He enjoyed power, used it to reshape society to his own allegedly Leninist vision, and promoted his own cult of personality.

The Khrushchëv Ascendancy, 1957–64

Once he had a free hand, Khrushchëv espoused Malenkov's policy of improving mass standards of living: forthcoming material prosperity should replace terror as a stimulus to mobilisation. In 1956 a bonus-based wage system and relatively relaxed approach to industrial discipline made urban life in a low-wage, shortage economy more bearable – as the joke went: 'They pretend to pay us, and we pretend to work.' Collective-farm procurement prices and peasant incomes continued to rise, although the size of private plots was reduced, and the authorities accelerated a process of amalgamating kolkhozy into larger units. Khrushchëv developed a major apartment-building programme begun after 1953. His prefabricated, poorly constructed tower blocks imposed a drab uniformity on Soviet towns, and were mocked as *khrushchëby* (a cross of 'Khrushchëv' with *trushchoby* 'slums') – more lasting but no less problematic than the 1960s tower-block flats of urban Britain. But while the living-space allowance per person remained very small, quantitatively the policy was very successful – between 1955 and 1964 the Soviet housing stock nearly doubled, and rent and utility charges were kept extremely low (Figure 16). This was particularly important since by 1960, for the first time in history, as many Soviet people lived in towns as in the countryside (rural dwellers constituted 52 per cent in 1959, 44 per cent in 1970, 38 per cent in 1980). Foodstuff production also gradually improved, and the Seven-Year Plan inaugurated in 1959 achieved notable results: GNP grew by 58 per cent, industrial output by 84 per cent, that of consumer goods by 60 per cent. De-Stalinisation was paralleled by the doctrine of international 'peaceful coexistence'; limited contacts with foreigners became possible, and even travel abroad for the favoured few.

In 1961 Khrushchëv presided over the new Programme for the Twenty-Second Party Congress, which declared the Soviet Union to be now a 'state of all the people': a further move away from Stalinism. Stalin's corpse was banished from the mausoleum to lie with lesser leaders by the Kremlin wall; Stalingrad was renamed Volgograd. The Congress went on to set precise consumer production targets, spoke of overtaking the USA, and proclaimed that full Communism would be reached by 1980. There was talk, too, of the emergence of a 'New Soviet Man' embodying higher civilisational virtues, as Soviet society matured. These goals would require greater

Figure 16 New apartment blocks, Moscow (1960s)
From the personal collection of the author.

social inclusion and engagement, and further development of socialist legality. The judicial system was accordingly revamped, empha-
sising due process of law and introducing lay elements such as
non-professional 'comrades' courts' and *druzhinniki*, auxiliary civilian street patrols; but strict controls and the informer system
remained – Russia was still a police state.

To restore the prestige and effectiveness of the Party, emasculated
by Stalin, and to pave the way for greater local administration in the
economic sphere, Khrushchëv reorganised industrial and Party structures. In 1957 the functions of central ministries were devolved to
105 regional economic councils (*sovnarkhozy*), to be headed by
Party committees, divided between agriculture and industry. This
displeased the ministry officials. It gave the Party a powerful role,
but cadres assigned to lower-status agriculture were inevitably
offended. More upsetting still was the ruling that all Party posts
should rotate: a move towards efficiency and accountability which,
however, threatened nomenklatura privilege and security of tenure.

Further improvement in agriculture (discussed below) was still
essential. Khrushchëv continued state support, with generally positive

effects. However, autocratic attempts to micro-manage the country-side from above, as in his misconceived maize campaign, which ignored expert advice and sowed maize in very unsuitable places, were counter-productive, as was his continued reliance on the charlatan Lysenko (Lysenko finally fell in 1965). Moreover, changes to the organisation of kolkhozy caused hardship, and disruption of production; although output of foodstuffs had increased considerably since 1953, two bad harvests in 1962 and 1963 took agricultural output below that of 1958. Price rises reflecting increased procurement costs were passed on in part to urban consumers; in 1962 in Novocherkassk they coincided with disadvantageous changes to worker pay rates, which caused riots – 23 protesters were shot; unrest also occurred elsewhere. Confronted by the working class it claimed to represent, the government was forced to import expensive foreign grain, an unpalatable measure which soon became a regular practice.

The government also faced problems in the field of ideology and expression. After the unofficial wartime concordat between the state and the various Churches, the ideological 1948 clamp-down had equally affected religion. Now the revelations of 1956 and release of camp prisoners sentenced for their belief led to an upsurge of religious activity. As a militant Communist atheist, Khrushchëv attacked such heterodoxy. From 1958 a wide-ranging campaign curtailed parish priests' jurisdiction, constrained Church incomes, closed numerous churches, repressed hierarchs and ordinary believers, and banned some confessions altogether, while civil ceremonies were devised to replace such religious rites as marriage and baptism: in 1959 a first Communist Palace of Weddings opened in Leningrad. Official treatment of Orthodox and non-Orthodox believers was not identical; and when the anti-religious drive slackened in 1963–4, dissident religious groups such as the Baptists remained a major focus of state attention.

Similar discipline was applied to the world of the arts. After 1954 the 'creative intelligentsia' had acquired new freedoms in the 'thaw'. Jazz musicians appeared, and experimental painters. Full censorship remained in place, but publication of literary works became slightly easier. The young poets Yevgenii Yevtushenko, Andrei Voznesenskii and Bella Akhmadulina produced verse which was excitingly political and apolitical. In 1956 Vladimir Dudintsev's novel *Not by Bread Alone* attacked industrial corruption and bureaucracy; and the war became a major and approved literary theme. But others such as Akhmatova and Pasternak remained in shadow, and the latter was pressured into refusing the Nobel Prize when it was awarded him in 1958 after *Dr Zhivago* (published in Italy in 1957). Solzhenitsyn's sensational novella *One Day in the Life of Ivan Denisovich* (1962), a brilliantly understated account of camp life, was the first direct publication on the GULag. It was allowed to appear because it bolstered Khrushchëv's policy of the moment, and was soon the subject of retrospective censorship. Policy was becoming stricter. A 'parasite law' of 1961 prescribed penalties for anyone deemed not gainfully employed – later used against the talented young poet and subsequent Nobel laureate Iosif Brodskii. In 1963 Khrushchëv personally visited a Moscow exhibition of modern art, and compared the canvasses to daubings with a donkey's tail. His successors were even less liberally inclined: after his fall in 1964, they staged show trials of uncompromising intellectuals, the first of a new generation of 'dissidents'. De-Stalinisation in the arts, as in other fields, ground to a stop.

Khrushchëv saw himself as a man of the people, and rejoiced in being a *praktik*, a do-er not an intellectual. He wished to create a more humane society; he presided over a lessening of internal repression and international tension, and considerable improvement in post-war standards of living. Nevertheless as leader he remained authoritarian and presumed to dictate his own opinion on all matters. His management was erratic, and autocratically wilful – he was accused of 'voluntarism' and of 'hare-brained schemes'. Khrushchëv alienated important constituencies. Rioting workers and displaced peasants were not his friends; more importantly, disgruntled industrial managers and insecure Party cadres withdrew their support. His attacks on Stalinism alarmed the KGB, while his consumerist policies and emphasis on nuclear rather than conventional defence offended the heavy industry and military lobbies. The nomenklatura were not getting what they wanted. He gained kudos from Russia's space achievements, and Yurii Gagarin's first manned space-flight in 1961, but his disruption of Party life, his style of management, his failures and coarseness, and elements of his foreign policy, dismayed the elite. The Praesidium finally moved against him in October 1964, and in a semi-*coup* he was voted out: his 'request to retire' was granted. He himself later claimed that his greatest success was to have produced a peaceable change of leader.

The Brezhnev Period, 1964–82: Stability and Stagnation

Khrushchëv was succeeded as First Secretary by Leonid Brezhnev, with Aleksei Kosygin as Chairman of the Council of Ministers. Many of Khrushchëv's changes were reversed. Brezhnev built up his own clientele in the (now renamed) Politburo, and emerged as *primus inter pares* among his colleagues. In his later years something of a personality cult developed; but Kosygin retained his position until his death in 1980, and the leadership remained largely collective or oligarchical. At the Twenty-Third Party Congress in 1966 Brezhnev was elevated to General Secretary (a title used by Stalin), and 11 years later he became Chairman of the Praesidium of the Supreme Soviet as well, titular head of state. He was showered with inflated military and civil honours, including the Lenin Prize for Literature following publication in 1973 of his ghost-written and egocentric memoirs. But his personal power was less than that of Khrushchëv, and Brezhnev made a point of leading from the middle and of conciliating his Party base. His watchword was 'stability of cadres'; turnover of officials at all levels of the Party was slow, and unlike Khrushchëv the leadership was increasingly content to leave specialists to work without interference. Brezhnev indulged in nepotism, and tolerated corruption; he and his colleagues grew old together, a gerontocracy. His health began to fail from 1973, and in his last years he was largely incapacitated; but he died in office in 1982. Neither of his next two successors, Yurii Andropov (1982–4) and Konstantin Chernenko (1984–5), survived their appointment by more than 15 months.

Brezhnev was above all an *apparatchik*; indifferently educated, 10 thinker, he was a talented organiser. Under his regime the leadership emphasised order, control and traditional priorities. De-Stalinisation was partially reversed. While huge investment in agriculture and food subsidies continued, military expenditure was increased and established economic patterns maintained: measures to promote greater economic flexibility introduced by Kosygin in 1965–6 petered out. Life for ordinary citizens who toed the expected lines was uneventful, and living standards rose gradually – political quiescence was bought with a modicum of material improvement: an unspoken 'social contract' between people and Party. By the 1980s, most households could aspire to a refrigerator and television set; but private cars remained scarce and there were periodic shortages of

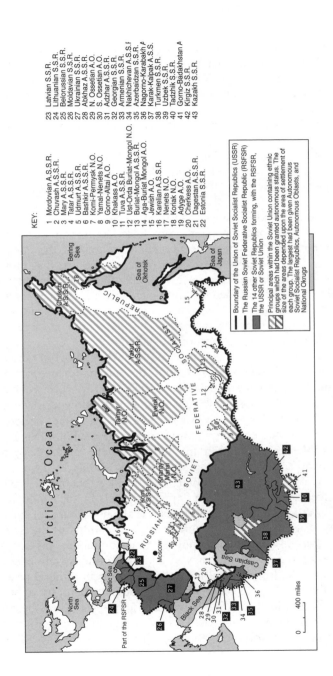

KEY:

1 Mordovian A.S.S.R.
2 Chuvash A.S.S.R.
3 Mary A.S.S.R.
4 Tatar A.S.S.R.
5 Udmurt A.S.S.R.
6 Bashkir A.S.S.R.
7 Komi-Permyak N.O.
8 Yamal-Nenets N.O.
9 Gorno-Altai A.O.
10 Khakass A.O.
11 Tuva A.S.S.R.
12 Ust-Orda Buriat-Mongol N.O.
13 Buriat-Mongol A.S.S.R.
14 Aga-Buriat Mongol A.O.
15 Jewish A.O.
16 Karelian A.S.S.R.
17 Nenets N.O.
18 Koriak N.O.
19 Adyge A.O.
20 Cherkess A.O.
21 Dagestan A.S.S.R.
22 Estonia S.S.R.

23 Latvian S.S.R.
24 Lithuanian S.S.R.
25 Belorussian S.S.R.
26 Moldavian S.S.R.
27 Ukrainian S.S.R.
28 Abkhaz A.S.S.R.
29 N. Ossetian A.O.
30 S. Ossetian A.O.
31 Adzhar A.S.S.R.
32 Georgian S.S.R.
33 Armenian S.S.R.
34 Nakhichevan A.S.S.R.
35 Azerbaidzan S.S.R.
36 Nagorno-Karabakh A.O.
37 Karak-Kalpak A.S.S.R.
38 Turkmen S.S.R.
39 Uzbek S.S.R.
40 Tadzhik S.S.R.
41 Gorno-Badakhstan A.O.
42 Kirgiz S.S.R.
43 Kazakh S.S.R.

|||	Boundary of the Union of Soviet Socialist Republics (USSR)
▬	The Russian Soviet Federative Socialist Republic (RSFSR)
▨	The 14 other Soviet Republics forming, with the RSFSR, the USSR or Soviet Union
▨	Principal areas within the Soviet Union containing ethnic groups which had been granted autonomous status. The size of the areas depended upon the area of settlement of each group. The largest had been given Autonomous Soviet Socialist Republics, Autonomous Oblasts, and National Okrugs

Map 11   The Soviet Union in 1970

© Sir Martin Gilbert, *The Routledge Atlas of Russian History* (London and New York, 2002), no. 144

different foodstuffs. The lot of the collective farmers was further improved. Religion and natural sciences, though not the social sciences or literature, gained more freedom of manoeuvre. In foreign affairs, despite the crushing of Czechoslovakia in 1968, '*détente*' with the West brought the triumph of the 1975 Helsinki Agreement, ratifying the post-war European settlement and the USSR's borders, and lasted until the invasion of Afghanistan in 1979. At home, Khrushchëv's promise of Communism by 1980 was quietly forgotten, and the USSR was said to be at the – indeterminate – stage of 'developed socialism'. In 1977 a new constitution was promulgated to reflect this stage of development; among other things it re-emphasised the leading role of the Party in Soviet life. The leadership sought to coopt the population by encouraging Party membership – numbers of members rose dramatically, making the Party as an organisation, however, more heterogeneous and less disciplined, and encouraging the further growth within it of networks and patronage chains. As terror receded, dissenting and dissident voices became louder; but they had more resonance abroad than at home and were easily contained by police methods. The population at large was preoccupied in making the best of the daily grind.

However, apparent tranquillity masked decline. Not only did the Soviet Union fall increasingly behind the international economic and technological leaders, despite its successes in space, rocketry and military technology, but economic growth slowed to almost nothing: the later Brezhnev years became known as the 'period of stagnation' – in the economy and in society as a whole. Domestic social problems and inter-ethnic tensions were suppressed; but international comparisons, the rise of the 'Solidarity' workers' movement in Poland, and military failure in Afghanistan eroded confidence. Social dysfunction expressed itself in such indicators as corruption, cynicism, high rates of alcohol abuse or infant mortality. The fundamental problem was the inability of the Soviet system – Party, society and economy – to accommodate productive change. By the time of Brezhnev's death these issues were becoming pressing. Andropov, intelligent, though with an illiberal past as head of the KGB 1967–82, attempted to address them by tightening social discipline, but died before any long-term results became apparent; Chernenko, untalented, conservative and sick, did nothing. The task of resolving the crisis fell to his successor, Mikhail Gorbachëv.

The Post-Stalin Economy

The 'Stalin revolution' had generated a centrally planned 'command' economy based upon state ownership of all material resources and upon discipline and coercion in implementation: a system particularly suited to rapid deployment of resources for extensive growth. Its brain was Gosplan, and its nervous system the Party chain of command: the political and administrative network of the Party was essential to its functioning. Its fundamental mechanism was fulfilment of the centrally defined targets of the Five-Year Plans, usually set in measures of number, weight, size or volume. Consequently it provided few incentives to optimise other desirable goals – product quality, consumer satisfaction, cost efficiency or elimination of waste and pollution. It rejected competition and choice, although in practice elements of market relations remained within it. Such elements were to be found in employment, or in private individuals' consumption decisions, and most markedly in foreign trade, also in the domestic 'private sector', those areas of domestic economic activity where individuals could operate outside the planned system – the black or shadow economy, personal services, peasant household plots. In the 1970s–1980s the 'private sector' accounted altogether for perhaps 10 per cent of GDP.

Such domestic 'market relations' remained in fact an essential factor without which the command system would not have functioned; and they had far-reaching social as well as economic effects. Informal mechanisms developed parallel to and parasitic upon the official economy. From the outset, many enterprises had found it essential to even out defects of official coordination and raw material supply by employing 'fixers' (*tolkachi*), who bartered and made unofficial deals with other economic units. Individuals likewise turned to *blat*, the 'economy of favours', to acquire goods and services which were ostensibly available but in practice simply unobtainable through official retail and service channels. Access to such things largely depended upon personal connections and the ability to reciprocate favours received, usually by diverting state property or resources from the workplace. This semi-legal economic activity matched the social-political situation where ostensible high principles masked the reality of non-legal police control. In both social and economic life, therefore, personal networks were essential: these relationships privileged private friendships and trust, and unofficial connections, over public mechanisms and state channels, and fostered cynicism and mistrust towards official law and public values. These factors continued to operate up to and beyond the end of the Soviet Union.

The Soviet planned economy worked (with varying success) from the 1930s until the 1980s, providing macro-economic stability, continuous growth of output, full employment and job security, and the bare essentials of daily life. The colossal central planning exercise involved some million production units producing 20 million categories of goods – for all its imperfections, a remarkable achievement. After 1953 terror was removed as an economic incentive, and the Soviet Union began to open up to the wider world, developing stronger commercial relations with both Comecon partners and Western economies. Material support for Third-World regimes (for example, buying Cuban sugar) likewise became a factor in economic activity. At home, successive governments became more responsive to social factors and consumer needs, and to consumer dissatisfaction; in the 1970s and 1980s they also showed themselves economically sensitive to political developments in the Comecon countries, particularly Poland. After Stalin systemic discipline gradually slackened, allowing marginally greater latitude to producers, something also necessitated by the growing complexity of the economy.

However, the Soviet economic regime was deeply inertial and inflexible, and systemically inefficient. It disregarded product quality and aptness for purpose, and encouraged extravagant inputs of labour and materials. It offered few incentives to innovation. Introduction of new methodologies, machinery and products usually brought ministries and plant managers only trouble – short-term diseconomies, disruption of production and therefore threats to plan fulfilment and attendant bonuses: most were correspondingly unenthusiastic. This disinclination to respond positively to change remained the case despite the growth of Soviet research and development, and the wide-ranging purchase of foreign technology and plant, widely practised in the 1930s and renewed on a large scale from 1958 by Khrushchëv, especially in his drive to modernise the chemical industry. Machine imports remained substantial, but direct foreign investment and licensing were excluded. The logical conclusion of technology importation was the 'turn-key' industrial project, complete plants supplied and installed by foreign contractors. In 1965–70, for instance, Fiat engineers built the vast Volga Automobile

Plant (*VAZ*) at Toliatti on the Volga (a brand new city named after the Italian Communist leader Togliatti), in the process training thousands of Soviet operatives in Russia and in Italy; the contractor finally handed over a fully operational industrial complex.

The VAZ project was constructed under Brezhnev's administration, which in its first years was not economically unsuccessful, building on the developments and investments of the 1950s. Only after 1973 did slowing growth become a matter of concern, and even then growth did not cease altogether: from 1973 to 1982 *per capita* GDP rose on average 0.9 per cent annually. Western economies also slowed around 1973, largely as a result of the savage OPEC oil-price increases of 1973–4. (The Soviet slow-down was, however, the more worrying because the USSR was a significant oil exporter and therefore a beneficiary of the price rise. The sharp fall in world oil prices of 1986 would become a factor in Gorbachëv's economic problems.) Hard-currency earnings from raw materials, especially oil, gas and gold, were a major part of the Soviet economic equation; and both resource depletion and Soviet reliance on volatile export markets have been suggested as contributory causes of the economy's difficulties in the 1970s and 1980s. Another crucial and endemic defect was the weakness of agriculture.

After 1953 the Stalinist focus on heavy industry was revised to give greater consideration to consumer needs, including food production and therefore agriculture – although the heavy-industrial and machine-tool sector, allied to military production, always remained a dominant interest group within the economy. The importance of food in Soviet consumption budgets must be emphasised. In a low-wage economy where basic urban utilities and services (housing, domestic power and water, medical care, transport, education) were provided by the state at low or no cost, food loomed very large in individual and family outlay; its provision, at reasonable prices, formed an essential part of the unspoken Soviet 'social contract'. And if more food was to be produced for the cities, the plight of the countryside had also to be addressed. The inhuman Stalinist exploitation of the peasantry was replaced by policies which sought to take some account of their needs, of their rights, and of rationality in economic exchange between countryside, town and state. Under Brezhnev, government finally gave collective farmers state benefits comparable to those long enjoyed by urban workers: in the 1960s (low) pensions were introduced, followed by a guaranteed minimum wage and health insurance – private-plot size restrictions were also reduced. A new Kolkhoz Charter promulgated in 1969 still denied kolkhozniki the right to own a horse, or automatically to receive an internal passport; but over the following decade the passport position improved, and by 1980 collective-farm workers had finally acquired the same legal status and right of movement within the Soviet Union as their urban neighbours.

This was not enough by itself, however, to transform Soviet agriculture. As we have seen, state investment in agriculture increased greatly after 1953, and went on rising throughout the post-Stalin period: in the late 1960s it stood at 18 per cent, a decade later over 25 per cent, of the total. This did achieve a considerable increase in production. Nevertheless, food imports had to be continued; by the late 1970s they absorbed some 40 per cent of hard-currency expenditure, and in 1981 Brezhnev declared 'the food problem' to be the central issue of the new Eleventh Five-Year Plan (1981–5). Extensive methods of increasing inputs were pursued to their limits in the 1960s and 1970s, with better farm inventory, improved seed, fertilisers, and more; but by the 1980s higher investment was producing diminishing returns. From 1950 onwards a policy of farm amalgamation into larger units was adopted – collective farm numbers fell from 250,000 in 1949 to 69,000 in 1958 and to 36,000 in 1965; many kolkhozniki were moved into state farms. But the increasing size of the units, dictated by hopes of economies of scale as well as considerations of political and logistical control, was too big for optimum production organisation within the existing system; at the other end of the scale, the extremely productive private plots were too small. In any case, as the economist Philip Hanson indicates, the agricultural sector suffered from the same inherent defects as its industrial counterpart:

> The running of Soviet state and collective farms was, with perhaps a handful of exceptions . . . , not concerned with good husbandry. It was all about coping with orders from above that were ill-informed and internally inconsistent, in an environment where there was no incentive to economise on inputs, skills shortages were desperate, the supervision of huge numbers of farm employees was unavoidably patchy, and most of the peasants found work on their private plots a prime necessity.

Moreover, this was accompanied from 1955 by appointment of a new generation of collective-farm chairmen, outsiders, usually ex-army or Party men, who became authoritarian professional managers, closer to the regional authorities than to the peasants. Relations between the new chairmen and their farm workers were compared in one 1960s eye-witness account to those of Imperial noble landlords and their barshchina serfs. The process of improvement in the countryside moved slowly: although catching up, the kolkhozy still lagged far behind in terms of welfare, amenities and education, and energetic young peasants left their villages for better career opportunities in the cities. The structure of Soviet agriculture, and the external *diktat*, bureaucratic micro-management and autocratic local leadership by which it was run, continued to deprive the peasantry of incentive and autonomy, and to undercut the state's ability to feed its people from its own resources. From 1981 the size of the grain harvest became a state secret.

Under Khrushchëv and Brezhnev the government of the 'peasant state' had thus become more benign, but only relatively so. As in Spittler's model (pp. 93, 103 above), peasants adopted attitudes, lifestyle and behaviour which best adapted their life to their circumstances and their continuing enforced subjection. They felt little responsibility for the property or the profitability of the collective and routinely resisted or negotiated the attempts at mobilisation of the farm chairman, who as the responsible manager had to run the kolkhoz as best he could and represent it to outside authority: a process vividly described in Fëdor Abramov's 1963 novella *The Dodgers*. The consequences of Stalinist dekulakisation, collectivist restructuring and coercive exploitation remained, until the end of the Soviet Union and beyond it, a grossly inefficient agricultural sector and a peasantry set apart from urban society, lacking motivation, initiative or entrepreneurial energy and concerned primarily with its own subsistence. The need to import food became a serious factor in Soviet international relations.

INTERNATIONAL RELATIONS OF A SUPERPOWER

During the war the Allied leaders had agreed to set up an effective international successor organisation to the League of Nations. The 1941 Atlantic Charter and the 1942 Declaration by United Nations presaged the drafting of the United Nations Charter in San Francisco in 1945. But neither the USA nor the USSR was prepared to rely only on the UNO for security and stability. The deadly rivalry of the two competing political and ideological systems asserted itself, and relative wartime cordiality gave way to Churchill's 'Iron Curtain', tensions in partitioned Germany, and the 1948–9 Soviet blockade of West Berlin. Russia's subjection of Eastern Europe and creation of Comecon (CMEA) was paralleled by the establishment of the North Atlantic Treaty Organisation in 1949; and the integration into NATO of the new West German state in 1955 prompted the setting-up of the Warsaw Pact organisation (1955–6). The Berlin crisis was resolved without 'hot' military action, and direct great-power relations subsided into the stalemate of the Cold War; but the Western presence in partitioned Berlin made it a permanent flashpoint and loophole, which the Soviet side was constrained to screen off in 1961 with the Berlin Wall. Over the next four decades the nuclear and conventional military confrontation between East and West would be mitigated by the doctrine of Mutual Assured Destruction and repeated steps to agree international limitations on military development and capacity. The nearest approach to war was the Cuban missile crisis of 1962, when Khrushchëv tried to station nuclear missiles on America's Caribbean neighbour, taken over by Fidel Castro in 1959; US pressure forced their withdrawal, in return for a promise not to invade the island. But fierce Soviet–Western competition for influence, resources, and regional and global dominance shaped world affairs, and found violent expression in proxy conflicts, of which the first was the Korean War, 1950–1.

The glacial late-Stalin years gave way to 'peaceful coexistence' under Khrushchëv, who faced once more the old Soviet dilemma of competing revolutionary and diplomatic objectives. The new leader undertook not to export revolution by military means, and declared that the USSR would 'bury' its capitalist rivals in peaceful competition. Improved US–USSR relations gave greater security and valuable commercial opportunities, and enabled Khrushchëv to modify domestic policy priorities. The USSR built up its military establishment in an effort to achieve and maintain parity with the USA, while also actively pursuing *détente* and international security through arms-limitation measures. In Europe the Kremlin had two specific security goals – consolidation of the post-war settlement which had redrawn international borders, and maintenance of control over the

USSR's new satellites. Soviet diplomacy worked towards the first goal by seeking to formalise the division of Germany, and maintaining pressure on Berlin: the German Federal Republic was recognised diplomatically, but so was the German Democratic Republic, which the Western Allies insisted on viewing simply as the Soviet zone of occupation. A breakthrough here came only in 1969, when the new *Ostpolitik* of Willi Brandt, Federal Germany's first Social Democratic Chancellor, opened the way to the Helsinki accords of 1975; these acknowledged existing European state borders and created a permanent Council for Security and Cooperation in Europe (CSCE), thereby completing the post-war settlement in Europe. Brezhnev's triumph was diminished by the inclusion in the accords of human rights as specified in the UN Charter – an irritation rather than a serious problem for the Soviet and Eastern European police states. The second goal, of control over the 'People's Democracies', was achieved by a combination of military force and economic integration: the Red Army put down opposition in East Berlin in 1953, Hungary in 1956 and (with Warsaw Pact allies) Czechoslovakia in 1968, while economic ties were developed through commercial exchange, pricing arrangements and Soviet supply of raw materials, especially oil – although individual Comecon countries retained control of their own economic planning. The Prague events of 1968 gave rise to the 'Brezhnev doctrine': a declaration that the Soviet Union reserved the right to intervene militarily wherever established Communist governments were under threat. The possibility of military intervention slowed changes arising in Poland from the 1970s onwards, and only the Kremlin's acknowledgement that it would not use force broke the dam holding back regime change in Eastern Europe in 1989.

The Brezhnev doctrine was also invoked in 1979, in support of the new Communist regime in Afghanistan: but the application of the doctrine outside of the Soviet 'outer empire' provoked a fierce Western response, including trade sanctions – the suspension of grain supplies – and the boycotting of the 1980 Moscow Olympics. The Afghan conflict soon became in any case a disaster, the Soviet Vietnam, an unwinnable war against Islamic guerrilla opposition which alienated opinion at home and finally had to be ended by Gorbachëv with the withdrawal of Soviet forces in 1988.

Czechoslovakia, the Brezhnev doctrine and Afghanistan were all aspects of Soviet relations with the rest of the Communist world. The most difficult partner in this respect was China. Mao Tsedong's revolution in 1949 was a great fillip to world Communism, but soon brought disagreements and rivalry with the USSR, since China was a potentially powerful direct neighbour with its own geopolitical interests, and a leadership not disposed to subordinate itself to Moscow either politically or ideologically. China acquired nuclear weapons in 1964. From 1958, as Khrushchëv pursued *détente* with what Mao called the American 'paper tiger', relations deteriorated, leading finally to a complete ideological break and serious Sino–Soviet border clashes in 1969–70. Things were only patched up in the 1970s and further *rapprochement* achieved under Gorbachëv, after the Chinese themselves had become more 'revisionist'. Soviet domination of the 'socialist camp' was equally challenged by the independent stance of Tito's newly-Communist Yugoslavia, which was expelled from the Cominform in 1948; partial reconciliation followed in 1955. Albania and Romania also refused total compliance, as did some elements of Western Communist Parties (notably Italy's) after 1968.

The other area of Soviet endeavour in this period was the unaligned Third World. Opposition to 'imperialism' involved support for national-liberation movements and socialist regimes, which might become clients as well as markets for Soviet exports and arms sales. No vital issues of Soviet security were at stake in these cases, only the larger competition with the capitalist world, and the projection of Soviet power across the globe. The post-war decolonisation of Africa and Asia offered favourable opportunities. The USSR gave some support to North Vietnam, patronised Patrice Lumumba in the Congo, supported the Marxist MPLA in Angola. India received particularly favourable treatment. In the Americas Soviet support kept Castro's Cuba afloat against US embargos; later, the Nicaraguan Sandinistas were well received in Moscow. Not all such relations were successful: Egypt, for instance, recipient of considerable aid, ultimately turned its back on its benefactor. With Israel the USSR initially had mixed relations. Having recognised the new state in 1948, Stalin briefly broke relations during the anti-Jewish campaign of his last years. They were definitively broken again after the Seven-Day War in 1967, when Moscow firmly adopted a pro-Arab, anti-Zionist stance, while Soviet Jewish dissidence began to grow. A movement for emigration, hindered by the Soviet authorities, soon became an issue in USSR–US relations.

Between 1971 and 1991 over 750,000 Soviet Jews emigrated, principally to Israel and the USA, especially after the lifting of restrictions under Gorbachëv.

REGIME AND SOCIETY

Dilemmas of Progress

The reining-in of the Stalin terror apparatus in 1953 confronted the Soviet leadership and elite with a new situation. From the beginning of Soviet power, the regime had imposed its authority, maintained order and mobilised society and the economy by a combination of ideology, idealism, control and coercion. Popular belief in and enthusiasm for Marxism-Leninism were never universal, and were widely shaken by Khrushchëv's denunciation of Stalin's abuses which promised to eschew such absolute repression for the future. To maintain its moral authority the post-Stalin regime had to demonstrate its practical competence as well as the reality of its ideological schema: hence the constant emphasis on material achievement and on growing world power. Soviet citizens, if otherwise sceptical, could be enthused by more and better consumer goods, and by superpower status and old-fashioned feelings of national superiority. When Gagarin triumphed over the laggard American space programme, in public the military significance of the achievement was overshadowed by the Soviet triumph over capitalist competitors, and few questioned whether the resources involved would have been better spent on terrestrial needs. Nevertheless, it became increasingly difficult to maintain Communist belief among the population, and the mature years of international Soviet power, the 1960s–1980s, were the period when scepticism and cynicism became established.

The growing problem was both practical and ideological. As a result of good Soviet educational provision, the population was becoming increasingly well educated. Better communications, and gradually expanding foreign travel, including to other Communist states, meant that external ideas and news sources became more accessible, despite official attempts to jam Western radio stations and restrictions on such things as copying machines. (During the abortive 1991 *coup* Gorbachëv listened to the BBC World Service to discover what was happening in Moscow.) Failed promises and the revelations of de-Stalinisation, limited though the latter was, had undermined the

Party's infallibility and its message. These factors together subverted the official line: there were ever-more troubled and questioning believers, and unbelievers – though Soviet citizens were well versed in necessary public forms of expression. Nomenklatura children were increasingly interested in Western pop music and 'cool', prestigious Western jeans, rather than reading Marx or building Communism. Pride in genuine Soviet achievements, the constant indoctrination of official discourse, continuing KGB omnipresence, and the exhausting daily grind, maintained conformity among the majority population. But the lessening of post-Stalin coercion made it possible – whether for undisciplined workers, local Party bosses, shadow-economy entrepreneurs, or independent-minded intellectuals – to flout regime expectations and still survive. Moreover, for the regime too, personal initiative and confrontation with the truth remained desirable within limits, for social and economic progress. Dudintsev's *Not by Bread Alone* (1956), with its deliberately metaphysical title and its depiction of the ultimately successful struggles of an idealistic inventor, showed that heroism consisted in confronting a corrupt and self-seeking local establishment in the cause of truth and technological advance. This local establishment itself had to find survival strategies in the new circumstances, in which it relied heavily on the established tradition of networking and patronage. The Soviet regime in some ways relived the cycles of 'revolution from above' experienced by its Imperial predecessors – great power status achieved through Petrine coercion and Catherine II's consolidation was followed by a failing struggle to combine the maintenance of authoritarian ideological control with the structural requirements of further social, technical and economic progress. The outcomes were those of Nicholas I: as we shall see, like Alexander II Gorbachëv inherited economic and social dysfunction, imperial overstretch, and an increasingly polarised and disenchanted elite, and both rulers sought to meet these challenges by wide-ranging but controlled change within the existing system. Gorbachëv was perhaps more enlightened and adventurous, but no less a prisoner of his own world-view than Alexander II. He has also been compared to the 'Enlightened Despots' – Soviet 'Enlightened Absolutism' was no more productive in the long term than that of the eighteenth century in resolving the tension between authoritarian social control and socio-economic prosperity and growth.

Dissident Values

The winding-down of terror allowed a resurgence of the critical intelligentsia tradition in the Soviet Union. It had in fact never been fully destroyed, but had fallen relatively silent in the Stalin years. Now, in the face of less fatal repression, dissenting voices re-emerged. The older generation still survived in such towering figures as Pasternak and Akhmatova, who had only ever minimally accommodated themselves to Soviet norms, while both rejecting emigration. Akhmatova lived an essentially non-Soviet morality, bound in with her personal ethics and Orthodox religious belief, often at great personal and material cost. During the Terror, in a despairing (and temporarily successful) attempt to help her imprisoned son, she had penned a letter to Stalin. Otherwise she stood aloof. When even manuscripts were vulnerable, her poems were learnt by heart, committed to memory by herself and her friends: this was how she preserved *Requiem*, her response to the Stalin terror years, published fully in the Soviet Union only in 1987. After her renewed public presence during the war, and Zhdanov's anathema of 1946, she remained a monument to integrity and alternative humane values, rehabilitated only shortly before her death in 1966.

From 1953 onwards, as already noted, cautious new voices were able to make themselves heard in official publications, while public literary politics reflected the political tensions between liberals and conservatives. But alternative publicity strategies soon appeared; increasingly from the mid-1950s hand- and typewritten works began to circulate, developing in the mid-1960s into the full-blown phenomenon of *samizdat*, 'self-publishing', through which dissidents pursuing a range of causes challenged authority. Perhaps the best-known samizdat journal was the 'Chronicle of Current Events', which from 1968 to 1982 regularly recorded events concerning human rights in the USSR, through 64 issues of up to 200 pages each. Significant works of literature and music (*magnitizdat*, 'magnetic [tape] publishing') which circulated in this way included the novels of Solzhenitsyn and the popular subversive ballads of Aleksandr Galich, Vladimir Vysotskii and Bulat Okudzhava.The parallel to samizdat was *tamizdat* ('publishing over there', i.e. abroad), which became increasingly possible as contacts grew with the outside world. The first major tamizdat case was Pasternak's *Dr Zhivago*. The conviction and sentence of Andrei Siniavskii and Yulii Daniel in 1966 for publishing abroad material deemed 'defamatory' to the USSR marked the ideologically repressive stance of the new Brezhnev regime, and the beginning of sustained dissidence which lasted in a variety of forms until Gorbachëv's perestroika. Such groups eschewed violence, and usually demanded that the regime honour its own proclaimed (but not observed) democratic and legal standards; and they were prepared to suffer for their actions. In the late 1960s a 'Human Rights Movement' developed in reaction to regime policies; it was further stimulated by the human rights prescriptions of the 1975 Helsinki Agreement and the terms of the 1977 constitution. Several active rights groups were established in the RSFSR and other republics, including Helsinki Monitoring Groups and a 'Working Commission to Investigate the Use of Psychiatry for Political Purposes'. Environmental damage provoked by careless industrial development gave rise to environmental groups, and unsuccessful attempts were made to advance the ideals of feminism and of free trades unions. Dissidents were active in other arts besides literature: the sculptor Ernst Neizvestnyi, the painter Oskar Rabin, the great cellist Mstislav Rostropovich.

These movements were almost all small in numbers, and largely confined to well-educated city dwellers. They were able to establish solidarity and networks with people of like mind, but they did not achieve wide popular resonance. Dissidents' stubborn nobility of purpose and of method, however, excited great interest and admiration in the West, where their causes were supported and their writings broadcast back to the USSR; and the Soviet authorities were restrained by potential adverse Western reactions and their possible material consequences from total repression. The regime rid itself of numbers of individual dissidents by forcibly deporting them to Western countries: Solzhenitsyn was prevented from accepting his Nobel Prize for literature in 1970, and ejected from the Soviet Union in 1974.

Religious and nationalistic dissent also emerged, among various confessions and in several republics, and involved larger numbers and segments of the population. In largely Roman-Catholic Lithuania religion and nationalism combined into an unusually powerful movement. Baptists sought freedom of worship. Ukrainians sought greater autonomy. The Crimean Tatars and

Georgian Meskhetians deported by Stalin agitated to return to their homelands; Jewish 'refuseniks' and Soviet Germans sought the right to emigrate to Israel and Germany respectively – finally, with success. Certain forms of less overt dissent were tolerated within the system. Some Russian writers championed a return to Russian pre-Communist national values: in particular talented members of the 'village prose' school such as Vladimir Soloukhin and Valentin Rasputin celebrated and mourned the simple virtues, closeness to nature and spiritual awareness of rural, peasant life. These writers did not oppose the regime and were published officially, but their ideological stance increasingly challenged Marxist-Leninist orthodoxy, and they later emerged on the nationalist 'right wing' of perestroika and post-Soviet politics.

One may also view the extensive shadow economy as a form of dissidence: its unofficial and sometimes gangster enterprises, which fed upon the defects of the official economy, naturally avoided direct confrontation with the establishment, but represented a powerful ideological as well as material challenge to it. The final fate of the Communist regime also showed how hollow the ideological underpinnings of the Soviet state itself had become. In 1991 few believed in Marxism-Leninism any more. Members of the nomenklatura elite effortlessly adopted other ideologies, principally liberal or nationalist, and cosied up to the resurgent Orthodox Church, many also ensuring themselves a handsome share of the old Union's material resources. When the ban on the Communist Party was lifted, it re-emerged as a significant political force, but as much a vehicle of protest as an ideological vanguard; and its political potential has steadily declined in the post-Soviet period.

In terms of systemic development and change, the dissident movements were not of great importance so long as the Soviet system was stable. The security forces were always able to contain them if they wished – under Andropov the KGB largely silenced active intellectual dissent. The regime was undermined not by dissidents' protests or even its own human-rights violations as such, but by the corrosive impact of the perpetually unreal official discourse, by economic dysfunction and imperial overstretch, and its ultimate inability to satisfy the desires of either the populations or the leaders and elites of its constituent republics.

PERESTROIKA AND THE END OF THE USSR: 1985–91

Gorbachëv and 'New Thinking'

In 1985 nobody (in East or West) was thinking in terms of Soviet collapse, only of reform. On Chernenko's death, finally, the Politburo accepted as General Secretary a member of the next generation: Andropov's protégé Mikhail Gorbachëv. The son of peasants from Stavropol in southern Russia, Gorbachëv had studied law at Moscow State University, where he also met his wife: legality would become an important concern. He made a high-flying political career in Stavropol before being called to Moscow in 1978 to take responsibility for agriculture, and succeeded Chernenko in March 1985, aged 54. The new General Secretary was a committed Communist who wished to maintain the Soviet system. He was fully aware of the need for deep reform, though he failed to grasp all the potential economic and political consequences. He had the support of a pro-reform consensus – majorities of the Central Committee, top administrators, KGB and military leaderships all now accepted the urgency of change. Gorbachëv was however more radical than many of his supporters in seeking new approaches to Soviet problems and in refusing fundamentally the option of a return to violent repression, whether at home or abroad. In foreign affairs he perceived that the endless development of more weapons was counter-productive, generating reciprocal enemy images which in fact undermined security, justifying a spiralling and increasingly unaffordable arms race. He therefore sought to break away from ideological competition and seek cooperation and arms reductions with the major powers. In 1985 he held the first Russo–American summit since 1979 with President Ronald Reagan, in Geneva, the first in a series which led to several arms-limitation agreements. In 1988 he ended the Soviet involvement in Afghanistan; relations with China were also improved. When political pressures reached crisis proportions in the outer empire in 1989, he let it be known that the Kremlin would not intervene by force: consequently Communist governments fell across the region. This stance made him very popular internationally – he received the 1990 Nobel Peace Prize – and initially at home as well; but Soviet opinion was alienated by growing domestic confusion, and by the loss of the outer empire and Soviet prestige. Falling popularity added to the difficulties of Gorbachëv's final years.

At home, Gorbachëv's refusal to countenance full-scale military repression eventually facilitated the break-up of the Union. But in 1985 he had as yet no clear blue-print for the Soviet Union's future. Initially he took forward Andropov's disciplinary and anti-corruption policies, while building a new team to replace the Brezhnevite appa-rat and Politburo which he had inherited – wide-ranging changes included the summons to Moscow from Sverdlovsk of Boris Yeltsin, as Moscow City Party First Secretary and candidate Politburo member. Calls to improve production by 'accelerating' work-place processes had little result. His anti-alcohol campaign, designed by Yegor Ligachëv, then effectively his deputy, addressed a real social problem, but produced unexpected consequences. It encouraged illicit distilling, seriously undercut state revenues, and in some places Stalinist mentalities led to blanket destruction of valuable vineyards. Popular humour made 'General (*Generalnyi*) Secretary' into 'Mineral-Water (*Mineralnyi*) Secretary'.

Political Issues

From the beginning of what came to be known as *perestroika* ('restructuring'), Gorbachëv used the term *glasnost*, 'openness', in his speeches – the term coined under Alexander II in the 1850s prelude to the 'Great Reforms'. He was harking back to early Soviet traditions of public whistle-blowing and denunciation of abuses, and (as under Alexander II) 'openness' was intended to operate within prescribed limits. But he soon found that the Party–state apparat in general was recalcitrant in defending its turf from unsettling enquiries and changes; the most entrenched opposition came from the personal power-bases and networks of the nomenklatura which had such deep roots in Russian political culture. Faced with these systemic obstacles, Gorbachëv sought a new consensus based upon legality and consent. He adopted a strategy of mobilising the rank-and-file against the Party establishment, and of engaging public opinion in the interests of uncovering the true state of affairs – the genie's bottle was uncorked. The April 1986 explosion at the Chernobyl power station in Ukraine – the world's worst nuclear acci-dent, a huge disaster with transcontinental and devastating local impact – came as a catastrophic demonstration of the ills of the system, a 'lightning flash' like Kronshtat for Lenin. It was caused by deliberate, irresponsible, flagrant disregard of prescribed safety procedures, and the authorities' initial instinct was to cover it up: it was made public by Scandinavian radiation monitors. As Gorbachëv recalled in his *Memoirs*, Chernobyl 'shed light on many of the sicknesses of our system as a whole. Everything that had built up over the years converged in this drama: the concealing or hushing up of accidents and other bad news, irresponsibility and carelessness, slipshod work, wholesale drunkenness.' Now glasnost was pushed wider, with new editorial appointments to key journals, release of previously banned works and of imprisoned dissidents, notably Gorbachëv's personal recall to Moscow in December 1986 of the exiled eminent nuclear scientist Andrei Sakharov.

In the following three years Gorbachëv worked with great skill and endurance to change the political landscape; but from 1989 he was increasingly responding to events running beyond his control. Initially he tried, not very successfully, to democratise the system from within by introducing multi-candidate competitive elections for Party and public posts. He also restarted the rehabilitation of victims of political repression, effectively stalled under Brezhnev. In the jockeying over policy changes, Yeltsin emerged as a radical voice. He attacked conservative influences (Ligachëv) and the slowness of perestroika, and lost his Moscow job and Politburo position as a consequence (though not his membership of the Central Committee; in 1990 he would go further and leave the Communist Party). When inner-Party democratisation hung fire, Gorbachëv's next step was to widen politics beyond the Party: in mid-1988, in the glare of television cameras, the Nineteenth Party Conference approved a new legislature or parliament, the All-Union Congress of People's Deputies (CPD). It was ratified by the Supreme Soviet in December; one-third of the 2250 delegates were to be elected on a national territorial basis, another third from constituencies reflecting population density, while the remaining 750 were to come from 'public organisations' such as the Komsomol and the Academy of Sciences, including 100 reserved seats for the CPSU. The CPD was to meet twice yearly, with interim affairs run by a smaller elected Supreme Soviet.

The much freer but still partly controlled All-Union CPD elections held in March 1989 caused some spectacular upsets of Communist candidates, but produced only a minority of reformist deputies: some 400 'democrats' including Sakharov and Yeltsin, who became a leader of the radicals. Gorbachëv occupied one of the reserved CPSU places, and was then elected to the Supreme Soviet and to its Chair, thus becoming the 'speaker' of the Congress. The

First CPD (25 May–9 June 1989) had exceptional impact: it passed important legislation tending towards establishment of a really 'law-based state', and its impassioned, uncensored debates received unprecedented Union-wide television coverage. However, it was not integrated into the state administrative structure. Despite internal Party reorganisations, the 'leading role' of the Party and its dominance over soviet posts and practical administration continued.

These developments were paralleled by growing public activity and activism; the lessening of control permitted emergence of multifarious 'informal organisations', a resurgence of civil society. This allowed expression of opinions across the spectrum: as early as May 1987, for instance, a new anti-Semitic Russian nationalist organisation, *Pamiat* ('Memory'), staged demonstrations in Moscow. Economic difficulties produced strikes; in 1989 striking miners brought their griefs to the capital, and the events of that year in Eastern Europe sharpened public discontent – demands for democracy and better material conditions, coupled with overt resentment of nomenklatura privileges, produced mass demonstrations and forced out unpopular regional Party leaders. A 'Democratic Russia' 'bloc' (proto-political party) coalesced in many towns in early 1990, supporting a growing though still minority democratic electoral vote. Gorbachëv steered through further crucial moves against Party inertia: a CPSU Central Committee proposal, ratified in March 1990 by the Third CPD, amended the Constitution and finally removed the Party's political monopoly. Complete freedoms of election and of speech followed; local constituencies began to make their presence felt in unprecedented ways in decision-making at local and regional levels. The CPD also ratified a simultaneous proposal for the creation of an executive Union Presidency: besides controlling the government (Council of Ministers), the newly named President of the USSR would preside over an appointed Presidential Council (effectively a replacement for the now emasculated Politburo, but abolished as ineffectual in November), and a Council of the Federation, composed of the republican leaders. At the same time, the long-time ban on factions or separate 'platforms' within the Party was relaxed. Rather than standing for public election, Gorbachëv became All-Union President, unopposed, by CPD secret ballot, while remaining CPSU General Secretary. The Chairmanship of the Supreme Soviet (speakership of the CPD) was separated from the new Presidency. Gorbachëv now possessed a base outside of, as well as within, the Party; but he did not have the sanction of victory at the public ballot box.

The authority of the CPSU continued to decline. The establishment of an alternative Presidential governing structure and the dethroning of the Party from its 'leading role' marked a turning point. The entire Soviet system had rested on the Party-based leadership's ability to maintain and justify its forcible domination of society by appeal to a universalist ideology of which it was the custodian. The Party's 'leading role' was a logical corollary. Its disappearance struck at the essential linkages which held together both the economic and the political structures of the Union.

Economic Issues

Gorbachëv had inherited an economy increasingly inadequate to the requirements of superpower status. The Twelfth Five-Year Plan (1986–90) nevertheless set extremely optimistic targets, so optimistic as to cause a creeping budget deficit and suppressed inflation. His first two years brought no radical economic reform measures. Glasnost fuelled public and increasingly heterodox debate on economic options, but there was no dominant consensus in elite circles on how to proceed. In 1987–8, paralleling his widening of the political process, and spurred by alarming new economic statistics, Gorbachëv's administration undertook serious changes. They decreed decentralisation of decision-making and extension of local plant autonomy, extension of economic links (especially joint ventures) with the outside world, and legalisation and incorporation of the shadow economy, notably through 1988 laws legalising individual economic activity and private cooperatives. Like the anti-alcohol campaign, this slackening of central controls had unforeseen results. Partial economic devolution proved problematic. In tune with the rise of 'informal groups', independent cooperatives mushroomed: from 13,921 in 1988 employing 155,000 people, they rose to 245,356 employing 6 million in 1991. They answered a great social need. But they were soon being used as vehicles for plan evasion and then state asset stripping by sly officials and plant managers, and they were accompanied by the rise of mafia protection rackets, corruption among officials operating state controls, and by financial confusion, since the new organisations (like joint ventures too) were not harmonised with, but competed against, the traditional supply and financial structures. Far from improving over-all economic performance, these developments hastened economic breakdown and also encouraged further heterodoxy. The growth of grass-roots political influence had similar economic effects, as local politicians sought to defend their constituencies: when the city government of Moscow defensively blocked retail sales to non-Muscovites, officials in its supply regions, whose voters habitually travelled to shop in Moscow, retaliated by withholding delivery of goods to the capital. In 1989 some administrative attempts were made to win back central control over economic activity. But the high-powered State Commission on Economic Reform created in July 1989 to find an economic way forward moved inexorably further towards a mixed economy. Nevertheless, amid a plethora of economic reform proposals and growing political difficulties, the Gorbachëv government could not bring itself to embrace the undoubted hardship and dislocation that immediate radical reform would bring, and only palliatives and partial measures were undertaken. The abolition of the Party's leading role and its rapid loss of status compounded this situation: the Party apparatus was the transmission belt through which economic information and commands were disseminated. Without it the planned economy threatened to collapse.

The Union Question

The removal of the CPSU's political monopoly likewise posed a fundamental threat to the Union. If the Party was now to be just one competing party among others, without the charisma of divine right or the sanction of coercion, then only conviction, persuasion or material interest could hold the USSR together; and Gorbachëv had vastly underestimated the pent-up conflictual and centrifugal forces latent in the Union republics. The loosening of controls and the events of 1989 in Eastern Europe – the Berlin Wall fell in November – encouraged nationalistic movements towards autonomy, if not independence, in Georgia, Moldova and Ukraine, and ethnic clashes occurred between Armenians and Azeris, and in Uzbekistan. In the Baltic republics, Estonia, Latvia and Lithuania, where Soviet occupation and control had been re-established after World War II, just before the creation of the Soviet 'outer empire', pro-independence 'popular fronts' had emerged in 1988; all three republics declared their sovereignty within the Union. These developments prompted other republican leaders, and the RSFSR leadership too, to examine their own position within the Union. Uniquely in the USSR, Russia had no Party institutions of its own; the All-Russian Communist Party had transmuted into the All-Union Party in 1925. Russians had always dominated the All-Union Party and Soviet institutions – 58 per cent of CPSU members were Russian – but they had no separate control over their own affairs, and much of the wealth generated in the RSFSR was administered by All-Union bodies. Now a movement emerged to create separate RSFSR institutions. A Russian CPD was created in 1990; it narrowly elected Yeltsin as its first Chairman. Other bodies followed: an RSFSR Communist Party, which became the stronghold of hard-line anti-Gorbachëv conservatives, then a Russian Academy of Sciences, and RSFSR KGB and trades unions. In June 1990, moreover, to Gorbachëv's dismay, the Russian CPD passed its own declaration of RSFSR state sovereignty, asserting the primacy of Russian over All-Union law, and Russian right of control over republican institutions. The Russian example was soon followed by most other Union republics, starting a *de facto* devolution of power to the republican level. The Baltic republics had already gone further, and issued provisional declarations of independence; other republican leaderships increasingly courted their home constituencies by adopting nationalistic attitudes, something facilitated by the relaxation of Party discipline. They also became increasingly wary of the new pretensions of the Russian Republic.

Gorbachëv now found himself between the rock of conservative opposition and the hard place of radical liberalism and republican separatism. In 1990, control of economic assets on RSFSR territory became an issue between the Russian and All-Union administrations. Gorbachëv was finally persuaded of the desirability of rapid transition towards a market economy, and his advisers attempted to mend fences with the Russian republican leadership and economic radicals by working on far-reaching plans for economic change, the so-called '500 Days Programme'. But under pressure from powerful interest groups, Gorbachëv temporised in favour of a less radical solution; the radical alignment broke up, and the economic situation did not improve. In late 1990 he moved back to conciliate the threatening 'right', and appointed a number of conservative figures to key positions in government and in the armed and security services. Consequently, in December the liberal Foreign Minister Eduard Shevardnadze resigned, warning of a coming dictatorship; in January

1991, following urgings from anonymous pro-Union 'National Salvation Committees'in Lithuania and Latvia, Soviet special troops occupied official buildings in separatist Vilnius and Riga, and killed several civilians in confrontations with mass opposition; 100,000 demonstrators protested in Moscow, and Yeltsin called for Gorbachëv to step down; the special troops were called off. A new wave of economic unrest showed further the dangers of repression and incompetent economic conservatism, and Gorbachëv veered back towards the centre. Hoping to defuse the union and nationalities question, he held a referendum in March on the desirability of maintaining a union at all. Six republics boycotted it; in Russia it was linked to the creation of a directly elected Russian presidency. In those republics which participated, large majorities were in favour, and in April talks were instigated with all those willing to listen, including Russia's representative Yeltsin, on revision of the existing (1922) Union Treaty. These constitutional discussions produced a draft Union Treaty for a new, looser, 'genuinely voluntary' 'Union of Sovereign States'; finalised on 23 July 1991, it was published on 14 August, to be signed formally on 20 August by nine of the existing republics. Meanwhile in direct elections to the newly created RSFSR Presidency in June 1991 Yeltsin won a landslide, giving him an exceptional political and moral position – the first Russian leader ever to be popularly elected. Vice-President was Aleksandr Rutskoi, leader of the 'Communists for Democracy' bloc. Capitalising on his strength, Yeltsin issued a decree in July banning all political parties from operating in Russian places of work: a stroke against the Communist Party, which was based upon primary work-place organisations.

The August Coup and the End of the USSR

With the new draft Union Treaty ready, Gorbachëv took a holiday break in the Crimea. But his hopes of resolving the union issue were undercut by a *coup d'état* mounted on 19 August, by die-hards desperate to forestall the break-up of the USSR. The leaders, the self-styled 'State Committee for the State of Emergency', were his own appointees, the conservative figures he had so recently placed in power: the Vice-President, Prime Minister, Defence Minister, Head of the KGB. When he refused cooperation, they placed him under house arrest at his Crimean dacha, announced in Moscow that he was incapacitated, and declared a state of emergency. But they lacked widespread support, were woefully indecisive, and had made neither serious plans nor adequate preparations. Crucially, they failed to detain Yeltsin and his colleagues, Russian Vice-President Rutskoi and the Speaker of the Russian Parliament (CPD) Ruslan Khasbulatov, who made a stand at the 'White House', the Moscow seat of the Russian CPD and presidency. It was surrounded by putchist tanks, but bodily defended by thousands of unarmed Muscovite civilians. From the top of a tank, Yeltsin (who had a cameraman with him) appealed dramatically to the people and the world. Mass demonstrations against the *coup* in former Leningrad – by now renamed St Petersburg – were led by the reformist mayor Anatolii Sobchak.

The *coup* collapsed within three days; Gorbachëv returned and the plotters were arrested. The Communist Party had played no direct part, but it was tainted by association, and on 23 August Yeltsin humiliated General Secretary Gorbachëv by formally suspending the CPSU on Russian territory. Gorbachëv initially protested, but resigned his Secretaryship. The USSR CPD, associated with the CPSU, dissolved itself in September; in November Yeltsin banned the Party altogether in Russia. In the second half of 1991 new transitional Union institutions were created, but they and Gorbachëv as President were increasingly marginalised by Russian republican structures, which progressively took over the powers of the All-Union regime; the economic situation went from bad to worse, prompting the republics to go their own economic way too. Yeltsin failed to use his huge moral authority to make decisive changes, for fear of provoking complete social breakdown and a repetition of October 1917. The effect of the August *coup* was nevertheless the reverse of the plotters' intentions: the final discrediting of the CPSU and the collapse of the Soviet Union. Power had passed decisively to the republics, which were now highly suspicious of the centre, and of Yeltsin's powerful Russian Republic as well. Moreover, while republican leaders' separatist nationalistic rhetoric found an appreciative mass audience, independent status promised the republics' nomenklatura elites a power and a prestige to which otherwise they could never aspire. Lithuania and Georgia had already formally declared their independence; the failed *coup* brought a cascade of similar declarations, and by November only Russia and Kazakhstan remained in the Soviet Union. Although Moscow celebrated the *coup*'s failure as a triumph for democracy, attempts by Gorbachëv and Yeltsin to revive negotiations for a revised union failed completely. The independence of the Baltic, though not of other, republics was formally recognised by the centre. However, Ukraine, a crucial player, refused to accept any new union with authoritative central bodies; finally in December 1991 the leaders of the Slavic republics, Belarus, Russia and Ukraine, three of the original signatories of the 1922 Union Treaty, jointly declared the USSR at an end and announced the formation of a toothless Commonwealth of Independent States (*SNG*, CIS), which maintained a common economic space and some common military controls, but otherwise left the republics independent. Eight other republics (Armenia, Azerbaijan, Kazakhstan, Kyrgyzstan, Moldova, Tadjikistan, Turkmenistan, Uzbekistan) acceded to the new accord; the Baltic States and Georgia remained outside it. Gorbachëv resigned as Union President, and on 31 December 1991 the USSR ceased to exist.

8

· · · · · · · ·

The Russian Federation after 1991: Free Market and Democracy?

The break-up of the Soviet Union was accompanied by the demise of Communism as its guiding value system, to be replaced by free-market democracy. Yeltsin pushed ahead with a flawed economic transition, bringing great hardships to the mass of the population and huge wealth to a few 'new Russians', although a new economy gradually took shape. While 1991 provided a basis for democratic development, Yeltsin's relations with the Parliament deteriorated, resulting in armed confrontation in 1993. A consequent new constitution gave him sweeping presidential prerogatives, allowing the entrenchment of government power and control over society; war in Chechnia soon followed. The new situation also brought radical social and cultural change, challenging both long-established patterns of daily life and Russians' self-image and identity. Yeltsin's search for a successor ended with the emergence of Vladimir Putin as Prime Minister and his party's electoral success in 1999; Putin won election as President in 2000.

IDENTITY, DEMOCRACY AND THE MARKET

The Coming of a Market Economy

The demise of the Union and the CP gave Yeltsin the freedom he wanted to push ahead with radical economic reform in Russia. He chose to postpone further elections and the new Russian constitution required for the new circumstances. His new Prime Minister, 35-year-old Yegor Gaidar, a disciple of Hayek and Thatcher, advocated 'shock therapy' to take Russia straight to a market economy. In January 1992 price liberalisation was introduced (though not for housing or domestic utilities), as a first step towards comprehensive change. Prices rocketed; the population immediately began to feel the pinch. Over the following years of transition, economic reform became a battleground. Yeltsin ruled in Soviet style, relying on small coteries. The government reformers he appointed were increasingly opposed by those angered at the effects of rapid and sometimes ill-considered change.

In June 1992 the government proceeded to the privatisation of state industries, to be achieved by giving all citizens resources with which to buy shares: 10,000-rouble vouchers, one for each citizen, could be invested in newly privatised enterprises. Management and workforce were also allowed to acquire majority shares on favourable terms, which enabled many managers to accumulate controlling interests in their former enterprises, buying out workers, especially since 10,000 roubles was a small sum in strongly inflationary times and many vouchers were bought up by speculators: the old administrative elites often became the new owners, and skilful financial operators could make huge fortunes. Even so, many industrialists feared that withdrawal of state subsidy would cause collapse – a critical social as well as economic question, since Soviet enterprises had traditionally supplied numerous material services and benefits to their workforces. Supreme-Soviet ratification of 'voucherisation' was therefore conditional on continuation of state support for major industries. For the same reason the Central Bank maintained large and inflationary industrial credit accounts. In this way many wholly unprofitable enterprises staggered on, maintaining a workforce they could scarcely pay: unemployment remained low, despite raging inflation. Collective farms likewise continued to receive state subsidies, and the majority of them resisted privatisation and break-up into smaller units, preferring to reinvent themselves as agricultural cooperatives. This was a rational decision in the extremely unfavourable circumstances of the time where private investment credit was unavailable, contract law unenforceable, prices and payment mechanisms wholly unreliable, and the promised land-privatisation law a subject of bitter contention; but it also reflected traditional risk-aversion and the crushing of initiative among collective-farm workers, and offered few solutions to the problems of agriculture.

In December 1992 Yeltsin found it necessary to replace the uncharismatic and unpopular Gaidar by the less radical Viktor Chernomyrdin, former chairman of the state energy giant *Gazprom*, who soon placed some restrictions on profits and price rises. The economic turbulence of the reforms had disrupted established economic relationships and wage and salary payments, and for a while plunged many people into deep poverty. In 1992–4 moonlighting, barter, begging became commonplace; professionals, their salaries unpaid, spent their time growing vegetables and chickens at their dachas (country summer-houses). Criminality and violence rose, as criminals nested in official and commercial operations; illegal exports of precious metals and anything saleable became commonplace, as did capital outflows to Swiss bank accounts – some money transferred came from large-scale embezzlement of IMF loans. On the other hand the beneficiaries of the system could buy increasingly available imported and locally produced goods of all descriptions, and the most successful 'new Russians' developed a lifestyle of crudely conspicuous consumption. Moreover, wages slowly recovered, and privatisation was taking hold: by late 1994 nearly half of all workers were employed by private enterprises. However, the state presence still remained very strong, especially in agriculture.

Economic change continued. Chernomyrdin's moderate line favoured big industry; in 1995–6 further privatisation enabled wealthy firms to acquire shares cheaply and form conglomerates. A number of super-wealthy 'oligarchs' emerged, some of them improving their position further by supporting Yeltsin's 1996 presidential campaign. Violence and criminality remained the order of the day: the conglomerates ran their own security armies, while lesser operations routinely paid mafia gangsters protection money for a 'roof' over their business. Foreign investment under such conditions was extremely cautious, and much of what there was was predatory, seeking to make a fast buck in troubled conditions. The economy relied heavily on IMF loans, often misapplied or misappropriated. To make up for lost revenues from privatised state industries, the government instituted a punitively heavy tax regime, which inevitably encouraged tax evasion – the vast Gazprom, for instance, simply refused to pay. Another source of revenue was sought in government bonds, issued at interest rates sufficient to attract buyers both domestic and foreign. But such interest payments proved unsustainable. In 1998 Russia was compelled to default on its debts, producing a banking and industrial crash and currency devaluation, and wiping out savings. To some extent, however, the 1998 crash allowed the Russian economy to find a more even and durable keel: the decline bottomed out. By 2001 the World Bank had removed Russia from its 'crisis list' – although major structural problems remain.

The Growing Pains of Democracy

Yeltsin's presidential electoral victory in 1991 gave him unprecedented political authority. Most political controls of the Soviet era were abolished with the Union. But the painful reform programme over which he presided caused growing discontent, and his relatively autocratic style of government, as well as his policies, brought him increasingly into conflict with the Russian Parliament (CPD and Supreme Soviet), which also possessed an electoral mandate. Unreconstructed since its election back in 1990, the Parliament included many hard-liners and critics and became a focus of opposition, now led by Yeltsin's former ally Khasbulatov, with the support of Vice-President Rutskoi. Tension grew: the President found his policies increasingly obstructed. Finally in 1993 a presidential decree dissolved the Parliament, announcing new elections. The Parliament declared the decree illegal and Yeltsin deposed, and in his place swore in Rutskoi, who called for popular mass action against the Kremlin. Both sides claimed a popular mandate. The stand-off was only resolved when Yeltsin declared a state of emergency and on 4 October persuaded his reluctant Defence Minister to attack the White House, in which the Parliamentarians were ensconced and which he himself had defended only two years before. When tank shells holed its walls, the defenders surrendered; they were imprisoned with some of the plotters of 1991.

In the elections which followed in December, voters approved a new Constitution proposed by Yeltsin, which gave him exceptionally sweeping presidential powers; but they showed their distaste for the violence at the White House by giving a large block of the new State Duma's 450 seats to the ultra-nationalist Liberal Democratic Party of the populist Vladimir Zhirinovskii and the newly reconstituted Russian Federation Communist Party (CPRF) under Gennadii

Ziuganov. This constellation continued into the 1995 Duma elections, when Ziuganov and his allies became the largest grouping. In the 1996 presidential elections a second-round run-off between Yeltsin and Ziuganov produced a clear Yeltsin majority – a result achieved, however, by presidential monopoly of the crucial televisual media, vicious PR work, economic favours to wealthy key backers, and possibly also by gerrymandering. This was scarcely a celebration of democracy, and accorded with other manifestations of authoritarianism on the part of 'Tsar Boris', although Yeltsin's re-election was widely welcomed in the West.

Yeltsin was fortunate after 1993 in having no heavyweight opponents. Major national institutions were dependent on him, or quiescent. The Orthodox Church, newly risen once more to authority, relied upon the state for income and for support against other confessions; the Patriarch, Aleksii II, gave Yeltsin consistent backing. The armed forces, underfunded and demoralised, unable to provide for the large contingents being withdrawn from Eastern Europe, had no united leadership and had lost the ability to oppose policy. The new media spent more time attacking Yeltsin's personal foibles than his politics; the elites largely benefited from his regime. The CPRF became his most dangerous rivals. The party's ideology was increasingly conservative nationalist, and Ziuganov declared himself a Christian. In the years 1995–2001 the CPRF dominated the Duma, but after a strong electoral performance in 1995 it showed few signs of capacity to form an alternative government. Nor were any of the numerous other, smaller political parties capable of this: they possessed little organisational depth, and represented no serious social interest. Despite Yeltsin's ill health after 1995, despite rumours of corruption around his family, his falling popularity and conflicts with the Duma, his position remained relatively stable.

Yeltsin's strengthened political position also enabled him in 1994 to launch an invasion of Chechnia. The break-up of the Union had been accompanied by serious armed hostilities in some union republics – Georgia, Azerbaijan and Armenia, Moldova, Tadjikistan. Russia had largely avoided such conflicts, and remained peaceful and intact; but the Caucasian Chechen Republic, part of the RSFSR, had declared independence in 1991 under its shady nationalist leader Dzhokar Dudaev, and succeeded in maintaining its position against a Moscow show of force. Yeltsin, who had loosened the bonds uniting the USSR, would tolerate no secession from Russia: after negotiations and clandestine operations failed, and against considerable opposition within his government, he sent in the army. However, while his poorly constituted forces took the Chechen capital Groznyi, acting in the process with great brutality, they proved quite unable to bring the Chechens to heel. This use of major force, with little restraint and without real justification, contrasted sharply with Yeltsin's professed democratic ideals. Nor was it successful. To bolster his position during the 1996 presidential campaign, a deal had to be struck and a truce arranged, which allowed both sides in the conflict to avoid losing face.

Cultural Change and National Identity

Besides the problems of economic and political transition, the collapse of the Soviet Union precipitated a crisis of other values: rapid social and cultural change, and challenges to the population's established self-image and sense of identity. Many aspects of the previously dominant ideology were turned upside down; and however hollow the official line had become for many by 1991, adapting to life on radically different principles is painful, especially in times of economic upheaval. Glasnost and the opening of archives have revealed political crimes, but brought little redress for victims or repentance from perpetrators: neither government nor society has fully confronted that Soviet legacy. Entrepreneurship and wealth accumulation, previously excoriated, became positive goals, while the majority fell further into poverty. State planning constraints and deficiencies, bureaucratic checks and balances, were replaced by the uncertainties and financial exigencies of an ill-regulated market. The order and stability of ordinary life in the Soviet police state gave way to fluctuating supplies of goods, inflation and erosion of savings, sharp and illegal practices, and criminal violence. Industrial decay brought a decline in services (child care, health provision, social facilities) for which funding was becoming increasingly scarce. Women were disproportionately affected: as wages collapsed and jobs shrank, they were the first to suffer, and also had to bear the brunt at home – the 1990s saw growing alcohol abuse and domestic violence (sometimes fatal), rising divorce rates and an increasing number of one-parent (mother-only) families.

The cultural elite ('intelligentsia' in Soviet usage), producers and custodians of cultural and social values, had hitherto enjoyed state-funded support through organisations such as the Union of Writers and the Academy of Sciences; they had been especially courted by Gorbachëv. After 1991 their organisations continued to exist, but were now largely stripped of funding. The duty to 'speak truth to power', or to tell well-paid lies for it, was replaced by problems of basic survival. Old artistic norms were confronted by consumer demand, by new commercial media requirements for advertising and scandal, and by the saleability of such new genres as the erotica of the ultra-nationalist writer Eduard Limonov. At the same time the new freedom gave unprecedented opportunities, of which many took advantage. The fall of censorship and return of expatriates – Solzhenitsyn came home in 1994 – offered the marriage of Russian *émigré* with domestic culture. A varied, busy and humane new culture has emerged, with important figures such as the writer Viktor Pelevin. Nevertheless media freedom, and especially the politically crucial television channels, fell once again under domination, by wealthy 'oligarchs' and latterly by government, while the FSB (successor to the KGB) has clapped charges of treason on individuals – the environmental commentators Aleksandr Nikitin and Grigorii Pasko, or the journalist Andrei Babitskii – who brought lawful but unwelcome publicity to areas of official mismanagement.

Religion and the Orthodox Church have enjoyed resurgent popularity, authority and prestige. The 1988 millennium of Vladimir's conversion was a great opportunity, the abolition of the Soviet Council for Religious Affairs in 1991 brought freedom of belief and worship, and all leading political contenders have courted Church support. (The ideological vacuum left by the collapse of Communism encouraged credulous belief in general, in the most varied and wildest ideologies, ideas and phenomena.) Despite its past collaborations with the Soviet regime, the Orthodox Church has become one of the most trusted Russian institutions. However, it has failed to shake off its long tradition of reliance on state power to buttress a monopoly position and limit rival creeds (now, especially, well-equipped foreign proselytisers). There has been conflict with the Greek Catholic Church; other Christian confessions have experienced difficulties in registering themselves under new state regulations; and even a case of book-burning – the destruction of works by Western and liberal Orthodox theologians – has been reported.

The post-1991 territorial reconfiguration has seriously challenged established identities. Large numbers of Russians have found themselves living in sovereign former Soviet territories outside the Russian Federation, in the so-called 'Near Abroad'; for many Russians Ukraine in particular is an essential part of their community, and its secession subverts their sense of national integrity. On the other hand, in its post-Soviet form the Russian Federation still remains multi-ethnic – it has some 200 nationalities; in the new dispensation its federal structure, the history of its ethnic relations, can arouse controversy. So far the dominant approach to the reconstruction of national identity has been civic – equal legal status for all regardless of ethnic affiliation – but dissent has expressed itself both in the continuing support for the CPRF and in the strong rise of right-wing and sometimes anti-Semitic Russian nationalism.

Problems of identity are also linked to the official style of rule. Yeltsin's tenure was beset with tussles over both order and law. Among other things the post-Soviet definition of property rights, especially in land, excited enormous controversy: a Federation-wide land law eluded Yeltsin altogether. A result of his victory over the Parliament was the widening of Presidential prerogatives, which permitted the resurgence in government practice of the hallowed principle of *gosudarstvennost*, the dominance of state power. Nevertheless, despite his personal failings, Yeltsin seemed genuinely committed to an idea of democracy; he moved, however, in a rather traditional way in the matter of his successor.

THE YELTSIN SUCCESSION AND THE PUTIN YEARS

In 1995 Yeltsin's health began to deteriorate, exacerbated by heavy drinking; in 1996 multiple heart by-pass surgery was performed. During his second term his succession became an increasing preoccupation – his regime has been described as an 'electoral monarchy'. In March 1998 Chernomyrdin's indifferent success as Prime Minister led to his sacking; he was followed by a series of short-lived replacements. Sergei Kirienko (1998), a young technocratic reformer, was destroyed by the August 1998 crash. Yevgenii Primakov (1998–9), a former head of the SVB,[††] favoured by the Duma, was sacked for wishing to challenge the political monopoly of Yeltsin and his dubious entourage. Sergei Stepashin (1999),

---

[††] *Sluzhba Vneshnei Razvedki*, External Intelligence Service, equivalent to MI6 or CIA.

another former security chief, also proved to be too independent-minded for the Kremlin power game. Yeltsin finally found what he wanted in Vladimir Putin (1999). An unknown career KGB man before he joined the St Petersburg city, and then the presidential, administration, Putin briefly became head of the FSB before appointment as Prime Minister. Putin received unusually strong support from Yeltsin and soon made his mark on government, achieving exceptional political command. He was helped by renewal of war in Chechnia. The causes were Chechen incursions into Dagestan, and especially four large explosions in September 1999 in housing blocks in Moscow and other towns. These were blamed on Chechen terrorists, although the weight of evidence led some observers to label them FSB provocations; but Putin's uncompromising response, and his reassertion of Russian territorial integrity and power, brought him great popularity. The new Chechen war matched the first one in brutality and indeterminacy; however, in 2001, after the twin-towers atrocity of 11 September in New York, Putin declared his alignment with the American 'war on terror', thereby deflecting international criticism. In international relations generally Putin's measured pursuit of Russian interests was also seen to restore national dignity. In December 1999 his newly founded party, Unity, scored great success in parliamentary elections. On 31 December Yeltsin skilfully and unexpectedly resigned; Putin as Prime Minister correctly succeeded him as Acting President – a smooth and constitutional but essentially patrimonial political transition, pre-empting popular or Parliamentary participation. One of Putin's first acts was to guarantee all Presidents, including Yeltsin and his family, immunity from criminal investigation or prosecution. In the ensuing presidential elections of March 2000 Putin was uniquely well placed, and won a clear first-round victory.

The deep changes which have taken place in Russia in all fields since 1991 – economic, social, cultural and political – suggest that return to the former Soviet order is impossible. The Russian government professes its allegiance to democracy and market economics in the Euro-American image, and the prerequisites of an open and pluralist modern society have been created. At the same time the deeply rooted Russian principle of gosudarstvennost, a strong state power, remains politically attractive to many among the population, and habits of patriarchy and patronage persist; the Parliament has failed to provide a serious counterweight to the executive. President

Putin's government has made clear its intolerance of alternative political power bases and its intention to control crucial televisual media, and the integrity of law is by no means yet universally assured. Putin has declared his goal to be a 'dictatorship of law', strict legality: there seem however to be no real barriers to the dictatorial appropriation of law by ruling structures, a possible reversion to older practices. Neither the government nor the courts have shown determination to act against abuses and illegalities committed by the armed and security forces, and by organised crime. The FSB retains significant internal power, and many of its personnel are integrated into government and industry. Presidential discourse is couched in Western categories, but government instincts appear to remain authoritarian; favourable attention has recently been drawn to Putin's Soviet predecessor Yurii Andropov, another head of the KGB, who sought to improve society without loosening authoritarian control. It is uncertain, too, whether current economic structures will provide essential long-term competitiveness and prosperity and, despite the eventual passing of the elusive land law, how the divide between town and country will be bridged.

At the same time, Russians now officially enjoy rights and freedoms comparable to those of their European neighbours (including the right of travel and emigration: a huge Russian diaspora is now spread across Europe and America). Changes in culture and communication have transformed expectations. Despite its economic troubles Russia is endowed with natural resources and human talent, and with the ending of the Cold War it no longer faces powerful hostile states and the burden of great-power military provision. It remains to be seen how these different factors will shape the Russia of the twenty-first century.

Further Reading

Those in search of fuller accounts of Russian history may consult the admirable though ageing *Longman History of Russia* (7 vols, 1981–96); longer single volumes include those of P. Dukes, G. Freeze, N. Riasanovsky and most recently G. Hosking. M. Gilbert, *The Routledge Atlas of Russian History*, London and New York 2002, and J. Channon, *The Penguin Atlas of Russia*, London 1995 are invaluable geographical aids. D. Shaw, *Russia in the Modern World: A New Geography*, Oxford 1999, offers an excellent overview of historical and social geography. Broad analyses of Russia as empire and multi-ethnic state include D. Lieven, *Empire: The Russian Empire and its Rivals*, London 2000; J. LeDonne, *The Russian Empire and the World, 1700–1917: The Geopolitics of Expansion and Containment*, New York 1997; and A. Kappeler, *The Russian Empire: A Multiethnic History*, Harlow 2001. C. Obolensky exhibits *The Russian Empire: A Portrait in Photographs*, London 1980. On the frontier see M. Khodarkovsky, *Russia's Steppe Frontier: The Making of a Colonial Empire, 1500–1800*, Bloomington, IN, 2002; on military history see F. Kagan and R. Higham, eds, *The Military History of Russia and the Soviet Union*, 2 vols, New York and Basingstoke 2002–3, and E. Lohr and M. Poe, eds, *The Military and Society in Russia, 1450–1917*, Leiden 2002. For culture, art, architecture, literature and science see J. Billington, *The Icon and the Axe: An Interpretive History of Russian Culture*, New York 1970 (still useful); O. Figes, *Natasha's Dance: A Cultural History of [Imperial and Soviet] Russia*, London 2002; W. Brumfield, *A History of Russian Architecture*, Cambridge 1993; G. Hamilton, *The Art and Architecture of Russia*, Harmondsworth 1983; V. Terras, *A History of Russian Literature*, New Haven, CT, 1991; L. Graham, *Science in Russia and the Soviet Union: A Short History*, Cambridge and New York 1993. On the peasantry see T. Scott, ed., *The Peasantries of Europe from the Fourteenth to Eighteenth Centuries*, London and New York 1998 (E. Melton on Russia), and D. Moon, *The Russian Peasantry, 1600–1930: The World the Peasants Made*, London and New York 1999; G. Spittler's analysis of peasant society can be found in his 'Peasants and the State in Niger (West Africa)', *Peasant Studies* 8 (1979), 30–47 and is applied to early-modern Prussia in id., 'Abstraktes Wissen als Herrschaftsbasis. Zur Entstehungsgeschichte bürokratischer Herrschaft im Bauernstaat Preussen', *Kölner Zeitschrift für Soziologie und Sozialpsychologie* 32 (1980), 574–604.

On the geographical setting see D. Christian, *A History of Central Asia and Mongolia, 1: Inner Eurasia from Prehistory to the Mongol Empire,* Oxford 1998; the Mackinder theory is developed in the older W. Parker, *An Historical Geography of Russia*, London 1968. Besides Christian, the early historical period (Chapter 1) is covered by P. Dolukhanov, *The Early Slavs: Eastern Europe from the Initial Settlement to the Kievan Rus*, London and New York 1996; S. Franklin and J. Shephard, *The Emergence of Rus, 750–1200*, London and New York 1996; J. Martin, *Medieval Russian History 980–1584*, Cambridge 1995; M. Perrie and A. Pavlov, *Ivan the Terrible*, London 2003. On the political system see N. Kollmann, *Kinship and Politics: The Making of the Muscovite Political System, 1345–1547*, Stanford, CA, 1987, the same author's *By Honor Bound: State and Society in Early Modern Russia*, Ithaca, NY, and London 1999; and M. Poe in *Comparative Studies in Society and History* 38 (1996), 603–18.

The latest work on the Time of Troubles (Chapter 2) is C. Dunning, *Russia's First Civil War: The Time of Troubles and the Founding of the Romanov Dynasty*, Pennsylvania 2001. On the Godunov story see C. Emerson, *Boris Godunov: Transpositions of a Russian Theme*, Bloomington, IN, 1986; the pretender phenomenon is well discussed in M. Perrie, *Pretenders and Popular Monarchy in Early Modern Russia*, Cambridge 1995. D. Raleigh, ed., *The Emperors and Empresses of Russia: Rediscovering the Romanovs*, Armonk, NY, 1996, gives an overview of the new dynasty. J. Kotilaine and M. Poe, eds, *Modernizing Muscovy: Reform and Social Change in Seventeenth-Century Russia*, London and New York 2004, present the latest seventeenth-century scholarship. Essential for the schism is G. Michels, *At War with the Church: Religious Dissent in 17th-Century Russia*, Stanford, CA, 2000, and for the rise of serfdom R. Hellie, *Enserfment and Military Change in Muscovy*, Chicago and London 1971. Siberia occupies W. Lincoln, *The Conquest of a Continent: Siberia and the Russians*, London 1994; J. LeDonne treats the broad Imperial dimension in *The Grand Strategy of the Russian Empire: 1650–1831*, Oxford 2004. On social history see J. Hartley, *A Social History of Russia, 1650–1800*, London 1998, and B. Mironov, *A Social History of Imperial Russia, 1700–1917*, Boulder, CO, 1999; on Cossackdom P. Longworth, *The Cossacks*, London 1971. Longworth's *Alexis, Tsar of All the Russias*, London 1984, is a vivid biography. L. Hughes, *Russia in the Reign of Peter the Great*, New Haven, CT, and London 1998 is the modern standard on Peter I. See also recent contributions from P. Bushkovitch and J. Cracraft, and the Russian perspective of E. Anisimov, *The Reforms of Peter the Great: Progress through Coercion*, Armonk, NY, and London 1993. On the eighteenth century in general see S. Dixon, *The Modernisation of Russia, 1676–1825*, Cambridge 1999. E. Anisimov presents *Empress Elizabeth: Her Reign and Her Russia, 1741–1761*, Gulf Breeze, FL, 1995.

Chapter 3: I. de Madariaga's *Russia in the Age of Catherine the Great*, New Haven, CT, 1980/1990, remains unsurpassed; S. Dixon's briefer *Catherine the Great*, Harlow and London 2001, is excellent. On the nobility and administration see M. Raeff, *The Well-Ordered Police State [. . .] in the Germanies and Russia 1600–1800*, New Haven, CT, and London 1983; R. Jones, *The Emancipation of the Russian Nobility, 1762–1785*, Princeton 1973; J. LeDonne, *Absolutism and Ruling Class in Russia, 1700–1825*, Oxford and New York 1991. H. Scott, ed., *Enlightened Absolutism: Reform and Reformers in Later 18th-Century Europe*, London and Basingstoke 1990, provides the best account of Enlightened Absolutism. For Pugachëv see J. Alexander, *Emperor of the Cossacks: Pugachëv and the Frontier Jacquerie of 1773–75*, Lawrence, KS, 1973, and H. Landsberger, ed., *Rural Protest: Peasant Movements and Social Change*, London 1974; the beginnings of Russian abolition are addressed broadly by J. Blum, *The End of the Old Order in Rural Europe*, Princeton 1978, and specifically by D. Moon, *The Abolition of Serfdom in Russia, 1762–1907*, Harlow 2001. On Potëmkin and the south see S. Montefiore, *Prince of Princes: The life of Potemkin*, London 2000. W. Rosslyn, ed., treats *Women and Gender in Eighteenth-Century Russia*, Aldershot 2003; see also her *Anna Bunina (1774–1829) and the Origins of Women's Poetry in Russia*, Lewiston, NJ, 1997. A modern history of eighteenth-century Russian culture and the Court is lacking; but see H. Rogger, *National Consciousness in Eighteenth-Century Russia*, Cambridge, MA, 1960, *Canadian-American Slavic Studies* XIV/3, XVI/3–4 (1980, 1982, including J. S. Carver), and I. de Madariaga, *Politics and Culture in Eighteenth-Century Russia*, London 1998. P. Roosevelt provides a delightful account of *Life on the Russian Country Estate: A Social and Economic History*, New Haven, CT, and London 1995. J. Hartley and W. Lincoln offer good biographies of Alexander I and Nicholas I respectively. On the Decembrists, besides older standard works of A. Mazour and M. Raeff, see P. O'Meara, *The Decembrist Pavel Pestel: Russia's First Republican*, Basingstoke and New York 2003. N. Riasanovsky, *A Parting of Ways: Government and the Educated Public in Russia, 1801–1855*, Oxford 1976, maps the wider growth of dissent. For foreign policy see H. Ragsdale, ed., *Imperial Russian Foreign Policy*, Cambridge 1993. M. Anderson's older study of *The Eastern Question, 1774–1923*, London 1966, is still useful; J. Lukowski gives the latest account of *The Partitions of Poland 1772, 1793, 1795*, Harlow 1999, and D. Goldfrank of *The Origins of the Crimean War*, London 1994.

   The 'Great Reforms' (Chapter 4) are discussed by W. Lincoln, *The Great Reforms: Autocracy, Bureaucracy and the Politics of Change in Imperial Russia*, DeKalb, IL, 1990, and B. Eklof, ed, *Russia's Great Reforms, 1855–1881*, Bloomington, IN, 1994. On the emancipation, see Blum and Moon cited above, and S. Hoch in *Slavic Review* 62/2 (2004), 247–74. A. Gleason gives a highly readable account of *Young Russia: The Genesis of Russian Radicalism in the 1860s*, Chicago and London 1983; E. Clowes, S. Kassow and J. West, eds, *Between Tsar and People: Educated Society and the Quest for Public Identity in Late Imperial Russia*, Princeton 1991, examine the growth of civil society. V. Shevzov, *Russian Orthodoxy on the Eve of the Revolution*, Oxford and New York 2004; R. Stites, *The Women's Liberation Movement in Russia . . . 1860–1930*, Princeton and Oxford 1991; and A. Jones, *Late Imperial Russia: An Interpretation. Three Visions, Two Cultures, One Peasantry*, Bern etc. 1997, explore three other critical constituencies. Further on the peasantry see C. Worobec, *Peasant Russia: Family and Community in the Post-Emancipation Period*, Princeton and Oxford 1991; E. Kingston-Mann and T. Mixter with J. Burds, eds, *Peasant Economy, Culture and Politics of European Russia, 1800–1921*, Princeton and Oxford 1991; R. Bartlett, ed., *Land Commune and Peasant Community: Communal Forms in Late Imperial and Soviet Russia*, Basingstoke and London 1990. The best study of the last Tsar is D. Lieven, *Nicholas II, Emperor of All the Russias*, London 1993. The course of revolution is well charted in O. Figes, *A People's Tragedy: The Russian Revolution, 1891–1924*, London 1996, and C. Read, *From Tsar to Soviets: The Russian People and their Revolution*, London 1996. Lenin is anatomised by R. Service, *Lenin: A Political Life*, vols 1–3, Basingstoke and New York 1985–95, and id., *Lenin: A Biography*, Basingstoke and Oxford 2000.

In general on the Soviet period (Chapters 5 and 6) see R. Service, *A History of Modern Russia from Nicholas II to Putin*, Penguin 2003, and A. Nove, *An Economic History of the USSR, 1917–91*, Harmondsworth 1992. E. Mawdsley, *The Russian Civil War*, Boston, MA, 1987, should be supplemented by O. Figes, *Peasant Russia, Civil War: The Volga Countryside in Revolution, 1917–1921*, Oxford 1989. Other dimensions of revolutionary upheaval are shown by E. Wood, *The Baba and the Comrade: Gender and Politics in Revolutionary Russia*, Bloomington, IN, 1997, and R. Stites, *Revolutionary Dreams: Utopian Visions and Experimental Life in the Russian Revolution*, New York and Oxford 1989. Lenin's afterlife entertains N. Tumarkin, *Lenin Lives! The Lenin Cult in Soviet Russia*, Cambridge, MA, and London 1997. On the nationalities see T. Martin, *Affirmative-Action Empire: Nations and Nationalism in the Soviet Union, 1923–1939*, London and Ithaca, NY, 2001. A. Graziosi chronicles *The Great Peasant War: Bolsheviks and Peasants, 1918–33*, Cambridge, MA, 1997, and R. Conquest its worst results in *The Harvest of Sorrow: Soviet Collectivisation and the Terror Famine*, London 1986. Industrialisation is analysed by Nove, in the numerous works of R. Davies, and by H. Kuromiya, *Stalin's Industrial Revolution: Politics and Workers, 1928–32*, Cambridge 1988. S. Fitzpatrick's excellent *Stalin's Peasants: Resistance and Survival in the Russian Village after Collectivisation*, New York and Oxford 1994, is complemented by her *Everyday Stalinism: Ordinary Life in Extraordinary Times: Soviet Russia in the 1930s*, New York 1999; L. Siegelbaum, *Stakhanovism and the Politics of Productivity in the USSR, 1935–41*, Cambridge 1988, and S. Kotkin, *Magnetic Mountain: Stalinism as a Civilisation*, Berkeley etc. 1995 investigate more heroic discourses. R. Conquest, *The Great Terror: A Re-Assessment*, Oxford 1990, restates his earlier position; J. Getty (with O. Naumov, eds) revises his revisionism in *The Road to Terror: Stalin and the Self-Destruction of the Bolsheviks, 1932–1939,* New Haven, CT, and London 1999. Since Solzhenitsyn's *Gulag Archipelago, 1918–56: An Experiment in Literary Investigation*, 3 vols London 1978/1 vol. abridged 1999, the GULag has been dissected by A. Applebaum, *Gulag: A History of the Soviet Camps*, New York and London 2003. The controversy over the nature of Stalinism is summarised by H. Shukman, ed., *Redefining Stalinism*, London and Portland, OH, 2003; the thesis of N. Vakar, *The Taproot of Soviet Society*, New York 1962, deserves greater acknowledgement. The opening of the archives has brought much new writing on Stalin, as on other Soviet topics: the latest study is R. Service, *Stalin: A Biography*, London 2004. Other solid modern biographies include S. Cohen on Bukharin (1980), I. Thatcher on Trotskii (2003), A. Knight on Beria (1993), W. Taubman on Khrushchëv (2003), A. Pyman on Blok (1979–80), R. Reeder on Akhmatova (1994). The period is also rich in memoirs; see especially those of purge victims Ye. Ginsburg, N. Mandelshtam, A. Larina.

The standard on the Great Fatherland War is R. Overy, *Russia's War*, London 1998. On the times of the principal post-war leaders see M. McCauley, *The Khrushchev Era, 1954–1964*, London 1995, and E. Bacon and M. Sandle, eds, *Brezhnev Reconsidered*, Basingstoke 2002. On the economy see P. Hanson, *The Rise and Fall of the Soviet Economy: An Economic History of the USSR from 1945*, London 2003; on the informal economy, S. Lovell, A. Ledeneva and A. Rogachevskii, eds, *Bribery and Blat in Russia: Negotiating Reciprocity from the Middle Ages to the 1990s*, Basingstoke and London 2000, and A. Ledeneva, *Russia's Economy of Favours: Blat, Networking and Informal Exchange*, Cambridge 1998. On the Church see N. Davies, *A Long Walk to Church: A Contemporary History of Russian Orthodoxy*, Oxford and Boulder, CO, 2003, and on the elite M. Voslensky, *Nomenklatura: Anatomy of the Soviet Ruling Class*, London 1984. The later leadership – Khrushchëv, Brezhnev, Gorbachëv – have all written memoirs or autobiographies (as have Yeltsin and Putin). M. Galeotti treats Russia's Vietnam in *Afghanistan: The Soviet Union's Last War*, London 1995. A. Brown introduces *The Gorbachëv Factor*, Oxford 1996. Later societal developments are surveyed in G. Hosking, J. Aves and P. Duncan, *The Road to Post-Communism: Independent Movements in the Soviet Union, 1985–1991*, London 1992, and R. Sakwa, *Gorbachev and his Reforms, 1985–90*, London 1990. The fall is examined by R. Suny, *The Revenge of the Past: Nationalism, Revolution and the Collapse of the Soviet Union*, Stanford, CA, 1993, and in Sakwa's text-book, *Russian Politics and Society*, London 2002.

Sakwa, *Russian Politics* brings the story up towards the present. See further A. Steen, *Political Elites and the New Russia: The Power Basis of Yeltsin's and Putin's Regimes*, New York 2003; A. Aslund, *How Russia Became a Market Economy*, London 1995; A. Barker, ed., *Consuming Russia: Popular Culture, Sex and Society Since Gorbachëv*, Durham, NC, 1999; and R. Service, *Russia: Experiment with a People, From 1991 to the Present*, London 2002. J. Ellis, *The Russian Orthodox Church: Triumphalism and Defensiveness*, London 1996, and G. Smith, ed., *The Nationalities Question in the Post-Soviet States*, London and New York 1996, analyse two crucial constituencies. Yeltsin sets out his own stall in *Midnight Diaries*, and Putin his in *First Person*, both London 2000. (Martial arts lovers may also wish to consult V. Putin et al., *Judo: History, Theory, Practice*, Berkeley 2004.)

Index